Explorer
New Zealand

Nick Hanna

 Publishing

Written by Nick Hanna
Updated by Michael Mellor

Published by AA Publishing, a trading name of Automobile Association Developments Limited, whose registered office is Southwood East, Apollo Rise, Farnborough, Hampshire, GU14 0JW. Registered number 1878835.

ISBN-10: 0 7495 4379 5
ISBN-13: 978-0-7495-4379-2

A CIP catalogue record for this book is available from the British Library.

Colour separation by Fotographics Ltd
Printed and bound by Printer Trento Srl

Find out more about AA Publishing and the wide range of travel publications and services the AA provides by visiting our website at www.theAA.com/bookshop.

Reprinted June 2005
Revised fifth edition 2005
First published 1997

Titles in the Explorer series:
Australia • Boston & New England • Britain • Brittany California • Canada • Caribbean • China • Costa Rica • Crete Cuba • Cyprus • Egypt • Florence & Tuscany • Florida France • Germany • Greek Islands • Hawaii • India • Ireland Italy • Japan • London • Mallorca • Mexico • New York New Zealand • Paris • Portugal • Provence • Rome San Francisco • Scotland • South Africa • Spain • Thailand Tunisia • Turkey • Venice • Vietnam

Opposite: White-water rafting, Rotorua

A02703

How to use this book

ORGANIZATION

New Zealand Is,
New Zealand Was
Discusses aspects of life and culture in contemporary New Zealand and significant periods in its history.

A–Z
An alphabetical listing of places to visit. This section is divided into North and South Island and is then split into geographical regions. Places of interest are listed alphabetically within each section. Suggested walks, drives and Focus On articles, which provide an insight into aspects of life in New Zealand, are included in each section.

Travel Facts
Contains the strictly practical information that is vital for a successful trip.

Hotels and Restaurants
Lists recommended establishments.

KEY TO ADMISSION CHARGES
Standard admission charges are categorized in this book as follows:
Inexpensive   less than NZ$5
Moderate   NZ$5–20
Expensive   more than NZ$20

ABOUT THE RATINGS
Most places described in this book have been given a separate rating. These are as follows:

▶▶▶   **Do not miss**

▶▶   **Highly recommended**

▶   **Worth seeing**

MAP REFERENCES
To make the location of a particular place easier to find, every main entry in this book is given a map reference, such as 176B3. The first number (176) indicates the page on which the map can be found, the letter (B) and the second number (3) pinpoint the square in which the main entry is located. The maps on the inside front cover and inside back cover are referred to as IFC and IBC respectively.

Contents

5

*Dinghy racing on Lake Wakatipu, South
Island (below); sheep market (above)*

After completing his studies in social anthropology at Sussex, Nick Hanna set off to travel the world, and he has been a tireless globe-trotter ever since. His travel articles and photography have appeared in several national newspapers and magazines, and he is the author of seven guidebooks.

My New Zealand

Like many visitors to New Zealand, my first impressions were of the warmth and friendliness of the people, many of whom went out of their way to be helpful and hospitable during my travels. Another thing that strikes you as soon as you head out of the cities is the great open spaces—the empty road rolling onwards, and isolated farmsteads nestling in valleys in the middle of nowhere.

New Zealanders themselves are inveterate lovers of the Great Outdoors, and thousands now work in tourism as adventure guides—their enthusiasm and dedication make them among the most professional guides to be found anywhere in the world.

A myth demolished as soon as you hit a town or city of any size is that the country is a cultural backwater; the sheer variety of arts, entertainment and music on offer may come as a surprise. I also found myself spoilt for choice when eating out, with standards of food and wine that compare well with more exalted gourmet destinations. That doesn't mean you won't occasionally find yourself stuck in the wopwops (the back of beyond) where family-run tea rooms have nothing left but a stale meat pie—but you can compensate for it later elsewhere.

New Zealanders are acutely conscious of their colonial heritage, and with only 230 years of European settlement behind them, every plough, Victorian utensil or other material scrap of history has been preserved. At the opposite extreme, the heritage sector has produced some outstanding attractions that are at the cutting edge of museum design internationally: Two fine examples that I particularly enjoyed were Auckland's National Maritime Museum and Kelly Tarlton's Antarctic Encounter and Underwater World. Te Papa in Wellington has rapidly gained a world-class reputation too.

Above all, New Zealand gives the impression of openness: of opportunity for those who have settled there, from New Zealanders towards visitors, and open spaces to roam in. Rare qualities in an increasingly crowded world.
Nick Hanna

Mitre Peak, Milford Sound (above)

New Zealand Is

Considering its modest size, New Zealand has an astonishing diversity of landscapes and natural attractions, ranging from geysers to glaciers, rugged peaks to rushing rivers, and endless beaches to ancient beech forests. In this beautiful and unspoiled country, it is impossible to resist the call of the wild.

Highest mountain: Aoraki/Mount Cook (3,754m/12,317ft)
Longest river: Waikato River (425km/264 miles)
Largest lake: Lake Taupo (606sq km/234sq miles)
Largest glacier: Tasman Glacier (29km/18 miles)

❑ In order of popularity, the most frequently visited natural attractions in New Zealand are:
1   Whakarewarewa Thermal Reserve, Rotorua
2   Waitomo Caves
3   Milford Sound
4   Aoraki/Mount Cook National Park
5   Fox and Franz Josef glaciers ❑

10

DISTANT ISLANDS Over 2,000km (1,243 miles) away from the mainland of Australia, New Zealand has the South Pacific to the north and east, the Tasman Sea to the west and the Southern Ocean to the south.

The two major land masses are the North Island (115,777sq km/44,702sq miles) and the South Island (151,215sq km/58,384sq miles), with Stewart Island (1,746sq km/674sq miles) lying off the southern tip of the South Island. To the south and east there are also six remote and uninhabited island groups (many now wildlife refuges), plus the inhabited Chatham Islands.

The North Island is the more heavily populated of the two main islands and the chief focus for commerce and business, while the South Island has the lion's share of majestic scenery and unspoiled wilderness. With about three-quarters of the population of 3.6 million living in urban areas, there is no shortage of space.

New Zealand is both volcanic and sedimentary in origin, with geothermal springs and geysers (and active volcanoes) found mostly in the North Island. Mountain ranges and rugged hills are characteristic of both main islands; the Southern Alps (South Island) are the most impressive mountain chain, with 223 named peaks rising above 2,300m (7,546ft). The country's high rainfall, combined with the steep landforms, has created fast-flowing rivers and many superb inland lakes.

The 15,808km (9,825 miles) of coastline encompasses mighty fiords, semitropical beaches and hundreds of bays and harbours.

The Bay of Islands, looking over Motuarohia Island

Much of New Zealand is volcanic, like flat-topped Mount Tongariro in the central North Island

MOA'S ARK This group of islands drifted away from the ancient super-continent of Gondwanaland somewhere between 80 and 100 million years ago, long before the appearance of mammals on other land masses. In this isolated environment (which has been dubbed 'Moa's Ark'), numerous species of flightless bird evolved; the moa is now extinct, but kiwi, takahe and other flightless species still exist. You can also see many visiting waders and the royal albatross. Around the shoreline seals, dolphins, penguins and even whales abound.

❏ New Zealand's Department of Conservation is acknowledged as one of the top environment conservation authorities in the world. Operating through a network of field units and 13 conservancy offices, it uses its annual budget of just NZ$180 million to look after and protect more than 8 million hectares (20 million acres). Vital recovery projects are focused on rare and threatened species such as tuatara, kiwi, native frogs, giant weta, kakapo and land snails. ❏

Originally 80 per cent of New Zealand was covered in forest; just under a quarter of this is now left, most of it protected. The majority of native trees are evergreens, including giant conifers such as kauri, totara and rimu. There are some 2,500 native plant species (including 1,450 flowering plants). Some of the more common and distinctive plants include nikau palms, ponga (tree ferns), epiphyte orchids and the 'cabbage tree', which is a lily though it looks like a palm. In coastal areas native flax and toi toi (pampas grass) are common, and this is also the environment of the pohutukawa or 'New Zealand Christmas Tree', which blooms deep crimson in December.

Around one-third of the country is controlled by the Department of Conservation Te Papa Atawhai (DoC), which administers 14 national parks, 16 maritime reserves, 20 conservation parks and more than 1,000 regional parks or reserves. Among these are two natural World Heritage Areas: Tongariro National Park and Te Wahipounamu.

Sometimes referred to as 'the world's biggest farm', New Zealand is heavily dependent on agriculture and horticulture. Around 10 per cent of the work force is employed in agriculture, which has become remarkably efficient since the removal of subsidies in the 1980s.

SCIENTIFIC FARMING Meat, dairy products and wool are among the principal export earners in New Zealand and, despite diversification into other areas, agriculture and horticulture still account for around 60 per cent of export earnings and 11.5 per cent of gross domestic product. As befits a farming nation, agricultural research is well established, and efficient management of grasslands enables even sparse, hilly terrain to support high stock numbers. In order to achieve this, New Zealand pioneered the use of aircraft for spreading fertilizers and seed; it was also one of the first countries to develop mechanical milking for dairy herds.

SHEEP, SHEEP, SHEEP There are some 24,000 sheep farms in New Zealand, containing about 40 million sheep. This rises to 70 million at the height of the lambing season, with around 90 per cent of the 26 million lambs born each year being exported.

❑ Horticulture is a boom area for exports, with overseas sales rising from NZ$30 million in the 1970s to over NZ$1,500 million in the 1990s. Apart from the famous kiwifruit, the other principal earners are apples, pears and fresh and processed vegetables. Exotics such as ginseng, valerian and angelica are also exported to meet the growing demand for medicinal herbs. ❑

The first flocks in New Zealand were merinos, introduced in the 1830s for their fine fleeces, but these were gradually replaced with other breeds that adapted better to the warm, humid climate. Refrigerated shipping (which started in 1882) led to a shift of emphasis towards breeds that produced both meat and wool,

There are around 17 sheep to each New Zealander

such as the more hardy Romneys from Britain. Cross-breeding has produced sheep suitable for different areas, and a wide variety of sheep is now farmed—even the merino has made a comeback.

New Zealand wool is noted for its length and colour as well as for its high yields. The country is the second-largest producer in the world (after Australia) of clean, scoured wool, about 90 per cent of which is exported. But the high cost of sheep farming is forcing farmers to turn to cattle or deer farming and forestry; the national flock has fallen from its peak of some 70 million sheep in 1981.

MILK AND CHEESE Dairy farming is concentrated mainly in the North Island, with around 14,500 dairy herds (approximately 4.4 million cattle) in the country as a whole. Herds are large compared to those elsewhere (averaging about 140 milking cows), and most farmers belong to dairy co-operatives that manufacture and market dairy products.

New Zealand has been exporting cheese since the 1840s and now manufactures over 60 varieties, including some developed in New Zealand (such as blue supreme, aorangi and akronia) as well as high-quality versions of European cheeses (such as cheddar, brie, parmesan, edam and mozzarella). Other dairy exports include milk powders, butter and ghee (clarified butter). The country accounts for about 25 per cent of world trade in dairy products, and the industry provides 11 per cent of New Zealand's export earnings.

DEER FARMING Deer are considered a pest, and until the 1970s it was official policy to kill them because of

Dairy farming is a large part of agriculture in the North Island

the damage they caused to upland grazing areas. Helicopters were used extensively to hunt them in the wild, with the venison then being exported (principally to Germany). When deer farming started in the 1970s, the hunters switched to capturing live animals, which were kept in enclosures with strong, high fences. Now there are around 1.1 million farmed deer, although they are still classified as noxious animals and special licences are needed to farm them. As well as venison, antler velvet is also exported, principally to the Far East.

❏ Fur farming includes possum skins, rex and chinchilla rabbit fur, and ferret fur. Possums (which are killed by cars on almost every road in the country), like deer, are classed as noxious pests, and are subject to an official eradication policy. Around two million possum skins are exported annually. ❏

While New Zealand enjoys a high-profile environmental image, it also has one of the worst records in the world for wiping out native species. More than 500 plants, birds and animals are said to be still under threat.

❏ It is known that moa were still alive in Fiordland when the first Europeans arrived on the west coast, because a bone from a moa found in a midden in Takahe Valley had a mark on it made by a steel implement. Maori used to split the bones to get at the marrow, and the steel tool was probably obtained from sealers camping in nearby Dusky Sound. ❏

THE END OF THE MOA These colossal flightless birds (rather like ostriches, up to 4m/13ft tall) were wiped out by hunting (early Maori were referred to as 'moa hunters'), along with another 20 species of birds. One of these was the New Zealand eagle (*Harpagornis moorei*), the largest eagle ever known, with a wingspan of more than 2.5m (8ft); it vanished because its prey, including the moa, was also disappearing. The burning and clearing of forests by early Maori, and the introduction of predators such as the Polynesian rat (*kiore*) and the Maori dog (now also extinct), likewise had a significant effect on native species.

DISASTROUS INTRODUCTIONS
Worse was to come with the arrival of the Europeans, who began bringing animals into the country at an unprecedented rate. Some were liberated for sport, others were introduced for their fur or simply as pets. By the first decade of the 20th century more than 50 species had been introduced, including rabbits, possums, hares, weasels, stoats, deer, goats and even wallabies.

Some introduced species (such as cows and sheep) now form a mainstay of the nation's economy, but other animals had devastating effects. Possums ate kiwi eggs, stoats ate their young chicks and dogs attacked the adults. Rabbits, deer, goats and possums gnawed away at native trees and plants, drastically altering the vegetation and soil ecology. The clearing of farmlands led to the loss of yet more native habitat and the extinction of a further nine species of bird.

THREATENED BIRDS Around 57 native bird species are currently considered threatened, including the kiwi, the national emblem (see pages 236–237). Other flightless birds currently under threat include the kakapo, a strange nocturnal parrot

that retains a precarious hold on Little Barrier Island and Codfish Island—only 250 individuals are still known to exist. Another Fiordland native, the bright blue and green takahe, was regarded as extinct before a small colony was discovered in 1948; just 200 of these birds are now left. The taiko, a large white-bellied sea bird, was also thought to be extinct until an amateur ornithologist spotted two of them on Chatham Island; around 50–100 taiko have now been refound, but their survival depends on the offspring from just a few nesting burrows. The native black stilt, or kaki, is another threatened species, with fewer than 100 left in the wild. And the inquisitive kea, the world's only alpine parrot, is also declining in numbers.

MAMMALS AND INSECTS The only native land mammals in New Zealand are bats. One species became extinct as recently as 1965,

and the other two (the long-tailed and short-tailed bat) are both uncommon and under threat. The country's largest insects are the weta (a group of wingless crickets) and these too are in retreat, with the giant weta (which can grow up to 10cm/4in long) currently found only in offshore sanctuaries and one mainland site. The huge black ground beetle (*Mecodema punctellum*) is similarly endangered. Thousands of insects in the country have yet to be classified, and many more may be disappearing without us even knowing it.

15

The kea, a native parrot (right), is under threat, but the introduced possum (below) is a pest

It is no exaggeration to claim that New Zealand is probably the best country in the world for adventure tourism. The choice of activities is enormous—and growing all the time.

OUTDOOR ATTRACTIONS New Zealanders prefer to spend a large amount of their recreational time in the open air, and given that most overseas visitors are also drawn to the country by the many outdoor attractions (such as lakes, mountains, glaciers and forests), it is perhaps only to be expected that New Zealand should have developed a sophisticated infrastructure for adventure tourism.

Nearly three-quarters of the 1.5 million visitors to the country each year take part in some kind of outdoor adventure, and there are now well over a thousand

Try rafting for a thrill

guides or companies in the adventure tourism business. For many New Zealanders, making a living from sharing their natural environment with visitors has now become a way of life. Courteous, well-trained and enthusiastic guides will add enormously to your enjoyment of exploring wilderness areas.

BUSH WALKS AND BUNGEE-JUMPING One of the most popular outdoor activities for visitors is a short bush walk (usually lasting less than half a day), and nearly every visitor information office or Department of Conservation (DoC) office has helpful leaflets and information on local walking tracks. Longer tramps on some of New Zealand's famous long-distance paths (such as the Abel Tasman, Routeburn, Heaphy, Milford and Hollyford tracks) are also popular.

Ballooning gives you a bird's-eye view of the countryside, and is mainly focused around Christchurch. Sea kayaking is a wonderful way to see the coast—try the Abel Tasman National Park. Jet-boating gives you a noisier, faster perspective on the great outdoors (see pages 210–211), and has become the third most popular activity for visitors (after short walks and scenic boat cruises). With its mountainous terrain and high rainfall, New Zealand is a perfect location for white-water rafting and as many as 50 companies operate on rivers in both the North and South Islands. Black-water rafting has also taken off in a big way: this mostly takes place around the Waitomo region.

Tandem hang-gliding, tandem parachuting and tandem parapenting (a mixture of parachuting and hand-gliding) are

Bungee-jumping in Queenstown, South Island

all good ways of experiencing these sports with little or no training, and bungee-jumping (spelled bungy in its native land, see page 245) has become virtually synonymous with New Zealand.

FLIGHTSEEING

Helicopter sightseeing is also very popular, with the busiest areas in Aoraki/Mount Cook National Park, Fiordland, Fox and Franz Josef glaciers and around the Queenstown lakes. Heli-fishing, heli-hiking, heli-skiing and heli-rafting are all popular. However, a spate of air crashes prompted a review by the Civil Aviation Authority (CAA) into aircraft safety in New Zealand. This resulted in a crackdown on operators who had been flying below minimum heights. If you are cruising around Milford Sound by boat, noise from the constant procession of light planes and helicopters above can be annoying.

❏ New Zealand is said to have more helicopters per head of population than any other country in the world. They were first used on a large scale during the 1960s for deer culling, with up to 50 culling as many as 200 deer each in a day; in the 1970s the pilots switched to recovering the deer for farming. In many remote areas, helicopters are used as daily work-horses for moving materials, surveying, fire control, drilling and crop spraying. ❏

DARE-DEVIL STUNTS As bungee-jumping and tandem parachuting are now so common as to be almost mundane, operators are constantly seeking even more daring skills to tempt the brave: If there is a new experience out there waiting to be invented, there is a good chance it will happen here first! Among the new thrills that have been proposed are wing-walking (in which passengers are strapped to the top wing of a Tiger Moth plane) and a simulated, low-level aerial top-dressing run. Latest crazes are 'zorbing' (rolling down Rotorua hillsides encapsulated in a large transparent ball); 'urban rap jumping' (abseiling down Auckland tower blocks) and 'Fly-by-Wire' ('flying' a 'plane' hanging from cables above a Wellington or Queenstown valley). These activities can change by the minute, check with the local Visitor Information Centre.

The resumption of nuclear testing by the French in the South Pacific in 1995 and 1996 caused outrage in New Zealand, which for a long time has been recognized as the standard-bearer of the movement for a nuclear-free Pacific.

ANZUS AND THE USA Despite the loosening of colonial ties, New Zealand dutifully supported Britain in foreign policy in the first half of the 20th century, sending 100,000 troops to Europe and the Middle East during World War I. During World War II it became clear that Britain was unable to reciprocate in defence matters, and politicians recognized the need to realign with the USA, whose Pacific fleet was at least based closer to home. In 1951 (during the Korean War) Australia, New Zealand and the USA together signed the ANZUS defence alliance.

As a result of this policy New Zealand deployed troops to support the USA in Vietnam in 1965, which led to widespread anti-war protests. With the election of a nationalistic Labour government in 1972 the troops were withdrawn, and New

Protestors keep up the pressure for a nuclear-free New Zealand

Zealand adopted an anti-nuclear stance, sending two warships to protest against French nuclear testing in the Mururoa atoll. This was partly a result of the greater role played by New Zealand in its Pacific backyard. At the same time, there was an outcry against nuclear-armed or nuclear-powered US warships using New Zealand ports, with a flotilla of 'peace boats' blockading Auckland Harbour to prevent nuclear submarines from entering it.

Further protests followed in the early 1980s, contributing to the election in 1984 of a Labour government that pledged to instigate a 320km (99-mile) nuclear-free zone around the country's shores. With the USA stating that it would 'neither confirm nor deny' whether its naval vessels were carrying nuclear weapons, it was unable to use New Zealand ports, and suspended its obligations to New Zealand under the ANZUS treaty.

18

THE RAINBOW WARRIOR In July 1985 the *Rainbow Warrior*, flagship of the international protest group Greenpeace, sailed into Auckland's Waitemata Harbour to join a flotilla of vessels on a protest voyage to the French nuclear-testing site in Mururoa. Just before midnight on 10 July a bomb blasted a hole in the ship; while most of the crew jumped to safety, a Greenpeace photographer, Fernando Pereira, went back to retrieve equipment. A second bomb exploded, and Pereira was drowned as the *Rainbow Warrior* sank.

It was the first ever act of international terrorism on New Zealand soil. Within two weeks the police had arrested two suspects, who proved to be agents for the French secret service.

RESUMED TESTING Given the anger and resentment caused by this act of sabotage by a foreign government in New Zealand territory, it was to be expected that New Zealand (with Australia) would lead the way in protesting against the resumption of French nuclear tests in Mururoa in 1995. The naval research ship HMNZS *Tui* was sent to Mururoa in August 1995, one of only two government-backed vessels to take part in

the protests (the other was a ceremonial canoe sent by the tiny Cook Islands). Although tests were still carried out in 1995 and 1996, worldwide protests forced France to concede that those would be the last, and to sign the Comprehensive Test Ban Treaty.

Meanwhile, relations between the USA and New Zealand had improved with a visit to Washington by the prime minister Jim Bolger in 1995. But diplomatic differences remain. With the hardening of attitudes caused by the French testing, there is little doubt that New Zealand will retain its nuclear-free policy.

❑ In November 1985 the two French agents responsible for the *Rainbow Warrior* bombing were sentenced to ten years' imprisonment, but the French pressed for their return and imposed a trade ban on New Zealand products in retaliation. The row eventually led to United Nations arbitration, under which France agreed to pay $13 million compensation and New Zealand handed over the agents. They subsequently spent just two years 'imprisoned' on the Pacific island of Hao before being repatriated to France. ❑

The bombing of the Rainbow Warrior *hardened public opinion against nuclear weapons*

The inherent flaws and misunderstandings over land ownership enshrined in the 1840 Treaty of Waitangi have led Maori to protest almost since the day it was signed. Bitter disputes over land rights still continue today, to the detriment of good race relations.

A DUBIOUS LEGACY Constitutionally New Zealand is perhaps unique in the world in that the legal basis for sovereignty and ownership over land is enshrined in a single controversial document, the Treaty of Waitangi (see pages 36–37). However, even if the Maori who 'sold' their land to the early settlers were fully aware of the consequences, the moral validity of these transactions has always been questionable. Disputes flared up from 1843 onwards, culminating in the New Zealand Wars and the Maori King Movement. A spate of occupations, sit-ins and other protests in the 1990s has once again brought the issue of land rights to the fore.

THE WAITANGI TRIBUNAL For much of the 20th century Maori mounted peaceful challenges to the provisions of the treaty, with numerous petitions to Parliament, court cases and even pilgrimages to London. In 1914 the Maori king, Te Rata, met King George V and Queen Mary at Buckingham Palace, but his deputation met with no response. In 1975 the government set up the Waitangi Tribunal to investigate land claims, but this was largely ineffectual until 1985, when its terms of reference were extended to include the investigation of grievances dating back to 1840. Critics claim it is too slow, and in fact by 1990 the tribunal had made recommendations on only seven substantial claims. Since then it has

❑ During a visit to New Zealand to attend the 1995 Commonwealth summit, Queen Elizabeth II formally signed legislation that apologized to Waikato Maori for the 'wrongful and unjust' land grab carried out by whites in the name of her great-great-grandmother Queen Victoria. On 2 November 1995, in the presence of the Maori Queen Dame Te Atairangikaahu and the then Governor-General Dame Catherine Tizard, the Queen gave the Royal Assent to an Act of Parliament compensating the Tainui tribe for its suffering 130 years ago, when they were wrongly branded as rebels, and troops were sent to fight them and confiscate their land. The Act admits that the British violated the Treaty of Waitangi and offers 'profound regret and apologies for the loss of lives'. Under the Act, the Crown handed back nearly 16,200ha (40,000 acres) of land, valued at NZ$100 million, with around 30,000 Tainui benefiting from the settlement. ❑

produced 70 reports, but another 800 are still outstanding.

THE FISCAL ENVELOPE

THE FISCAL ENVELOPE The backlog of outstanding claims and growing frustration among the Maori led the national government, in 1994, to propose an all-embracing package that (it was hoped) would resolve all outstanding claims before the end of the decade, with a ceiling of NZ$1 billion on the cost of all future settlements. To some Maori the idea of putting a ceiling on payments before claims are heard is equivalent to putting the cart before the horse; they also fail to see the logic in proposing a pan-Maori settlement when claims are dealt with on a tribal basis. The Labour government elected in 1999 dropped the idea of a 'fiscal envelope'.

PROTESTS AND SIT-INS Anger over government proposals boiled over in 1995, with protests in front of the Governor-General at the Waitangi Day celebrations marking the start of a round of sit-ins and occupations throughout the country.

Confrontations ensued in Hamilton, Tamaki (Auckland) and even in the tourist-orientated Whakarewarewa Thermal Reserve in Rotorua. One of the most controversial occupations was that of the Moutoa Gardens in Wanganui (see page 135), which dominated news headlines for several weeks as protestors squared up to the local council and refused to leave land which they claimed had been sold to the Crown illegally in 1848. In another confrontation, demonstrators burned down a school building near Kaitaia in protest at the time taken to hear their case.

RACE RELATIONS The 1995 protests played a crucial role in bringing the issue of land rights once again to the fore, although they did little for race relations in a country that generally prides itself on its harmonious biculturalism. It was a reminder to New Zealanders that good race relations cannot be taken for granted, and that (bearing in mind their warrior past) Maori have so far shown considerable restraint in their attempts to get their grievances from the 19th century addressed. Economic and social hardship among Maori have also fanned the flames of protest, and some radicals have used the protests as a platform to push the idea of Maori sovereignty—with their own judicial and political systems. One thing is certain—land claims will continue for some years yet.

21

Protestors disrupted the 1995 Waitangi Day celebrations

New Zealand has an abundance of natural produce, as well as different tastes, introduced by immigrant groups. It comes as no surprise to discover that a new generation of chefs is creating a culinary revolution in the nation's eating habits.

FROM STODGE TO SASHIMI Having inherited a tradition of stodgy, British Empire cooking, culinary culture in New Zealand has for a long time been epitomized by solid, no-nonsense fare such as steak, fries and coleslaw, pies, fish and chips, and roast meats. Even now, this may be all that you will find in country pubs or rural towns, but in cities and holiday havens such as Queenstown there is an abundance of new restaurants, bistros and urban cafés serving a cosmopolitan array of regional dishes from around the world.

This restaurant revolution has been driven by the demands of increasingly sophisticated visitors, by growing expectations as a result of wider international travel by Kiwis and also by the use of aromatic herbs and spices as well as the many different cooking styles introduced by immigrants from Asia and elsewhere.

In the 1960s good restaurants—and good chefs—were so few and far between that the Tourist Hotel Corporation was obliged to bring a squadron of chefs from Europe to work in local resorts. Now, Kiwi chefs are in demand in places such as London, and New Zealand has over 2,500 restaurants—Wellington is said to have more restaurants per person than New York.

Crayfish are among the superb ingredients of New Zealand cuisine

There are few national dishes as such, although *paua* (abalone) patties and whitebait fritters certainly come close, but it is the incredibly fresh produce, meats and seafood that make eating such a pleasure in New Zealand. Drawing on many different styles, the best New Zealand cooking today tends to lean towards the Mediterranean or the Pacific Rim, a fashionable fusion of East and West in a style perhaps best described as 'Californian'.

FROM FARM TO RESTAURANT New Zealand's farms produce superb beef and lamb (fed on pasture rather than grain, which gives meat a richer taste), and venison has become increasingly popular. Fresh seafood, good-quality dairy produce and an abundance of exotic fruits are just a few of the other natural ingredients available.

Some regions have their special dishes, and while most of the raw ingredients are available everywhere, these dishes are likely to be that much fresher in local restaurants. Oysters and mussels are farmed around the Coromandel Peninsula, and the Firth of Thames is noted for its scallops, flounder and crayfish. In the Bay of Islands, smoked kingfish and marlin are delicacies available during the game fishing season, and feijoas (similar to guava), passion fruit and tamarillos ('tree tomatoes') are grown in the Kerikeri area. Peaches, apples and pears are produced in abundance in Hawke's Bay, as are kiwifruit in the Bay of Plenty. The rich dairylands of the Taranaki region have numerous

> ❑ Traditional Maori delicacies include freshwater eels, mutton-bird (the young of the sooty petrel, with a strong, fishy taste), and seafood such as pipi and tuatua shellfish and kina (prickly sea urchins). A *hangi* is a feast of meat, seafood and vegetables (including the staple root crop, kumara), steamed over hot rocks buried in an earth oven (the *hangi*). Like many Polynesian foods, it is high in carbohydrates but well worth sampling. ❑

23

excellent cheeses, and Lake Taupo is famous for its massive trout—although you will have to hook it yourself, since restaurants are not permitted to sell trout.

In the South Island, Marlborough Sounds are noted for their farmed mussels (which are exported world-wide), and oysters and scallops are perennially popular in the port of Nelson. Blenheim produces garlic, cherries, apples, pears and much more besides, while the local crayfish in the seaside town of Kaikoura (its name is Maori for 'to eat crayfish') is not to be missed. Canterbury is famed for its lamb and is also known for its numerous duck farms. Across the Alps, tiny whitebait are a local delicacy along much of the west coast from September to November. Bluff oysters, Fiordland crayfish, salmon and blue cod are specialities from the south coast of the South Island.

Tasty green-lipped mussels are exported worldwide

In just two decades, New Zealand has moved from producing ghastly 'plonk' to internationally acclaimed table wines. More than 100 wineries now produce some 45 million litres (12 million gallons) of wine annually.

❑ The first vines in New Zealand were planted over 150 years ago by James Busby, the British Resident, who grew grapes in the back garden of his house in Waitangi. He was complimented on his 'delicious' white wine by the French explorer Dumont d'Urville in 1846, but fought a losing battle against intrusion by 'horses, sheep, cattle and pigs'. His little vineyard was finally destroyed by British soldiers during one of their battles with the rebel leader Hongi Hika. ❑

EARLY DAYS In addition to the vineyards around Auckland (see panel), other long-established winemaking areas include Gisborne, Nelson and Hawke's Bay, but output was traditionally small. The opening up of New Zealand to international influences in the 1960s led to a much greater demand for table wines, and the search began for fresh areas suitable for vineyards.

NEW VINEYARDS In addition to the new vineyards planted in the older wine-growing areas, other possible areas were also sought—principally in the Marlborough, Wairarapa and Canterbury regions. Of the numerous varieties of grape planted, one of the trail-blazers was the Sauvignon Blanc, which is ideally suited to the New Zealand climate, with its long, warm autumn days (helping to concentrate the sugar in the grape) and cool nights (providing a suitable acidic balance).

Among the pioneers in Marlborough were the Montana wineries, whose Sauvignon Blancs were the first New Zealand wines to gain international recognition. Another winery in the area is Cloudy Bay (established in 1985 by Australian winemakers), whose skilfully crafted Sauvignon Blancs are undoubtedly some of the best of each vintage. Sauvignon Blanc is produced in almost every winegrowing district, with those from the north being more lush and fruity and those from the south providing classic herbaceous overtones.

Chardonnay has also done exceptionally well in New Zealand, particularly in the Gisborne area. The Millton Vineyard, on the banks of the Te Arai River in Gisborne (the first certified organic producer in the country), produces some award-winning Chardonnays.

While winemaking in the Auckland region waned during the 1970s, it made something of a comeback in the 1980s with new plantings at Huapai, Ihumatao (near Mangere) and on Waiheke Island. Michael Brajkovich, whose family was one of the original producers in the area, took a giant leap from the old sherries and table wines of the mid-1980s to produce a

New Zealand wines hold their own with the world's best

Blenheim's sun and sparse soils are ideal for sparkling wines

❏ For most of this century, wine-making was dominated by sweet, highly alcoholic versions of forti-fied wines (such as sherry, port and Madeira) produced around the clay hills of West Auckland. Made largely by Dalmatian immi-grants, they were referred to as 'Dally plonk'. ❏

series of top Chardonnays of great flair and individuality; his Kumeu River Chardonnays and Sauvignon Blancs are of consistently high qual-ity. The 1993 vintages from around Auckland are also outstanding.

Neudorf Vineyard, near Nelson, is another great name to watch out for in Chardonnays, Sauvignon Blancs and Rieslings.

RED WINES The most famous reds are those produced at the Te Mata Estate in Hawke's Bay, revitalized by John Buck in the 1980s. Their Cabernet Sauvignon-based reds have been winning awards ever since: outstanding vintages include the 1982, 1989 and 1991 Coleraines. Other top producers in Hawke's Bay include Mission Bay and Kemblefield Estate. Waiheke Island in the Hauraki Gulf and the Wairarapa, east of Wellington, are also good for reds, especially Martinborough Pinot Noir.

SPARKLING WINES When Australia developed its first sparkling wines in the 1970s it did not take long for New Zealand to follow suit, although for many years the Montana vineyards were the only producers of *méthode champenoise* wines. Their Lindauer (first released in 1980) remains a classic. In 1989 Montana teamed up with the famous French Champagne house of Deutz and Geldermann, and their Deutz Marlborough Cuvée has established itself as a thoroughbred.

Cloudy Bay has followed a similar path, teaming up with the prestigious Champagne house of Veuve Clicquot Ponsardin to produce the stylish Pelorus sparkling wines that complement perfectly the local smoked salmon.

Visitor route sign on the 'Scenic Wine Tour', which takes in the famous vine-yards of Blenheim

From the earliest days New Zealanders have had to 'mend and make do', which has led to numerous inventions. Today, New Zealand is said to have more inventors per head of population than any other country.

A replica of Richard Pearse's first plane

(see pages 210–211). The physicist Sir Ernest Rutherford could be said to have 'invented' modern nuclear physics when he split the atom in 1919. New Zealanders also invented the first automatic milking, franking and stamp-vending machines, and the wrinkle in the humble hair-grip. An Auckland student, Edward Smith, invented the world's first mechanical railway crossing.

HOME-MADE REPAIRS There is a popular saying that given a length of No. 8 (4mm) fencing wire, New Zealanders can make anything. The do-it-yourself mentality arrived with the first European settlers, who had to learn to fix imported machinery themselves since the nearest spare parts depot was probably 20,000km (12,000 miles) away in Britain. Frequently they redesigned it as an improvement on the original.

GREAT INVENTIONS Pride of place for inventors goes to Richard Pearse, the South Island farmer who allegedly flew before the Wright Brothers (see panel, page 216). As well as designing his own planes, he also developed a machine for threading needles, a motorized plough and a bicycle that pumped up its own tyres as it went along. Another South Island farmer, Bill Hamilton, was responsible for inventing the jet-boat

MODERN TIMES A South Aucklander, Terry Roycroft, has designed and built the *Sealander*, the ultimate amphibian car, which has retractable wheels that allow it to achieve speeds of 30 knots (the previous maximum speed was 5 knots).

A Hamilton engineer has recently invented a solar-powered car driven by a revolutionary motor. It is capable of speeds of up to 40kph (25mph).

More off-beat is a device called the NightStar, a deflated star globe that fits in your pocket and functions as a miniature planetarium.

❏ The inventiveness of New Zealanders is celebrated in a book called *No 8 Wire, The Best of Kiwi Ingenuity*, by Jon Bridges and David Downs (Hodder Moa Beckett, 2000). ❏

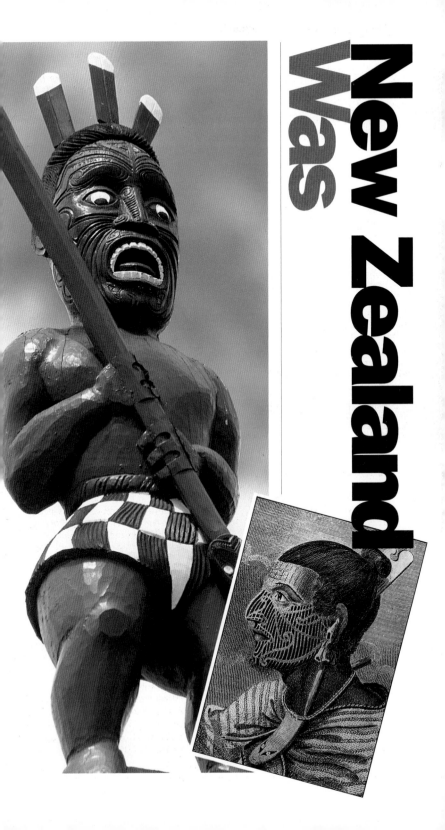

New Zealand Was

One consequence of New Zealand's geographic isolation was that it was one of the last countries of any size to be colonized. The first people to reach it were the Polynesians, who originated in Asia and spread out across the Pacific some 3,000 to 4,000 years ago.

❏ The homeland of 'Hawaiki', venerated in Maori culture, does not necessarily refer to a specific place. Hawaiki is a general term used throughout Polynesia to describe the ancestral homeland left behind in an onward migration, although in the case of Hawaii they may also have used it for the land they arrived in. Anthropologists believe the Maori originated in eastern Polynesia, possibly from the Marquesas in the Society Islands of French Polynesia. ❏

THE EXPLORER KUPE The Polynesians were expert sailors and often made long sea voyages, sometimes discovering new lands by accident and sometimes setting off on migrations in order to relieve pressure on their homeland. According to tradition it was the Polynesian explorer Kupe who first discovered New Zealand in around AD 950,

sailing from Hawaiki (see box). He explored the coast and sailed inland up the Whanganui River, before returning to Hawaiki with information on how to reach the land that his wife may have named Aotearoa— 'Land of the Long White Cloud'.

THE GREAT MIGRATIONS Some canoes undoubtedly landed in New Zealand after Kupe, but legend has it that the first great migrations took place during the 14th century, with a fleet of 12 canoes setting off from Hawaiki to escape overpopulation in the homelands. The existence of such a fleet has never been proved, but the names of all the canoes, with their occupants and landing places, form an important part of Maori genealogical history. Some of the canoes may have been lashed together to give greater stability on the ocean crossing, which would explain why they landed so close together. The voyagers brought food plants (including taro, yam and the sweet potato, kumara) as well as the rat and dog; pigs and domestic fowl were either eaten or lost overboard on the way.

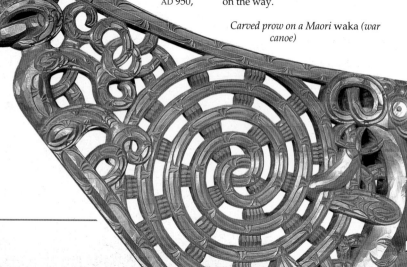

Carved prow on a Maori waka *(war canoe)*

ADAPTATION The people who arrived in Aotearoa had to adapt to a completely different climate from that of the tropical islands they had left. Food was at first plentiful: fish, shellfish, seals and an abundance of edible birds provided protein; one of the most easily tapped food supplies was the flightless moa, which had no predators before the arrival of humans.

Kumara, which is highly susceptible to frost, was difficult to grow as a perennial in New Zealand's temperate climate. Widespread cultivation only became possible with the discovery that kumara tubers could be lifted in the autumn and overwintered in pits (*rua*) in the earth for planting in the spring.

Other aspects of life also changed. The settlers brought the paper mulberry plant for making tapa cloth, but it grew only in the warmer north, so they learned to plait flax into fibre for clothes, cords and baskets. Rain capes were also made from flax, often decorated with feathers or dog skin. The country's forests provided huge trees for building much bigger canoes, and elaborate woodcarving became an established tradition. Bones were used for fishhooks, ornaments and spear heads, stone for tools such as adzes and axes, and volcanic stone such as obsidian for flake knives and other kinds of sharp tools.

In adapting to their new homeland, Maori developed one of the most sophisticated tribal cultures in the ancient world, with an elaborate social structure and a widespread trading system.

Elaborate carvings protect a marae *entrance*

❑ Studies of teeth and skeletons have shown that in the early days Maori had a varied and plentiful diet, but from the 15th century onwards the climate cooled considerably and populations became larger, with food becoming more scarce. People ate more shellfish such as pipi (clams, which usually contain some sand) and fern roots, both of which wore down teeth, so that by the time they were in their mid-20s their teeth were often worn down to the gum. With the introduction of the potato by Europeans, plentiful food supplies were once more assured. ❑

Over the centuries, Maori society evolved from the 'archaic' culture of the early moa-hunters into the sophisticated social system of the 'classic Maori' period. Kinship was of fundamental importance in Maori society, and inter-tribal warfare was a constant feature of this time.

SOCIAL HIERARCHY Maori society was and largely still is tribal, organized along strictly hierarchical lines, headed by the chiefs (*rangatira*), followed by the priests (*tohunga*), the commoners (*tūtūā*) and finally slaves (members of other tribes captured in battle). The family (*whānau*) and the subtribe (*hapū*) were part of the wider tribe (*iwi*), with this established social structure determining marriage and settlement patterns and, just as important, who fought whom. Tribal affiliations are still a vital part of life for many Maori.

The genealogy of the ancestors (*whakapapa*) is an essential element in the knitting together of tribes, and oral history still plays an important part in passing on information about the surrounding environment. A unified cosmology that venerated the gods of the natural elements was woven into the fabric of life, along with a series of concepts such as *tapu* (sacredness), *mana* (spiritual

Moko (tattoos) were a part of Maori fashion in 1880

authority or prestige) and *mākutu* (sorcery), which governed behaviour. Imaginative legends formed an important part of Maori oral heritage, and many of today's place-names derive from incidents taken from these elaborate tales.

INTER-TRIBAL WARS Maori tribes were constantly feuding, usually over territory or access to food sources, but also in order to avenge insults and extract *utu* (retribution). Sometimes these feuds would fester down the generations, but the consequent loss of life in pre-European times was probably negligible, as weapons were rudimentary and wars were usually only fought when the vital kumara crops did not need attention.

Young men sought honour in assaults with the *patu* (war club), gaining *mana* as warriors with each victory. The vanquished became slaves or were eaten. Although *hapū* would usually join forces to fight other *iwi*, there were also sometimes battles between *hapū* of the same *iwi*.

❏ Personal adornment in the form of tattooing (*tā moko*) was a striking feature of the classic period. The intricate patterns were purely for decoration, and tattooing had no relation to rank. It was a long, painful process undertaken with a bone chisel, with pigment rubbed into the incision. Men were often heavily tattooed on the face, body, buttocks and thighs; on women tattoos were usually confined to the chin and lips, and sometimes the ankles, wrists and forehead. ❏

VILLAGE LIFE Most families lived in small huts (*whare*), grouped together into villages (*kāinga*) that could range in size from a handful of individuals to more than 500 households, usually all members of the same *hapū*.

The focus of the community was (and still is) the *marae*, including an open space or village green where meetings and councils are held. Visitors are ceremonially bade welcome or farewell on the *marae*. An integral part of the *marae* is the *whare runanga*, or meeting house, which serves as a formal meeting place, for amusement and gossip at night or in bad weather and as a hostel for accommodating visitors. It is usually decorated with elaborate

A group of Maori displaying different costumes

carvings representing the ancestors, woven flax panels and symbolic paintings.

Within the village would also have been food storage pits (*rua*) and grain stores (*pātaka*), as well as bigger houses for the *tohunga* and *rangatira*, and sometimes a 'house of learning' or school (*whare wānanga*).

Often *kāinga* were grouped around a fortified hilltop village (*pā*). These hilltop forts were constructed using an elaborate system of ditches, banks and palisades, and in many cases proved impregnable to later attacks by European soldiers.

The first European to sail to New Zealand was Dutchman Abel Tasman, but after a bloody encounter with Maori he never set foot on land. Another 130 years passed before James Cook arrived, 'rediscovering' the country and placing it, literally, on the world map.

32

ABEL TASMAN

Geographers in Europe were convinced that somewhere in the South Pacific there must be a huge land mass (which they termed *Terra australis incognita*) to 'balance' the continents of the northern hemisphere. The explorers were to prove them wrong, but it was with the intention of discovering this unknown continent that Abel Janszoon Tasman set out from the Dutch trading post of Batavia (present-day Jakarta, Indonesia) in 1642. In command of two small ships, the *Heemskerck* and the *Zeehaen*, he sailed first to Mauritius and then doubled back eastwards to 'discover' Tasmania (which he named Van Diemen's Land).

After another seven days' sailing, on 13 December 1642, he sighted 'a land uplifted high' (the Alps in the South Island), but heavy seas precluded a landing. Instead he proceeded northwards along the coast, rounding Cape Farewell and anchoring in the shelter of what is today called Golden Bay.

Although he had been hoping to establish friendly relations with Maori, a fight broke out (see page 159) and he sailed on eastwards. Battling against headwinds in what was later known as Cook Strait, he turned around and headed up the west coast of the North Island; if he had continued a little further he would have found that this new land was two islands, and not the great *Terra australis incognita*.

❏ Tasman at first named the country he discovered Staten Landt, since he believed it to be connected to an island of that name off South America. But other explorers soon proved that the new land was an island, and the name was changed to 'Nieuw Zeeland', after the coastal province of Zeeland in Holland. It was probably an anonymous map-maker of the Dutch East India Company who thus gave the country its name, which was eventually anglicized to become New Zealand. ❏

Tasman then made another attempt to land, this time on what are now the Three Kings Islands (off Cape Reinga), but was again driven off by Maori. His journal and incomplete chart nevertheless helped to establish the new country on explorers' maps.

JAMES COOK Setting off from England in 1768 on the *Endeavour*, Cook's first goal was to sail to Tahiti to observe the transit of the sun by Venus—which helped astronomers to determine for the first time the distance from the earth to the sun. From there, he was to sail south in search of the unknown continent.

He first sighted the coastline of New Zealand on 6 October 1769, near Gisborne in the North Island. Cook eventually circumnavigated both islands (see pages 116–117), making highly accurate charts of the coastline, with just two glaring exceptions: he thought that Banks Peninsula was an island, and that Stewart Island was attached to the mainland. His accounts of his voyage, the detailed descriptions of the flora and fauna (compiled by the ship's botanists Joseph Banks and Daniel Solander) and the artist Sydney Parkinson's sketches of the land and its peoples brought New Zealand to the attention of the world. Cook returned to New Zealand in 1773 and again in 1777.

LATER EXPLORERS The French navigator Jean-François Marie de Surville anchored in Doubtless Bay just two months after Cook had arrived in New Zealand, but after a violent clash with Maori he sailed away after doing no more than chart the bay. He was followed two years later by a compatriot, Marion du Fresne, who believed that he was the first to rediscover the country after Tasman (Cook's data had not yet been published), and claimed it for France. After several weeks of friendly relations with Maori, du Fresne and 13 of his crew were killed and eaten—probably because of an infringement of the Maori system of behaviour (see pages 30–31). The remaining crew butchered nearly 300 Maori in revenge.

Several other expeditions followed, and by the end of the 18th century sealers and whalers were arriving on New Zealand's shores.

33

Abel Tasman (left) was the first European to sight New Zealand but Cook (right) was the first to land. Below: Cook's ships in Nootka Sound, Vancouver Island, British Columbia, on his third and final return from New Zealand

Hard on the heels of the explorers came the European traders, intent on profiting from natural resources such as flax, timber, seal skins and whale oil in this rich land. By the beginning of the 19th century, missionaries had also begun to settle in New Zealand.

❏ Cook introduced potatoes to New Zealand, and Maori quickly learned to cultivate them: They were easier to grow than kumara and gave bigger yields. Ironically, the time saved by growing potatoes also meant there was more time to fighting. Pigs (likewise introduced by Cook) were also reared for barter. Nails, blankets, axes and of course muskets were trading priorities for the Maori. Woodcarvings and shrunken human heads were much in demand by trading *Pakeha* (the Maori term for Europeans). ❏

SEALERS AND WHALERS From the 1790s onwards ships started landing shore parties around the coast of the South Island to hunt for fur seals. Often these men were marooned for months (sometimes years) in the harshest of conditions, but the seals were easy to kill and they could collect thousands of skins in a season. Within 30 years the seal population had been decimated and the trade was no longer profitable.

By the beginning of 1800s, whaling ships, hunting sperm whale offshore, were calling in at the Bay of Islands for provisions. In the 1820s this led to the establishment of the first permanent European settlement in the country, at Kororareka (Russell). At this time shore-based whaling stations were also being established, most of them in the South Island.

FLAX AND TIMBER New Zealand flax was much in demand for making ropes and cordage, and the flax fibre prepared by Maori was of good quality and attracted a high price. These traditional methods (which involved scraping away the fleshy part with a mussel shell) were unable to keep pace with demand, however, and mass production proved impractical. The trade lasted into the 20th century and was to prove far-reaching in its effects: It was largely through bartering flax for muskets that Maori first acquired firearms. Europeans had already introduced diseases (such as gonorrhoea, measles and smallpox) to which Maori had no resistance and which had a

A whaling ship, the Samuel Enderby, *departing for Auckland*

New Zealand's first missionary, the Reverend Samuel Marsden, lands at the Bay of Islands

devastating effect on the population. But worse was to come. The introduction of the musket added a lethal dimension to traditional inter-tribal warfare.

A longer-lived trade was provided by New Zealand's forests, which over more than a century of intensive exploitation yielded vast quantities of high-quality timber (see pages 76–77).

THE MISSIONARIES Although there were never large numbers of missionaries in New Zealand at any one time, their influence was considerable—not necessarily in converting the Maori, but in protecting them from the worst excesses of unlawful adventurers and teaching them new skills. They also supported the introduction of British jurisdiction and, eventually, sovereignty.

The first Anglican mission station was established in 1814 by the Reverend Samuel Marsden in the Bay of Islands, although it was well over a decade before any converts were made. Wesleyan and Roman Catholic missionaries soon followed. The first printing press was set up by William Colenso, and the Bible, prayer books and hymns were translated into

Maori. The missionaries succeeded in discouraging polygamy and cannibalism, but in changing Maori society they destroyed much that was of value in the traditional culture.

❑ In 1820, the Ngapuhi chief Hongi Hika sailed to England to help scholars compile a Maori dictionary. While there, he was presented to King George IV and showered with gifts, which he exchanged in Sydney on the return journey for 300 muskets. Once home, he embarked on a series of devastating campaigns against his old enemies in the Thames area and then the Waikato. The other tribes soon realized that they too must have muskets, and a series of battles left some 60,000 dead. By 1830 the fighting had died down and most tribes were once more at peace with each other. ❑

Despite the rich resources of New Zealand, the British Crown was reluctant to take it on as a colony. However, with the signing of the Treaty of Waitangi in 1840, Britain assumed sovereignty over the land. This turning point is still a source of contention today.

TOWARDS ANNEXATION The increasing lawlessness of many settlers led to calls for the imposition of law and order, and in 1823 the jurisdiction of the New South Wales courts was extended to New Zealand—though, given the difficulty of trying cases even in Sydney, this was largely a meaningless gesture. In 1833 the British government appointed James Busby as the first British Resident, but he had limited legal powers and no military backup; Maori dubbed him 'the man-o'-war without guns'.

Maori chiefs sign the Treaty of Waitangi, which they understood as a pact with Queen Victoria

❑ On 5 February 1840, over 400 Maori gathered on the lawns of Busby's house (now the Treaty House) in the Bay of Islands to hear the Treaty of Waitangi read out. Many powerful chiefs opposed it, and after some changes had been made, Maori withdrew to debate the issues. The next day they returned and, despite initial reluctance, 45 Maori chiefs eventually signed. Over the following months the treaty was carried throughout the land and signed by over 500 Maori chiefs. ❑

> ❏ French navy ships sometimes visited New Zealand to support the Roman Catholic missionaries. Anti-French fears were increased by a bizarre incident in 1837, when the self-styled Baron Charles Philip Hippolytus de Thierry proclaimed himself the Sovereign Chief of New Zealand and raised his own flag on land he had bought at Hokianga. The threat soon faded, however, when he ran out of money. ❏

Captain Hobson oversaw the transfer of sovereignty to the British

During this period immigration (particularly from New South Wales) was increasing, and speculators were 'buying' vast tracts of land in dubious deals with Maori; the threat from the French and the initiation of mass settlement schemes increased the call for action. Busby was replaced by Captain William Hobson, who arrived in the Bay of Islands on 29 January 1840 with orders to negotiate with Maori for the transfer of sovereignty to the British Crown.

THE TREATY OF WAITANGI Hobson and his staff quickly drafted an agreement which they hoped would protect the rights of both Maori and the settlers. The result was the Treaty of Waitangi, which was signed on 6 February 1840. Although this day has been celebrated ever since as the birth date of the nation, in fact the treaty was little more than a legal fraud. The ramifications of the errors contained in this document are still being felt in New Zealand today.

The text of the treaty was in English with a rough translation into Maori (signed by most of the chiefs), with considerable differences between the two. Essentially it assigned sovereignty (of which the Maori had no concept and which therefore could not be translated) over the country to the British Crown. In exchange, Maori would receive protection, full rights as British subjects and the full possession of their lands. The treaty also established a policy on land sales, granting the Crown exclusive rights to buy land and sell it on to settlers. This attempt at even-handedness went badly wrong as the government had only meagre resources at its disposal, and the agreement was in any case rarely upheld by land-hungry settlers.

LAND TENURE To Maori, land was *Papa*, the Earth Mother, and was closely tied in to their spiritual well-being. Land was held by the *hapū* or *iwi* rather than any one individual, and the concept of 'selling' territory was completely unknown (it could only be taken by conquest). It is clear that early land deals were considered by Maori more as leases. As settlers started arriving in large numbers they wanted more and more land, but Maori were becoming increasingly reluctant to sell. And the fact that land was soon changing hands at 20 times the price paid to the Maori naturally caused huge resentment.

Even before the Treaty of Waitangi had been signed, ships were setting sail from England with the first colonists destined for a series of 'planned communities' in New Zealand. These idealistic schemes brought a flood of new immigrants to the country.

Wakefield was a visionary who wanted planned communities

THE NEW ZEALAND COMPANY

The first of these schemes was organized by Edward Gibbon Wakefield, who in 1838 set up the New Zealand Company, with the aim of re-creating genteel farming communities in which workers knew their place and landowners were gentlemen of status and privilege. The plan was to buy up land cheaply from Maori and sell it on to capitalist investors, using the profits to pay the fares of the workers who would tend the newly established farms.

As stories grew of the British government's intention to conclude a treaty with the Maori, the New Zealand Company dispatched the *Tory* and its crew to buy land before the Crown acquired the sole rights to do so. One of their principal targets was Wellington, which was tipped to become the capital. But long before the *Tory* had reached New Zealand, Wakefield was already 'selling' land, recruiting settlers and sending off the first passenger ships.

DECLINE AND FALL

Between 1839 and 1843, the New Zealand Company sent 57 ships with over 18,000 immigrants from England. Settlements were established at Wellington, Nelson, Wanganui and New Plymouth, but many were beset by problems such as poor land, absentee landlords and disputes with Maori over ownership. Speculation eventually led to the collapse of the company in 1850; its remaining land was taken over by the government.

Although Wakefield's schemes did not work out exactly as planned (and he had not reckoned with the workers' desire to move out of the communities and farm their own plots), they did at least ensure a more orderly pattern of settlement than had been achieved earlier in Australia and Canada.

> ❏ Inspired by Wakefield's example (and in some cases supported by the New Zealand Company), other groups also tried to establish 'ideal communities'. Thus the Free Church of Scotland founded Dunedin in 1848, and the Canterbury Association established the Anglican community of Christchurch in 1850. ❏

Outwardly peaceful at the beginning of the 1840s, New Zealand was soon in the throes of a civil war (known variously as the Land Wars, the Maori Wars, or the New Zealand Wars—now the accepted term) that lasted for over two decades and led to over 1,000 deaths on each side.

❏ The injustices of land sales led directly to the formation of the Maori King Movement in 1858. Traditionally, Maori owed their allegiance to their *hapū* or *iwi*, but they hoped that by uniting under a paramount chief they would be able to protect their lands. Several North Island tribes proclaimed Te Wherowhero as their first king, Potatau I, but the movement was defeated in 1864. The Maori queen is still an important figure, however. ❏

TROUBLE AHEAD Following the signing of the Treaty of Waitangi in 1840, it was not long before the weakness of the agreement and its ineffective enforcement led to inevitable clashes over land.

The fighting broke out in the Wairau Valley near Blenheim in 1843, when settlers from the New Zealand Company started surveying land still under dispute with the Lands Commissioner. The chiefs, Te Ruaparaha and Te Rangihaeata, burned the survey huts and then repelled an armed party sent after them, killing 22 men.

BLOODY CONFLICTS Full-scale war broke out in June 1860, when the government tried to support a fraudulent land purchase in the Waitara area. The British troops were roundly defeated by the Te Ati Awa tribe at Puketakauere, a battle that marked the start of 21 years of conflict—and which confirmed to Maori that the government could not be trusted in land disputes.

War quickly spread across the central North Island. The outcome would have been far worse for the government but for the fact that many tribes joined the government forces in order to settle old scores. Troops were brought from Sydney, and although Maori fought ferociously and won many battles, they were eventually defeated by the force of artillery ranged against them.

Hostilities ceased in 1872, yet skirmishes continued until the surrender of the Maori king in 1881. To punish the rebel tribes, the government confiscated huge areas of land, disregarding the Treaty of Waitangi.

Rebel leader Hone Heke cuts down the British flagstaff at Kororareka (Russell)

At the end of the 19th century New Zealand was in the depths of recession, but as the economy improved, important social reforms were introduced, and it became the first country in the world to enfranchise women and introduce an old-age pension.

HARD TIMES During the 1860s, gold rushes brought prosperity to New Zealand (particularly in the South Island), but by the 1880s the gold rush was over, wool prices were low and the country was gripped by depression. Despite the introduction in 1882 of refrigerated shipping, which allowed meat and butter to be exported for the first time, farmers suffered. Unemployment was on the increase and factory conditions were appalling, with ruthless exploitation of child labour.

REFORMS In 1890, the Liberal Party was voted into power under the leadership of John Ballance, with a new mandate to improve living conditions. Large land-holdings were bought by the government and broken up into smaller farms in order to help more families to acquire land. Farmers were also lent money at low interest rates, and with a rise in overseas prices for farm products small family farms became profitable. Country towns began to flourish, and

as new communities grew, libraries and schools were built (free compulsory education had already been introduced in 1877). New laws were passed regulating conditions in factories, and in 1894 the world's first compulsory arbitration system for industrial disputes was introduced.

VOTES FOR WOMEN Alcohol was strong, cheap and widely available in the late 19th century, when it was said there were only two causes of death in New Zealand—alcohol poisoning and drowning as a result of riding home drunk from the pub. In 1885 the Women's Christian Temperance Union was formed; having stopped the sale of alcohol to children, its members went on to campaign for votes for women. Petitions were organized and politicians lobbied, and in 1893 New Zealand became the first country in the world to allow women to vote.

Women got the vote in New Zealand in 1893—a world first

In Christchurch in 1907, Dr. Truby King and his wife formed the Plunket Society, with the principal aim of training women in proper childcare. Although the infant mortality rate in New Zealand was half as high (75 per thousand births) as it was in Britain, it was still a matter of concern in a young nation with a small population. Plunket nurses established a unique support network, which still exists in New Zealand today: You will see signs to the 'Plunket Rooms' in almost every town in the country.

and much of what was left was too remote or too poor to farm. Life was hard and diseases introduced by immigrants took a heavy toll. The population fell from about 100,000 at the time of Cook's first visit in 1769, to an estimated 42,000 in the 1896 census, although by 1901 it had risen again to just over 45,000.

Clearing the forested land for farming was arduous work (below)

PENSIONS AND HEALTH CARE John Ballance was succeeded as leader of the Liberals by 'King Dick' Seddon, a popular politician whose concern for the lot of the poor led him in 1898 to introduce the world's first old-age pension for men (women's pensions followed in 1911). Other pioneering measures followed and New Zealand gained a reputation as an important innovator of social reforms.

TURN OF THE CENTURY At the turn of the century conditions improved greatly for *pakeha* (whites). The small family farm (averaging 40ha/ 100 acres) became the most common business. At the same time there was a drift to the North Island (whose population exceeded that of the South Island from 1896), and into the towns.

The Maori population, meanwhile, was in decline. Most families lived apart from *pakeha* in their own villages, but most of their land had either been sold or illegally 'confiscated' after the New Zealand Wars,

Although it was not to gain full independence until 1947, in the first half of the 20th century New Zealand gradually gained a sense of nationhood and of its own identity.

FIRST STEPS New Zealand was granted nominal self-government in 1852, but the British Crown still influenced legislation; it was not until the 1890s that the country gained proper control of its affairs (it would be another 50 years before full independence was achieved). In 1907, New Zealand was promoted from the rank of Colony to that of Dominion within the British Empire.

BIRTH OF A NATION In the 19th century the country was divided into six self-governing provinces (later expanded to ten), and people thought of themselves as Wellingtonians or Aucklanders rather than New Zealanders. The abolition of the provinces in 1876 broke down these barriers to some extent, but it was largely the introduction of telephones, the telegraph and roads and railways at the turn of the 20th

century that changed people's perception of New Zealand. From being a country of isolated coastal settlements it was now becoming a nation.

The first stirrings of nationhood came during the Boer War (1899–1902), when New Zealanders fought alongside British, Australian and Canadian troops. Used to long hours of riding and rough conditions, the New Zealanders made brilliant scouts and soon earned a reputation as 'the best soldiers in South Africa'.

WORLD WAR I New Zealanders gained a new sense of identity and pride during World War I, when some 100,000 troops joined the Australia-New Zealand Army Corps (ANZAC) in Europe and the Middle East. Their finest hour (and greatest losses) came during the Battle of Gallipoli in April 1915, when 2,700 New Zealand troops were killed and

42

❏ After World War I, over 90 per cent of New Zealand's exports came from agriculture, but a dramatic drop in world prices for wool, meat and butter in the early 1920s hit farmers hard. The solution seemed to lie in increased production, and during this period New Zealand became one of the first countries in the world to apply scientific principles to farming, introducing top dressing for pasture and selective breeding of dairy herds. By the end of the 1920s the average cow was producing 72 per cent more butterfat than it would have done at the beginning of the century. ❏

4,700 wounded during an ill-fated but heroic attempt to capture the Gallipoli Peninsula. By the end of the war 16,317 had lost their lives and 41,262 more returned home wounded. The casualties were the highest per capita of any Allied country.

Troops landing at Anzac Cove in 1915 during the ill-fated Gallipoli campaign

Labour Prime Minister 'Micky' Savage helped improve the lives of ordinary people

INTER-WAR YEARS Despite increased agricultural production in the 1920s, the economy foundered and the Great Depression of the 1930s had a profound effect. Unemployment rose and work initiatives were introduced under which thousands of hectares of pine forest were planted and many roads were built. In 1935, the new Labour Party swept to victory on a pledge of providing work, houses, schools and hospitals; as the world economy improved, bigger public projects (including hydroelectric schemes) were also funded. In 1938, Prime Minister Michael Savage announced a new comprehensive health care and social security system for those unable to work—another world first for New Zealand.

WORLD WAR II At the outbreak of war in 1939, New Zealand readily joined the Allies again. New Zealanders, including some 17,000 Maori (many in the famous Maori Battalion) fought with distinction in the Pacific, Crete, Italy and North Africa. Of the 200,000 who fought, 11,600 died and a further 15,700 were wounded.

Heavily dependent on agricultural exports, New Zealand has had to learn some painful economic lessons in recent decades. The prosperity it enjoyed after World War II gave way in the 1970s to severe recession. Despite drastic measures, this only deepened in the 1980s. There are, however, signs of recovery, with the tourist industry as a major contributor.

POST-WAR PROSPERITY After World War II the economy prospered, with prices for meat, wool and butter at a premium, and New Zealand enjoyed one of the highest standards of living in the world. Apart from a brief period (1957–60) when Labour was in power, post-war politics between 1949 and 1972 were dominated by the National Party. One of their first actions (1950) was to abolish the Legislative Council, Parliament's upper house, and although they promised to replace it with an elected body, this never happened.

PROTEST AND SURVIVAL Largely isolated and culturally stagnant in the 1950s, New Zealand was shaken out of its complacency in the following decade by the arrival of jet travel and television. The anti-war movement, calling for the withdrawal of New Zealand troops from Vietnam (sent there in 1965) gathered strength. The country's first big environmental protest took place in the 1960s, prompted by a controversial plan to raise the level of Lake Manapouri in order to produce inexpensive hydroelectric power for the aluminium smelter at Bluff. In 1972 a nationalistic Labour government was elected under Norman Kirk. It gained instant popularity by withdrawing troops from Vietnam, but the new mood of optimism was not to last.

RECESSION Until the 1970s, Britain had been New Zealand's main export market (taking some 90 per cent of all produce), but when it joined the

European Economic Community (EEC) in 1973, this market was effectively closed off. Combined with a steep rise in oil prices, this had a devastating effect on the economy. A decade of recession followed and unemployment, violent crime, bad

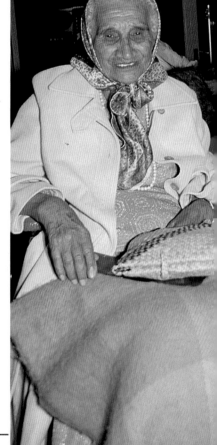

Dame Whina Cooper was an inspirational Maori leader

*Prime Minister David Lange oversaw
extensive reforms in the 1980s*

housing and other social
problems resurfaced.

This fragmentation of society
led to demands for change, and
to the growth of movements for
the rights of Maori, women and
gays. In 1975, Dame Whina Cooper
(later affectionately dubbed 'the
mother of the nation') led the Maori
Land March from Northland to the
capital in order to call attention to the
injustices of the loss of ancestral
lands, which resulted in the setting
up of the Waitangi Tribunal.

Also in 1975, Labour was ousted
by the National Party, led by the
abrasive Robert Muldoon. Strict
measures were imposed on immigration, imports and the dollar, but
by the end of the decade inflation
was running at 17 per cent, and the
government subsidized farm prices
heavily. With registered unemployment reaching 66,534 by 1984,
Muldoon was defeated in a snap election by a revitalized Labour Party,
under the leadership of David Lange.

THE LANGE YEARS New Zealand's
youngest 20th-century Prime
Minister David Lange initiated
a wide-reaching agenda of economic
reforms designed to put the country
back on its feet. These included
floating the New Zealand dollar,
deregulating the economy,
reducing tariffs, selling nationalized
industries and removing farm
subsidies at a stroke. This painful
medicine caused numerous business
failures and, combined with the
stock market crash of 1987, sent the
country's economy into a tailspin.

In August 1989,
David Lange unexpect-
edly resigned and Labour lost
power once more to the National
Party, led by Jim Bolger.

During the 1980s, New Zealand
was also re-orientating itself towards
the Pacific community, in particular
Australia. A free trade agreement had
been reached in 1965, but in 1983 this
was replaced with the more far-reaching Closer Economic Relations Trade
Agreement (CER). From 1 July 1990
this allowed unrestricted trade
between the two countries.

Jenny Shipley became New Zealand's
first woman Prime Minister in 1997
after a leadership coup in the National
Party. The following two General
Election was won by the Labour party,
led by Helen Clark—the country's first
elected woman Prime Minister. New
Zealand's Head of State, Governor-
General, Prime Minister, Chief Justice
and Attorney-General are all women—
perhaps appropriate in the first country
to give women the vote.

45

The office blocks of Auckland's business area cheek by jowl with Westhaven marina

Start of a yacht race by the Auckland Harbour Bridge with the cone of Rangitoto in the background

AUCKLAND The gateway to New Zealand for most international visitors, Auckland is the country's largest and most cosmopolitan city, with a plethora of prestigious museums and galleries, high-class restaurants and wine bars, excellent shops and numerous other attractions. Around a third of the country's population (just over a million people) live, work and play here. Aucklanders enjoy a lifestyle undeniably appealing to residents in a city that combines sophisticated culture with proximity to sheltered harbours and islands, countless surf or swimming beaches and outlying forests and parklands, but visitors may well find elsewhere the New Zealand that they are looking for.

Auckland sprawls across a narrow volcanic isthmus facing two huge natural harbours, **Waitemata Harbour** to the east (which opens out into the Hauraki Gulf) and **Manukau Harbour** to the west. The isthmus was formed as a result of the eruption of over 50 volcanoes; the oldest dates back 50,000 years, and the youngest erupted from the sea a mere 750 years ago.

The first Polynesians are said to have settled in the Hauraki Gulf after arriving in the canoe *Tainui* some 600 years ago. As other tribes descended on this fertile area they built numerous strongholds on the volcanic cones. By the 18th century nearly all of them were topped by *pā* (village) sites, but by the mid-19th century inter-tribal warfare and epidemics of introduced diseases had wiped out most of the Maori population.

After the signing of the Treaty of Waitangi in 1840, Governor Hobson moved the capital of New Zealand south from Kororareka (Russell) to Auckland, partly because of the advantages offered by its vast harbours and fertile soil. That year, the British bought 1,200ha (2,965 acres) of land from the Ngati Whatua tribe for a collection of blankets, clothes, pots, tobacco and pipes, plus a small cash sum; on 18 September 1840 the Union Jack was run up the flagpole and the settlement was proclaimed the capital. Hobson named the city after his former commander, Lord Auckland, then Viceroy of India. Auckland remained the capital until 1865, when the seat of government was moved further south again to the New Zealand Company settlement at Wellington.

Today Auckland's port handles much of the country's import and export trade and the city is one of its fastest-growing urban areas, with a highly cosmopolitan population that includes not only some 150,000 Pacific Islanders, but also a sizeable Asian community.

ORIENTATION The main artery of downtown Auckland is **Queen Street**, which runs south from **Queen Elizabeth Square**. In and around Queen Street you will find many of the major shops, hotels, airline offices, cinemas and other facilities. Flanking Queen Elizabeth Square are **Customs Street** and **Quay Street**, both parallel to the waterfront.

Viaduct Harbour is a lively area, with restaurants overlooking a constant procession of ferries and other craft; it is also home to the excellent **National Maritime Museum**. Arching across the harbour to the west is the Harbour Bridge, the main road link with the North Shore and the motorway up to Whangarei and Northland. About halfway up Queen Street lies Aotea Square, the site of the

Auckland

PACIFIC CAPITAL
In the 1950s Auckland began to attract thousands of Polynesian islanders, drawn by opportunities for work and education. There are now some 100,000 Samoans in New Zealand, with more people from the Cook Islands and Niue resident in the country than in their homelands. With good reason, Auckland has styled itself 'the hub of the Pacific'.

Aotea Centre (with convention and theatre facilities), the main **Auckland Visitor Centre** close by and the city's town hall (built in 1911 and restored in 1997). One block to the east is **Auckland Art Gallery**, backing on to **Albert Park** and the main **Auckland University** campus.

To the east of the central downtown district are the undulating grounds of the **Auckland Domain**, dominated by the **Auckland Museum**. Beyond are the trendy suburbs of **Parnell** and **Remuera**, spreading back down to the waterfront, which has attractions such as **Kelly Tarlton's Antarctic Encounter and Underwater World** and the popular beach at Mission Bay.

In 1997, Auckland's skyline gained a dramatic addition in the **Sky Tower**, part of the Sky City casino, hotel and shopping complex. The 328m (1,076ft)-high building has

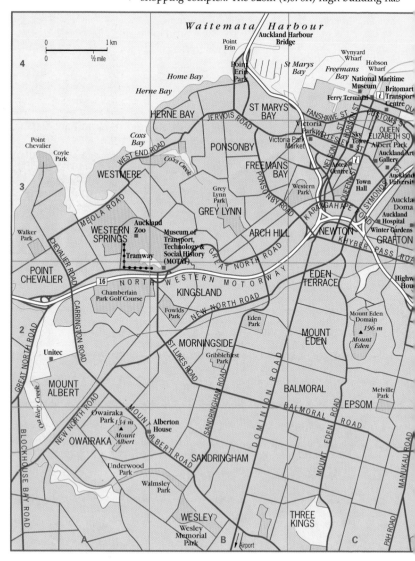

observation decks, and a revolving bar and restaurant with a 360-degree panorama of the city.

Auckland is said to have more boats per person than any other city in the world, and on any weekend a fleet of yachts, speedboats, dinghies, cruisers and catamarans fans out from the marinas, bound for the **islands and beaches** of the **Hauraki Gulf** and elsewhere. Numerous public ferries also ply the harbour waters, and there are said to be over a hundred mainland beaches within an hour's drive of the main city.

Auckland's attractions are widely spread out across the city; there is a reasonable bus network, including the frequent circular Link bus route and tourist buses that shuttle around the various sightseeing spots. But, despite the traffic, you may be tempted to rent a car.

Auckland's Town Hall

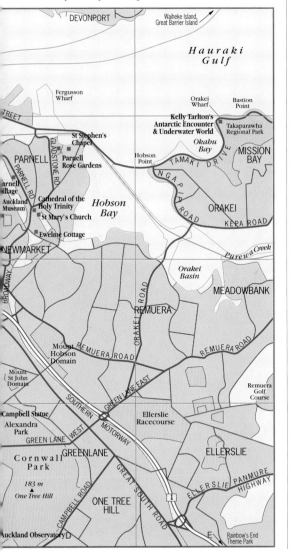

Auckland

50

HARBOUR SAILING

Every visitor to the 'City of Sails' should go on the harbour at least once. Fullers Harbour Cruise does a circuit at 10:30 and 1:30 (tel: 09 367 9111; www.fullers.co.nz); the Pride of Auckland Company (tel: 09 373 4557; www.prideofauck land.com) has a fleet of four monohulls and cata-marans that operate regu-lar 'Experience Sailing' trips as well as various other options, including lunch or dinner cruises (daily, according to demand). The square-rigged brigantine *Søren Larsen* (tel: 09 411 8755; www.sorenlarsen.co.nz) operates day-trips during the summer. Confident sailors can rent a sailing boat from Rangitoto Sailing (tel: 09 358 2324; www.sailingnz.co.nz) at Okahu Bay; the club also offers 14-hour learn-to-sail courses. Sea kayaking (Ferg's Kayaks, tel: 09 529 2230; www.fergskayaks.co.nz) is highly recommended.

MAORI SONG AND DANCE

Some of the best introduc-tions to Maori culture are the regular shows held at the Auckland Museum. Preceded by a guided tour of the Maori exhibits, the half-hour shows (daily 11AM and 1:30PM, plus 2:30 Jan–Mar *Admission: moderate*) take place in front of the Hotunui meet-ing house, with numerous *haka* (ceremonial war dances) with plenty of explanations and audience participation. The only tour company owned and operated by Maori within the Auckland region is Maori Heritage Tours (tel: 09 278 0932), which runs a range of interesting city and coun-try tours from a Maori perspective, including the 'twilight Maori experience' with a *hangi* and cultural show on a *marae*.

►► Auckland Art Gallery   48C3

Corner Wellesley and Kitchener streets, tel: 09 307 7700; www.aucklandartgallery.govt.nz
Open: daily 10–5. Admission: free

Opened in 1888, this was New Zealand's first permanent art gallery, and it now houses one of the country's most significant collections of national and international art. The international collection spans European art (from the 13th century to Impressionism and after), Japanese prints and contemporary American works, while the national collection has some of the earliest *pakeha* paintings in New Zealand (dating from Cook's voyages), and works by C. F. Goldie, Gottfried Lindauer, Frances Hodgkins and other celebrated New Zealand artists. Exhibitions in the Heritage Gallery change frequently; the ground-floor (free) exhibits are from the permanent collection; the first floor (a pay area) has touring exhibitions.

Across the road from the main building, the New Gallery extension *(Admission: inexpensive)* is housed inside the former central Auckland telephone exchange building. This interesting project has been designed as a 'walk through' space linking Wellesley Street and Khartoum Place, with shops and cafés alongside the exhibition areas. The New Gallery focuses on contempo-rary New Zealand and international art and includes a gallery devoted to Colin McCahon, regarded by many as the country's foremost 20th-century artist.

►►► Auckland Domain and Museum   49D3

Auckland's biggest park, between the heart of the city and the eastern suburbs, is 80ha (198 acres) of sports fields, landscaped gardens and wooded areas.

Crowning the central hilltop is the **Auckland Museum►►** (tel: 09 309 0443; www.akmuseum.org.nz. *Open* daily 10–5. *Admission: donation)*, housing extensive displays of Maori arts and culture, including the magnif-icent carved meeting house *Hotunui* (1878), elaborate gateways and storehouses and the great war canoe *Te Toki a Tapiri* ('Tapiri's battle-axe'). Built in about 1836, this was the last of the great Maori war canoes, capable of carrying up to 100 warriors. There are also interesting displays on Pacific canoes and the decorative arts of Asia, an extensive natural history section and a Weird and Wonderful children's discovery area. The upper-floor galleries devoted to New Zealand's military history include a Spitfire and Zero gallery (with one of the few surviving Japanese Zero planes), an armoury display and presentations on New Zealanders at war.

The excellent range of items in the ground-floor shop includes handcrafted jade, glass, ceramics and bone, as well as *paua* shell jewellery, knitwear and books.

Near to the museum, the **Winter Gardens►** *(Open* daily 10–4. *Admission: free)* are housed in a glass conservatory filled with tropical and subtropical plants and ferns.

►►► Auckland Zoo   48A3

Western Springs, tel: 09 360 3800; www.aucklandzoo.co.nz
Open: daily 9:30–5:30 (last admission 4:15). Admission: moderate

Established in 1922, the excellent Auckland Zoo houses around 900 bird and animal species, ranging from Asian elephants to tuatara and other unique New Zealand fauna. Like all the best modern zoos, it has moved away from the 'animals in cages' formula to embrace a much wider perspective on the environment and to provide more naturalistic enclosures for the animals.

Highlights at the zoo complex include a meerkat enclosure where you can crawl through underground tunnels and pop up for a ground-level view of these enchanting creatures, an elephant enclosure, the Tui farm (hands-on farm activities for children) and the Glade New Zealand Aviary.

The zoo's latest project is the vast McDonald's Rainforest, with five species of primate swinging free in the forest trees, and an adventure pathway including a platform in the tree canopy.

Future projects include Sealion Shores, a replication of New Zealand's coastal environment, where an abundance of native wildlife is found within the seashore habitat. A coastal trek, both above and below the water, will provide intimate views of the sea lions.

The zoo is served by bus 045 or Explorer satellite bus (see page 55) and is linked by tramway and vintage bus to nearby MOTAT (see page 53).

Auckland Art Gallery (below), where Lindauer's Maori portraits chronicle the meeting of two cultures

Some scenes from the film The Piano *(1993) were shot inside Ewelme Cottage*

MARKET DAYS
One of the best markets in the city is the Victoria Park Market (Victoria Street West; www.victoria-park-market.co.nz. *Open* daily 9–6), housed in a rambling old building with shops, cafés and stalls on several levels. On weekends there are outdoor performances and live music. In the heart of Auckland's Polynesian community, the Otara Market (Newbury Street, Otara. *Open* Sat 6AM–noon) has a lively atmosphere, with stalls selling food, clothing, arts and crafts, and plenty more besides.

►► **Historic Houses**   *48C2, 48B1, 49D3*
Open: Wed–Sun 10:30–noon, 1–4:30.
Admission: inexpensive
Auckland is not as well endowed with historic buildings as some other cities, but it does have several houses under the protection of the Historic Places Trust. One of the finest of these houses is **Highwic**►► (40 Gillies Avenue, Epsom, tel: 09 524 5729) a 'colonial gentleman's residence' in the timber Gothic style, built in 1862 by Alfred Buckland, a wealthy landowner and racing enthusiast.

Another impressive private mansion is **Alberton**►► (100 Mt. Albert Road, tel: 09 846 7367), which was built in 1863 and has exotic Indian-style verandas and towers. The more homely **Ewelme Cottage**►► (14 Ayr Street, Parnell, tel 09 379 0202. *Open* Fri–Sun 10:30–noon, 1–4:30) is a fascinating cottage, built in kauri wood, that remained in the same family for 105 years and still contains many of their furnishings and personal effects.

►►► **Kelly Tarlton's Antarctic Encounter and Underwater World**   *49E3*
23 Tamaki Drive, tel: 09 528 0603; www.kellytarltons.co.nz
Open: Dec–Feb 9–8; Mar–Nov 9–7, last admission one hour before closing. Admission: expensive
Built inside a series of underground storm-water storage tanks near Orakei Wharf to the east of the main city, Underwater World was developed by the diver and wreck expert Kelly Tarlton. Its main attraction is a vast aquarium with a moving walkway inside an acrylic tunnel, giving a fish-eye view of stingrays and reef fish, moray eels and several species of shark.

Linked to it is Antarctic Encounter. This starts with a replica—complete with sounds and smells—of the hut Scott used on his ill-fated expedition to the South Pole in 1912. A heated snow cat then carries visitors through a simulated snowstorm to an Antarctic landscape, complete with a breeding colony of king penguins.

Kelly Tarlton's Antarctic Encounter and Underwater World is 6km (3.5 miles) from central Auckland, and several buses run regularly from downtown.

►► Mount Eden 48C2

Auckland's highest volcanic cone (196m/643ft), Mount Eden is great for a panoramic view of the city and its isthmus and harbour, even though Sky Tower is 130m (427ft) higher. Mount Eden also has extensive earthworks and terracing that once protected this fortified site. The entrance is on Mount Eden Road, 15 minutes' drive from downtown (or take bus 274 or 275 from Britomart Transport Centre or the Explorer satellite bus).

► Museum of Transport, Technology and Social History (MOTAT) 48B2

Western Springs, Great North Road, tel: 09 846 0199; www.motat.org.nz. Open: daily 10–4:30. Admission: moderate
Close to Auckland Zoo, MOTAT contains a vast collection of vintage machinery and equipment, ranging from trucks, trains and trams to early computers, telephones, printing presses and much more. Of particular interest are the remains of the plane flown by Richard Pearse, the pioneering South Island aviator (see page 216).

The main site, MOTAT 1, is linked to MOTAT 2 (1km/0.5 mile away) by a tramway to near the Auckland Zoo entrance, where it connects with a vintage bus. MOTAT 2 houses the aviation collection, with a fascinating range of exhibits that includes the last Solent Mark IV flying boat left in the world, and a working steam railway. MOTAT 1 is ten minutes' drive from downtown (bus 045 from Britomart Transport Centre or Explorer bus, see page 55).

URBAN RAP JUMPING
For an urban thrill, try the latest in downtown adventure tourism—abseiling down Auckland's Mercure Hotel with Ground Rush (tel: 09 571 0521; www.groundrush.co.nz). No previous experience necessary!

Earthworks in Mount Eden's crater above the city

The marina at the National Maritime Museum

THRILLS AND SPILLS
A big attraction for children in the Auckland area is the Rainbow's End theme park, with its roller-coaster, flume rides, a pirate ship and numerous other rides and shows. Rainbow's End (tel: 09 262 2030; www.rainbowsend.co.nz. *Open* daily 10–5. *Admission: expensive*) is near the Manukau exit on the southern motorway, 15 minutes from the heart of Auckland.

▶▶▶ New Zealand National Maritime Museum, Hobson Wharf 48C4

Corner Quay and Hobson streets, tel: 09 373 0800; www.nzmaritime.org
Open: daily, summer 9–6; winter 9–5. Admission: moderate
This excellent museum, right in the heart of the city on the harbour front, is a must see for every visitor to Auckland. It's a dynamic and imaginative celebration of New Zealand's maritime heritage and the voyaging traditions and craft of the Pacific. You can easily spend several hours here watching craftsmen at work, admiring the many boats, taking a ride on a steam launch, listening to old mariners' tales in an oral history section, or exploring the interior of an immigrant ship. As well as a dockside restaurant, there is a nautical emporium with a good range of gifts.

Based around a marina, the museum includes displays on New Zealand yachting, whaling, Polynesian voyagers, seaports and much more. In the marina itself is a water-borne collection of Pacific Island canoes, veteran power and sail craft, and a massive 1926 steam floating crane. Grouped around the marina are workshops for boat-builders, sailmakers, riggers and wood-turners.

Outside the museum stands *KZ1*, the contender for the 1988 America's Cup. You can take harbour cruises on board the scow *Ted Ashby* or the steamboat SS *Puke* (most days. *Admission: moderate*).

▶ One Tree Hill   49D1
Manukau Road
Nearly all the extinct volcanic cones in the area surrounding Auckland were used by Maori as fortified hill settlements, but One Tree Hill was one of the biggest and most extensive, capable of sheltering up to 4,000 warriors. The crater was surrounded by a number of smaller 'satellite' *pā* (fortified hilltop village) sites, with the remains of the ditches and ramparts still visible today.

The hill is now sadly misnamed, since its summit tree had become dangerous following a chainsaw attack in 1994, and was felled in 2000.

▶▶ Parnell   49D3
On the east side of the Domain from the downtown area, Parnell is one of Auckland's oldest inner-city suburbs. At the beginning of the 20th century it was one of the most desirable addresses in Auckland, but then fell into decline until it was redeveloped in the 1960s and 1970s, with the accent on restoration of the many old family houses and shops in the area. Today it is a hive of activity, with dozens of trendy boutiques, restaurants, wine bars, art and craft galleries and a number of curio shops.

The main thoroughfare is **Parnell Road**, with restaurants and shops lining the hill on both sides of the street. Halfway down on the west side is **Parnell Village**, with wooden bridges and old brick pavements linking a series of little shopping enclaves in and around attractively restored Victorian houses.

Between the months of November and March, it is worth wandering down to the spectacular **Parnell Rose Gardens▶** (Gladstone Road. *Open* daylight hours. *Admission: free*), where thousands of roses bloom. Just across from the rose gardens is **St. Stephen's Chapel▶** (Judge Street. Interior viewable only when open for worship, 9AM most Sundays), in a lovely setting overlooking the harbour. Completed in 1857, this tiny wooden chapel is one of the best examples in the city of a Selwyn church, built in a Gothic style that evolved under Bishop Selwyn (1809–1878), characterized by steep-pitched shingle roofs, external timber buttresses and leaded windows.

At the top of Parnell Road is the **Cathedral of the Holy Trinity** (tel: 09 303 9500; www.holy-trinity.org.nz. *Open* Mon–Sat 10–4, Sun 1–5), which has been the subject of considerable controversy because of the use of virgin kauri wood (now extremely rare) in its construction. Just behind the cathedral is the lovely **Saint Mary's Church▶** (*Open* as above), another wooden church with some fine stained glass. The church was built in 1888, and was moved to this site in 1982.

BUSSING IT
Stagecoach Auckland operates routes to most major attractions, and a one-day Busabout pass gives unlimited travel from 9AM weekdays and any time at weekends (tel Rideline: 09 366 6400; www.rideline.co.nz). The Link bus circles the city every 10–20 minutes. More expensive is the United Airlines Explorer Bus, which does a circuit of all the major attractions, allowing you to hop on and off (departures on the hour May–Sep 10–4, and on the half hour Oct–Apr, from the Ferry Building, tel: 0800 439 756; www.explorerbus.co.nz). At Auckland Museum it connects with an hourly satellite bus (Oct–Apr 10:30–3:30) to Mount Eden, the Zoo, MOTAT and other sights.

55

Eat, drink and people-watch in trendy Parnell

The signal station on Mount Victoria above the waterfront suburb of Devonport

Auckland environs

►► Devonport   49D4

One of the most enjoyable ways to spend a day or an afternoon in Auckland is to hop on one of the frequent ferries to the suburb of Devonport, on the end of the North Shore peninsula.

Devonport was the landing place of the great canoe *Tainui* in the 14th century (the site is commemorated by a bronze sculpture on the King Edward Parade foreshore); it was later one of the first areas to be settled by Europeans, and has many interesting and well-preserved old buildings.

Stepping ashore on the redeveloped **Devonport Wharf** (with a host of shops and dockside eating places), you emerge at the bottom of **Victoria Road**, the main thoroughfare, lined with bookshops, craft galleries, outdoor cafés and gift shops and antiques shops.

At the top of Victoria Road, 500m (545 yards) from the ferry, a pathway leads to the top of **Mount Victoria**►►, an extinct volcanic cone with the outlines of Maori fortifications clearly visible around the summit. There are terrific views of the **Hauraki Gulf**, with an orientation table identifying offshore islands.

From the park with the huge Moreton Bay fig tree, near the wharf at the bottom of Victoria Road, it is a pleasant stroll along the seafront to **North Head Historic Reserve**► (tel: 09 445 9142. *Open* daily 6AM–10PM. Vehicle gates close at 6PM. *Admission: free*) at the very tip of the peninsula. This is another volcanic cone, riddled with gun emplacements (including a rare 'disappearing gun') and tunnels that were dug during the 19th century, when there were fears of a Russian invasion. On the other side of the headland is the long sweep of **Cheltenham Beach**, looking out to Rangitoto Island.

In the opposite direction along the seafront is **Anne Street**, with quaint Victorian houses. Farther along, Spring Street leads to the **Royal New Zealand Navy Museum** (tel: 09 445 5186. *Open* daily 10–4. *Admission: free*), that has exhibits tracing the Navy's development from the early days.

FERRIES TO DEVONPORT
Fullers Ferries run to Devonport from the Downtown Ferry Terminal (Pier 1) every half-hour between 6:15 and 9:15AM and 10AM and 6:30PM, Sun–Thu, 10AM–1AM Fri–Sat, then hourly to 11PM Mon–Thu and 10PM Sun. The crossing takes 10–15 minutes and costs NZ$8 return.

A movement that began some years ago and gained impetus by the film Once Were Warriors, *urban Pacific chic is a fusion of cultures that represents an upsurge in pride in the country's Maori and Polynesian heritage.*

From souvenirs to street chic Until recently, Kiwis (whether Maori or *Pakeha*) tended to look down on things with a Maori theme. Polynesian influences also seemed to be limited to bright floral shirts or shell necklaces. But now a new generation of young Maori and Polynesian designers, artists and musicians has sparked a revival in traditional culture, interweaving conventional styles and textiles, high fashion, rap music and street wear to forge their own look and create a new style: urban Pacific chic. The *lava-lava* (a Polynesian 'skirt' for men) may still take some bravado to wear, but *tapa* (a papery textile made from beaten tree bark) is increasingly being used for clothes, hats and bags.

Haka rap The ancient rhythms and chants of Maori or Polynesian music are being rediscovered and reworked into a distinctive contemporary sound. The arrival of hip-hop and rap music (which also rely on beats and chant-like deliveries) has been instrumental in the creation of a new hybrid, blending the beat with old songs, *poi* rhythms and the melodic Maori flute. Artists such as Maree Sheehan and Emma Paki are part of this new Pacific sound, while the popular New Zealand band Crowded House used a group of Cook Island log drummers and a Maori choir on one of their albums.

Tattoo you Tattooing is now in vogue again, a revival inspired partly by the film *Once Were Warriors*, which tells the stylized story of a Maori street gang, fully tattooed and proud to be Maori. Traditional curvilinear patterns are now combined with contemporary designs.

PACIFIC FESTIVAL
The annual Pasifika Games, with their sporting events and dance festivals, are a meeting place for Auckland's Pacific community, with the sights and sounds of the Pacific mingling in a blur of cultures from Maori, Samoan, Chinese, Cook Island and Niuean peoples.

Maori carving, here at Auckland Waterfront, gained impetus from Once Were Warriors *(1994)*

57

Auckland

ISLAND FERRIES

Marine transport throughout the Hauraki Gulf is dominated by the Fullers cruise and ferry company, with a fleet of vessels ranging from cargo and passenger monohulls to custom-built cruise catamarans. Departures to Rangitoto are four times daily, to Motuihe two/three times weekly, to Waiheke approximately hourly and to Great Barrier Island (holiday periods only) three/four times weekly. There are many more sailings in summer. Fullers also has a variety of packages including accommodation and tours on the islands. For full details contact Fullers Cruise Centre, Ferry Building, Quay Street (tel: 09 367 9111/fax: 09 367 9148; www.fullers. co.nz).

Rangitoto Reserve protects native trees, ferns and orchids

▶▶▶ Hauraki Gulf (inner)   49E4

It is no wonder that so many people in Auckland own boats, given the myriad of islands in the Hauraki Gulf within easy reach for beach barbecues, fishing jaunts, diving adventures, scenic walks and more. The islands are easily accessible for day-trips or overnight stays, with regular ferry services to many of them and small charter boat companies providing other options.

Sheltered by the long arm of the Coromandel Peninsula to the east and by the mainland to the south and west, most of the Hauraki Gulf lies within **Hauraki Gulf Maritime Park**, which embraces 47 islands and one mainland reserve (North Head in Devonport). Several of the islands are wildlife sanctuaries.

The nearest island to Auckland, and the youngest in the Gulf, is **Rangitoto▶▶▶**, which emerged from the sea in a series of volcanic explosions as recently as 750 years ago. Its distinctive cone is a familiar sight from downtown Auckland, and a climb to the top (2km/1.25 miles: allow one hour each way, or take a guided tour on the Explorer tractor-train) will be rewarded with a 360-degree panorama of the city and the Gulf from the summit (260m/853ft). The black basaltic lava rock of Rangitoto may seem like an inhospitable environment, but distinctive plant communities have developed here, including mangroves, and the island hosts over 200 species of native trees and plants, 40 kinds of fern and several species of orchid. There are also lava caves, black-back gull colonies and pohutukawa groves, linked by tracks from the DoC visitor centre by the wharf.

Reached by a causeway from Rangitoto, **Motutapu▶** is two-thirds the size and completely different in character. Mainly farmland, it has some superb beaches and several

On the viewing platform at Rangitoto Island

popular walking tracks, including the Motutapu Farm track from Islington Bay to Home Bay (90 minutes each way) across the south of the island, which is part of the New Zealand Walkway system. South of Motutapu, **Motuihe►** is a much smaller island (covering 180ha/445 acres) but it also has excellent beaches and is popular on weekends with boating enthusiasts and swimmers.

The largest and busiest island in the inner Gulf is **Waiheke►►►**, just 35 minutes from Auckland by ferry. The most populous of the islands, it has a thriving arts and crafts community with many galleries and craft shops. A good starting point is **Artworks►** (2 Korora Road, tel: 09 372 1234. *Open* daily 10–5), which runs craft courses. The island is fringed by terrific beaches, while inland there are walkways through native bush and farmlands. One of the most popular walks is the 90-minute track to Stony Battery at the east end of the island, where a World War II gun emplacement overlooks the Gulf, or take a bush walk through the Forest and Bird Reserve at Onetangi.

There is a wide choice of accommodation and plenty of restaurants and cafés. With average temperatures said to be 5°C (41°F) warmer than the mainland, Waiheke also has no fewer than 25 vineyards and wineries. Mountain-biking, horseback-riding and sea-kayaking are other options on the island. Buses connect with the ferries, and taxis and rental cars are available, or you can bring your own vehicle on the car ferry from Pakuranga in Auckland's eastern suburbs. For visitors on foot, it is a pleasant 20-minute walk from the ferry wharf to Oneroa.

FROM *PĀ* SITES TO PICNIC SITES
Before the arrival of the Europeans, the islands of the Hauraki Gulf were extensively settled by Maori, who called them *motu whakatere* ('the floating islands'), and the trenches and terraces of Maori *pā* sites can be seen on many island hillsides. During the 19th century some of the islands were traded to the colonists in exchange for gold, guns, gunpowder and blankets. In the early 20th century the first ferry services started, bearing the families of Auckland city to the islands for Sunday picnics—Browns Island (Motukorea) and Motutapu were two of the most popular destinations.

A kauri dam on Great Barrier Island: The flood released by 'tripping' the dam carried the kauri logs downstream to the mill

SEA-KAYAKING
An excellent way of getting up close and personal with Waitemata Harbour is to go sea-kayaking. It's neither difficult nor dangerous, and professional guides will escort you round the harbour, to Rangitoto (including at night) or even up the river to the Puhoi pub, north of Auckland. Operators include Ferg's Kayaks (tel: 09 529 2230; www.fergskayaks.co.nz) and Outdoor Discoveries (tel: 09 813 3399; www.nzkayak.co.nz).

▶▶▶ Hauraki Gulf (outer)　　　49E4

Although slightly harder to reach, the islands in the north of the Hauraki Gulf are also worth visiting if you have the time. The most remote is **Great Barrier Island▶▶▶**, 80km (50 miles) from Auckland and the largest island in the Gulf. There is an enormous number of things to see and do on Great Barrier, which has just 572 residents distributed across its 280sq km (108sq mile) area. Over half of the island is conservation land, with vast tracts of native bush containing several rare species of flora and fauna—including the largest populations of brown teal duck left in the country.

Great Barrier, named by Captain Cook because it appeared to bar the entrance to the gulf, was one of the first islands to be colonized by Europeans, who mined for gold and copper and milled its extensive kauri forests for timber. There are old kauri dams, the remains of whaling stations and a network of tramping tracks to explore.

The west coast's sheltered beaches are good for swimming, while the more exposed east-coast beaches are popular for surfing, diving and fishing. Horseback-riding, kayaking and safari tours are also on offer, and with 200km (125 miles) of unsealed hill roads, the island is perfect for mountain-biking. Accommodation includes backpackers' hostels, motels, fishing lodges and homestays.

Great Barrier is not wired for electricity (power is supplied by generators, solar cells, windmills and gravity pumps), and the telephone system was modernized only recently, thus doing away with Barrier residents' main source of information—the party line.

To the west of Great Barrier, **Little Barrier Island** is an important nature reserve, with the only area of rain forest in the country to have remained unaffected by introduced browsers (such as deer) or predators (such as possums). About a third of the island was logged in the past, but these areas are now regenerating bushland. Access to the island is strictly controlled: To apply for a permit, contact the DoC office at Warkworth (tel: 09 425 7812).

Close to the mainland shoreline, 26km (16 miles) south-west of Little Barrier Island, is **Kawau Island▶▶▶**, reached via ferries from Sandspit. Manganese was found here in the 1830s, and a Scottish company mined the deposits until a node of copper was discovered in 1842, when it switched to mining copper instead. In 1862 the island was bought by Sir George Grey (an early governor and later premier for a brief term), who converted and extended the former mine manager's house into stately **Mansion House▶▶**, which has been restored and opened to the public (tel: 09 422 8882. *Open* daily 9:30–3:30. *Admission: moderate*). Grey planted many exotic trees and introduced non-native wallabies, peacocks, pheasants, quail, geese and even tree kangaroos to the island: Peacocks still strut across the mansion's lawns and wallabies are a fairly common sight.

From the Mansion House walking tracks lead to beaches, Maori *pā* sites and the remains of the old copper and manganese mines at Miners Bay.

To the north of Kawau Island, just 100m (110 yards) from the shore across a narrow channel, lies the scientific reserve of **Goat Island**. Access to the bush-clad island is restricted, but snorkellers and divers are allowed to explore the marine reserve that surrounds it.

To the south of Kawau is **Tiritiri Matangi▶**, another scientific reserve, but this time run as an 'open sanctuary' in which visitors are free to wander the walkways around the island. It is particularly popular with bird-watchers because of the large number of native species (many of them endangered) that live here: You may be able to see or hear bellbirds, North Island saddlebacks, brown teal ducks, black robins and red-crowned parakeets. The flightless takahe has also been introduced.

FERRIES TO KAWAU
Ferries to Kawau Island operate from Sandspit, just outside Warkworth, one hour's drive north of Auckland. There are about three departures daily, journey time 45 minutes. You can also join the historic Mail Run, leaving Sandspit at 10:30AM daily, which cruises around the bays delivering mail and supplies before reaching the Mansion House (there is time to visit the house and gardens before the return trip). Contact The Kawau Kat, PO Box 931, Warkworth (tel: 09 425 8006; www.kawaukat. co.nz).

61

Elegant Mansion House on Kawau Island

Lion Rock at Piha Beach

Drive
& Forest Walk

Waitakere Ranges

The Waitakere Ranges Regional Park is a 10,000ha (24,710-acre) wilderness area within easy reach of the city, with waterfalls, beaches and rain-forest walks. This tour takes you right through the park to the Tasman coast and back, with opportunities for several short walks on the way. Allow the best part of a day.

From Auckland, follow SH16 to the northwest, taking the Waterview exit and then following Urban Routes 19 and 24 through Titirangi; 6km (3.5 miles) later you reach the Arataki Visitor Centre to the left.

You are now on the eastern fringes of the **Waitakere Ranges**▶▶▶. This hilly area, rising to 470m (1,542ft) above sea-level, is volcanic in origin, and is most notable for its huge expanses of regenerating forest, crisscrossed by nearly 250km (155 miles) of walking and tramping tracks.

The modern **Arataki visitor centre**▶▶ is superbly designed to blend into the surrounding bush; elevated platforms provide stunning **views**▶▶ over the forest, with Manukau Harbour to the southeast and Auckland beyond to the east.

The boardwalk leads past native trees (such as rimu, young kauri and maukoro) to displays inside the visitor centre (tel: 09 817 0077. *Open* Sep–Apr Mon–Fri 9–5; May–Aug 10–4, Sat–Sun 9–5. *Admission: free*) on the inhabitants of the rain forest, such as geckos, rare frogs, tui and kereru. On the lower level, an excellent wide-screen audiovisual presentation recounts the history and ecology of the ranges (presentations every 20 minutes. *Admission: inexpensive*).

As well as the distinctive architecture of Arataki (which means 'pathway to learning'), you will notice the powerful **carvings**▶▶ of Maori ancestral figures. The *pou* (guardian post) that fronts the building represents the ancestors of the local Te Kawerau a Maki, and is carved from two kauri that were felled with full protocol and *karakia* (rituals) offered to Tane, the god of the forest. Inside, four more carvings represent other ancestors.

From the visitor centre, follow the Nature Trail and then the Upper and

Lower Loop Trail (a one-hour round trip walk) through the forest, where vines and climbers festoon trees and perching epiphyte plants hang from every branch. At the far end of the Loop Trail steps lead up to a mature kauri plantation; although by no means as awesome as the tremendous forest giants of the Waipoua Kauri Forest (see pages 74–75), the biggest tree here still manages to impress: some 600 years old, it has a girth of nearly 8m (26ft) and a height of 37m (121ft).

Leaving Arataki, follow the Scenic Drive signs, turning left at the first main junction down to **Piha**▶▶. As you crest the ridge, this huge black volcanic sand beach is laid out before you, with the 100m (328ft)-high Lion Rock proudly standing sentinel where the stream meets the sea.

Piha is primarily a surfers' beach, so be extremely wary of rips and other hazards if you decide to swim; alternatively, you can climb and scramble up the track on Lion Rock (one hour return trip) or tackle the Tasman Lookout Track at the south end of the beach (40 minutes round trip).

Drive back up Piha Road, turning left to rejoin Scenic Drive. After just under 1km (0.5 mile) you will come to the **Rose Hellaby House**, one of the earliest guest-houses in the area, which now contains a display on the history of the region (*Open* Sun and public holidays 11–5 in summer; 1–4 in winter; Sat 1–4 all year round. *Admission: donation*). From the gardens (*Open* daily 9–6. *Admission: free*) there is an astonishing **view**▶▶ over West Auckland, Manukau Harbour, Waitemata Harbour and beyond to the Hauraki Gulf and the Coromandel.

Continue on to a short loop road, climbing to the summit of Pukematekeo (336m/1,102ft) which has a beautiful **panorama**▶▶, this time extending right up the west coast to Kaipara Harbour and back across the city and its harbours.

Follow Scenic Drive until it ends on the outskirts of Swanson, continuing through the township to take the motorway back into Auckland.

Maori ancestral figures at the Arataki visitor centre

63

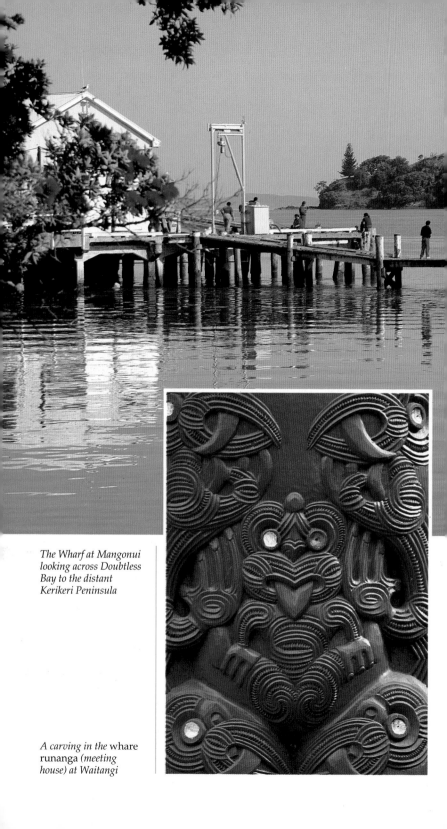

The Wharf at Mangonui looking across Doubtless Bay to the distant Kerikeri Peninsula

A carving in the whare runanga *(meeting house) at Waitangi*

NORTHLAND This peninsula, 240km (149 miles) in length, runs north from Auckland towards the equator. Its mild climate year-round has earned it the sobriquet 'the winterless North'. The east coast is indented with numerous bays and harbours with islands, and its sandy beaches provide a base for adventure activities such as sailing, diving, sea-kayaking, swimming and surf-casting.

It is not just its climate that makes Northland a busy tourist region; it also has many historical attractions, including the **Waitangi National Reserve**, where the Treaty of Waitangi was signed in 1840. The reserve forms part of the **Bay of Islands Historic and Maritime Park**, a hugely popular holiday area with most facilities concentrated in the seaside town of **Paihia**: it is advisable to reserve accommodation in advance for weekends or public holidays in high season. A short ferry ride from Paihia is the tranquil township of **Russell**, which takes great pride in its heritage as the earliest European settlement in the country.

Northland

DEPARTING SOULS
Cape Reinga is traditionally revered by Maori as the last stepping stone for the spirits of the dead on their journey back north to 'Hawaiki', starting from the gnarled roots of the ancient pohutukawa tree on the eastern side of the headland.

The west coast, by contrast, is lined with sweeping beaches pounded by surf from the Tasman Sea—perfect for beach walks or surf-casting. Inland, the magnificent **kauri forests** are not to be missed.

The bulk of Northland tapers off to a narrow finger jutting out into the ocean, with **Doubtless Bay** on the east coast providing a convenient base from which to explore. On the west coast, **Ninety Mile Beach** sweeps in a single unbroken stretch of shimmering sand up towards Cape Reinga, at the very tip of the peninsula.

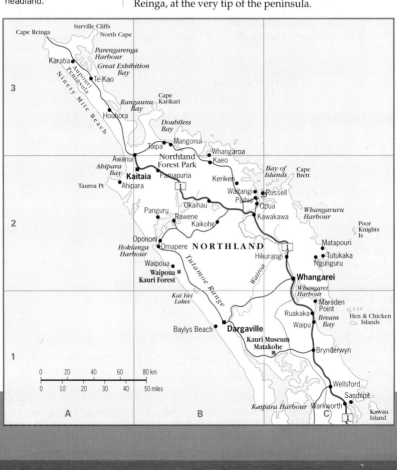

►► Cape Reinga   66A3

Almost at the northernmost tip of the North Island, Cape Reinga has breathtaking sea views, stretching as far as the Three Kings Islands on a clear day. To the right of the lighthouse you can also see the Surville Cliffs on the adjoining North Cape—the most northerly point on mainland New Zealand. From the cape, a 90-minute walk will take you to either Sandy Bay, on the way to North Cape, or south to Te Weraki Beach.

Trips to Cape Reinga (see panel) run from the Bay of Islands, Doubtless Bay and Kaitaia, with one leg of the journey by road and the other passing along **Ninety Mile Beach►►**, a huge expanse of sand (which is in reality 90km/50 miles long).

On the eastern side of the peninsula is lovely **Houhora Harbour**, excellent for kayaking, surfing or just sitting on the beach. Near by is the **Subritzky/Wagener Homestead**, an unusual pioneer cottage built between 1860 and 1862.

►► Doubtless Bay   66B3

Doubtless Bay has plenty of good beaches and makes a convenient base for visiting the Far North and Cape Reinga. It got its name when, sailing past in 1769, Cook declared it was 'doubtless a bay', and continued on his circumnavigation.

The main settlement is the charming and historic port of **Mangonui►►►**, a significant Maori settlement classified as a Conservation Zone. In the mid-18th century whaling ships called in here to pick up supplies, and by the end of the century it had become an important port for the shipping of kauri timber and kauri gum.

It has a handful of hotels, craft shops, cafés, a bank and the famous Mangonui Fish Shop, next to the wharf. It is also popular for fishing, diving and other water sports. A good view of the harbour and sea can be had from the **Rangikapiti Pā Historic Reserve►**, just past the end of the village.

Continuing westward the next bay is **Coopers Beach►**, fringed by pohutukawa trees, followed by **Taipa**, where the explorer Kupe is said to have made his first landfall in about AD 950.

CAPE REINGA TRIPS

Both Fullers (tel: 09 402 7421; www.fullers-bay-of-islands.co.nz) and Kings (tel: 09 402 8288; www.kings-tours.co.nz) run trips to Cape Reinga from Paihia in the Bay of Islands, but this 500km (300-mile) round trip makes for a long, exhausting day. You will get more time to stop at other places of interest if you leave from Kaitaia or Doubtless Bay, and the service tends to be more personalized, with smaller buses. From Kaitaia tours are operated by Sand Safaris (tel: 09 408 1778; www.sandsafaris.co.nz); from Mangonui, Nor-East Coachlines (tel: 09 406 0244) runs similar trips with daily departures.

67

Northland's Ninety Mile Beach is officially designated a road

THE FIRST PLOUGH
The Kerikeri soil yielded an abundance of kumara and potatoes, which the Maori traded (along with pigs and flax) with visiting whalers. In the early days of the mission station, Reverend Butler introduced the first plough and bullock team to the country, unloaded from the naval ship *Dromedary*. 'The agricultural plough was for the first time put into the land of New Zealand,' he wrote on 3 May 1820, 'and I felt much pleasure in holding it after a team of six bullocks.' The settlement thereafter acquired its name, *keri*, meaning 'to dig', and then *kerikeri*—'to keep on digging'.

Rewa's Village, showing a raised storehouse

▶▶ Kai Iwi Lakes   66B1

These three freshwater lakes 25km (15 miles) northwest of Dargaville have been developed as a recreation reserve, with plenty of opportunities for swimming, boating, camping and fishing.

▶ Kaitaia   66B2

The main commercial hub in the Far North, Kaitaia is a busy base for tours heading up to Cape Reinga, but its drab main street has limited appeal as somewhere to stay—Doubtless Bay is a much better prospect. Just off the main street, the **Far North Regional Museum** (tel: 09 408 1403; www.northland-museums.co.nz. *Open* summer, Mon–Fri 10–5, Sat–Sun 10–4. *Admission: inexpensive*) has many examples of polished and worked kauri gum, as well as displays on natural history and Maori objects.

To the east of Kaitaia (18km/11 miles farther on at Beckham Road, Fairburn) is the **Nocturnal Park▶** (tel: 09 409 4100. *Open* summer 9AM–10PM; winter 9–9. *Admission: moderate*), which has a kiwi house and a glow-worm grotto.

▶▶▶ The Kauri Museum Matakohe   66C1

Tel: 09 431 7417; www.kauri-museum.com. Open: daily, winter 9–5; summer 8:30–5:30. Admission: moderate

On the way to the Waipoua Kauri Forest when heading north from Auckland, this wonderful museum provides information on absolutely everything associated with kauri, from the history of logging and gum-digging to superb items of kauri furniture. The kauri gum display in the basement is particularly noteworthy, with its numerous elaborate carvings. One wing is almost completely filled by the enormous trunk of the Balderston Kauri, a giant that was felled for the museum after it had been struck by lightning.

▶▶▶ Kerikeri   66B2

Kerikeri lies at the heart of a rich horticultural district and is surrounded by citrus and kiwifruit orchards. Around the main township there are also a number of workshops and co-operatives selling ceramics, woodcarvings, jewellery and other arts and crafts.

Just beyond the township is the delightful **Kerikeri Basin▶▶▶**, a picturesque inlet with numerous historical associations. It was here that the Reverend Samuel Marsden established the country's second mission station in 1819, with the Reverend John Butler appointed as superintendent. Three years later Butler had finished building his home, the oldest surviving building in New Zealand and

now known as the **Kemp House**▶▶▶ (tel: 09 407 9236. *Open* daily, summer 10–5; winter 10–4. *Admission: moderate*). The interior of the house, which was restored in 1989 provides a fascinating insight into the lives of the early missionaries.

Next door to the Kemp House is the **Stone Store**▶▶ (same opening times as Kemp House), from which James Kemp dispensed rations to the other mission stations in the area. Completed in 1836, it is the oldest surviving stone building in New Zealand and has been restored. A

small museum contains the original plough (see panel page 68).

Also in the Basin, **Rewa's Village**▶▶▶ (tel: 09 407 6454. *Open* daily, summer 9–5; winter 10–4. *Admission: inexpensive*) is well worth a visit. It is a replica of a pre-European Maori fishing village (*kāinga*) on the riverbank, built in 1969. The village has a chief's house, raised storehouses and typical thatched houses (*whare*). Access is via a visitor centre, where there is also an audiovisual display on the early history of the Kerikeri Basin (*Open* on demand. *Admission: donation*).

Across the inlet from the village is the fortified *pā* site to which the villagers would have retreated when threatened by raiding parties. Now a historic reserve, **Kororipo Pā**▶▶▶ (*Open* at all times. *Admission: free*) was the power base of the famous warrior chief Hongi Hika (see page 35). Signboards explain the various features of this elaborately terraced hilltop site, which is reached via a wooden footbridge from the tea rooms across from the Stone Store.

Missionaries built Kemp House (top); the church at Matakohe's Museum (above)

HELL-HOLE OF THE PACIFIC
When Captain Cook sailed into the Bay of Islands in 1769, there was a thriving Maori settlement here known as Kororareka. With the arrival of the European whalers it degenerated. A visiting surveyor described it as a 'vile hole, full of impudent, half-drunken people', and its reputation earned it the title 'Hell-hole of the Pacific'.

Exploring the rock pools at Russell

DOLPHINS IN THE BAY
Resident pods of bottlenose dolphins live in the bay throughout the year, and since 1991 Dolphin Discoveries has been taking small groups out to view them or (in calm conditions) swim with them. Snorkelling equipment and wetsuits are provided. Sei whales, minke whales and orcas can also be spotted along the coast at different times of year. Contact: Dolphin Discoveries, Marsden Road, Paihia (tel: 09 402 8234; fax: 09 402 6058; www.dolphinz.co.nz).

▶▶▶ Paihia   66B2

The main tourist town in the Bay of Islands, Paihia is the most convenient base for cruises or other activities in the Maritime and Historic Park, and for visiting Russell, Kerikeri and Waitangi. It is not an especially attractive town, but it does have a wide range of motels, hotels and other accommodation, as well as plenty of restaurants, cafés and shops, so it's good for exploring the area.

Your first stop should be the Maritime Building on the quayside, where there are several booking and information offices, including the visitor centre (tel: 09 402 7345. *Open* daily 8–5), Fullers Travel Centre, King's Dolphin Cruises and Tours, and deep-sea fishing operators. Behind the Maritime Building, Paihia wharf is busy with charter vessels, dolphin-watch boats, launches and the Russell ferries.

Just next to the wharf is an aquarium, **Aquatic World▶** (tel: 09 402 6220. *Open* daily 9:30–6; extended hours in summer. *Admission: moderate*), which gives an insight into marine life in the Bay of Islands.

If you're driving to Russell, a car ferry leaves every 10 minutes from Opua, 6km (4 miles) to the south. As well as the road, there is a community-built Paihia-Opua coastal walkway round the beaches and mangroves. The walk will take you about 2 hours 30 minutes in one direction.

▶▶▶ Russell   66B2

This delightful tranquil town with a long history is less than ten minutes across the bay from Paihia, by local ferry, and is well worth visiting for the day.

Soon after the signing of the Treaty of Waitangi, Hobson purchased a block of land at nearby Okiato—renamed Russell after Lord John Russell, then British Colonial Secretary—with the aim of establishing the country's capital there. Nine months later, in March 1841, the capital was transferred to Auckland, and in 1844 the village of Kororareka was given the name of Russell.

The economic decline that followed the shift of the capital to Auckland fuelled resentment among local Maori, who sacked the town in 1845. Rebuilt the following year, by the turn of the century it had become a quiet summer holiday destination. In 1930 a road between Whangarei and Russell was built, allowing access by car for the first time.

Much of the history of Russell is covered in the **Russell Museum▶** (tel: 09 403 7701. *Open* daily, summer 10–5; winter 10–4. *Admission: inexpensive*).

Next door, the **Bay of Islands Maritime and Historic Park Visitor Centre▶** (tel: 09 403 7685. *Open* Mon–Fri 8:30–5, Sat–Sun 9–5. *Admission: free*) has displays and a free audiovisual presentation (every half-hour from 9AM) on the natural and human history of the park.

One block away is **Christ Church▶▶▶**, the country's oldest surviving church, built in 1835 by the local citizenry who were horrified by Kororareka's debauched reputation (see panel page 69). The churchyard contains the graves of Maori chiefs and six sailors from HMS *Hazard* who died in a pitched battle with Hongi Hika's forces (the church walls still bear the scars of musket shots and cannonballs).

Pompallier▶▶▶ (tel: 09 403 7861. *Open* daily, Dec–Apr 10–5; May–Nov guided tours at 10:15, 11:15, 1:15, 2:15, 3:15. *Admission: moderate*), almost on the seafront, was built by French Roman Catholic Marist missionaries to house their printing press. They used the *pisé de terre* (rammed earth) technique that was common in their native Lyon, and the result is an elegant and unusual two-storey building, completed in 1842. Extensively restored, it once more houses a printing press and book-bindery, as well as a display on the Marists and a small shop selling superb handcrafted books and other items. Tapeka Pā Historic Reserve (2.4km/1.25 miles north) has excellent views over the bay, and Long Beach (1km/0.5 mile east) is good for swimming—and is unofficially clothes-optional at the northern end.

BAY OF ISLANDS CRUISES
A bay cruise is a good way to see the islands and places of interest (such as the site where Cook landed in 1769). Fullers (tel: 09 402 7421; www.fullers-bay-of-islands.co.nz) and Kings (tel: 09 402 8288; www.kings-tours.co.nz) both run a variety of trips. Take the 5-hour Fullers 'cream trip', which began in the 1920s to collect milk and cream from outlying farms (daily departures at 10AM in summer; Mon, Wed, Thu and Sat in winter). Bay cruises also visit the Hole in the Rock at Cape Brett at the mouth of the bay (weather permitting). You can also zip through in a fast open boat such as Fullers' *Excitor*.

71

The architecture of Pompallier shows its French origins

Walk

Historic Russell

This is an easy walk up to the top of Flagstaff Hill and then around historic Russell township, with lovely views from the top of the hill and many interesting places to visit. Allow around two to three hours, including visits to the Museum, Christ Church and Pompallier.

From the ferry jetty turn left and follow The Strand. Immediately on your right is the **Duke of Marlborough Hotel▶** (tel: 09 403 7829; www.theduke.co.nz), the fourth hotel on this site (earlier ones were sacked or burned) and the proud possessor of New Zealand's oldest liquor licence, issued in August 1840. This is a good place to stop for coffee or refreshments on the outdoor terrace before heading up the hill.

Continue to the end of the beach and go on around the rocks into **Watering Bay** (at high tide, when this route is impassable, continue up Wellington Street and follow the high tide detour), used for reprovisioning ships in the early days. Take the signposted track up through the **Kororareka Scenic Reserve** to find a concrete dam. This is on the site of the original dam built by sailors so that they could collect water from the creek.

Emerging from the bush, follow the road until you see a track on the right up through the bush again to **Flagstaff Hill▶▶**. From here there are panoramic views across the Bay of Islands, with Cape Brett visible to the

72

east. At the end of the peninsula you can see **Tapeka Pā**, a fortified site which is now a historic reserve. A sea battle between rival tribes fighting for dominance in the region took place just off this point in the early 19th century.

Erected after the signing of the Treaty of Waitangi in 1840, the flagstaff has long been a symbol of English domination, and as such was cut down four times by local Maori in 1844 and 1845. As a peace gesture organized as 'a voluntary act by those directly connected with cutting it down', it was replaced in 1857 with 'a noble spar, cut from the bush and dragged up the hill by four hundred men'. The following year the British flag was again hoisted on the mast, dubbed *Whakakotahitanga* ('being at one with the Queen'), the remains of which form the present flagstaff. On a hillock opposite is a **mosaic** of the Bay of Islands, commissioned in 1988. From Flagstaff Hill take the track sign-posted behind the parking area, which cuts down through the bush to Wellington Street. On the corner of Wellington and Queen streets stands the **Bakers'**

View from Flagstaff Hill (left); cannon set up in Russell in 1847 (below)

House, built in the 1880s for Ernest Ford, merchant and son of New Zealand's first surgeon Dr. Samuel Ford. For almost a century since then it was home to generations of the Baker family.

Bear left, following Wellington Street, then turn right on to York Street. Immediately opposite the Methodist Church (built in 1913) is an **Immigrant Cottage**, the last of a group of five prefabricated cottages erected by the government in 1857; this one was the home of the signal-man at the Flagstaff.

Turn left on to Chapel Street and right on to Church Street, at the end of which stands **Christ Church▶▶▶**, the oldest church in New Zealand. Head back down to the seafront along Robertson Street towards the **Russell Museum▶**, turning left at the shore to reach **Pompallier▶▶▶**.

As you return towards the wharf, the DoC visitor centre and headquarters of the Bay of Islands Maritime and Historic Park lies to the right, in a building that was Russell's post office and courthouse from 1875 to 1969. On the grassy foreshore just beyond it is an old **cannon**, one of two that were set up to defend the town against Hika's attack in 1847. Several historic buildings line the foreshore, among them the **Swordfish Club** (www.swordfish.co.nz), established in 1924.

Northland

POOR KNIGHTS ISLANDS MARINE RESERVE

Poor Knights Islands Marine Reserve, 24km (15 miles) off the east coast of Northland, is New Zealand's most famous scuba-diving destination. Established in 1981, the reserve consists of two main islands—Tawhiti Rahi and Aorangi—with a narrow passage between them. Warmed by currents from the Coral Sea, its sheer submarine cliffs, tunnels and caves are home to tropical and subtropical species not normally seen around New Zealand. Tutukaka (north-east of Whangarei) is the nearest port, but trips also depart from Paihia. Contact: Dive! Tutukaka, Marina Road, Tutukaka (tel: 09 434 3867; www.divenz.co.nz) or Paihia Dive, PO Box 210, Paihia (tel: 09 402 7551; www.divenz.com).

The war canoe Ngatokimatawhaorua *joins the annual Waitangi Day celebrations*

▶▶▶ Waipoua Kauri Forest   66B2

The last remnant of the extensive forests that once covered much of the North Island, the Waipoua Kauri Forest is well worth a visit to see some of the mightiest trees in New Zealand. Saved from the loggers at first by its very remoteness, Waipoua Forest was purchased by the Crown in 1876, but its new owners were unsure what to do with it. The threat posed by the demand for wartime boat-building supplies in the 1940s sparked off a well-organized preservation campaign. This was the country's first great conservation battle and resulted in the creation of the Waipoua Sanctuary in 1952.

The largest living tree in New Zealand is **Tane Mahuta** ('the God of the forest') in the northern section of the forest; this hugely impressive kauri tree is thought to be around 1,200 years old and has a height of 51m (169ft) and a girth of 14m (45ft). To the south, a side road leads to a parking area with access to several more remarkable kauri, including the second largest in the forest.

There are extensive displays on kauri and forest flora and fauna in the **Waipoua Forest Visitor Centre** (tel: 09 439 0605. *Open* daily 9–5. *Admission: free*).

▶▶▶ Waitangi   66B2

The road bridge across the river from Paihia leads into the **Waitangi National Reserve▶▶▶** (tel: 09 902 7437; www.waitangi.net. *Open* daily 9–5. *Admission: moderate*). It was on the foreshore here that the signing of the Treaty of Waitangi took place between the Maori tribes and the British Crown on 6 February 1840, and this site is considered in effect the birthplace of modern New Zealand. In the visitor centre are portraits of many of the principal figures involved and copies of treaty documents. There is also a theatre with an audiovisual presentation (every 30

minutes from 9AM) on the events surrounding the treaty.

At the heart of the reserve is the **Treaty House▶▶▶**, one of New Zealand's oldest surviving buildings (1834) and the home of James Busby, the British Resident at the time. A fine example of Georgian design, it contains displays on the treaty and the Busby family.

In front of the house, lawns sweep down to the water's edge, with a massive kauri **flagstaff** marking the spot where the treaty was signed. To one side is a splendid *whare runanga*▶▶ (meeting house), built in 1940 to celebrate the centenary of the signing, which contains elaborate panels and carvings from major Maori tribes.

In the other direction from the visitor centre, on the foreshore at Hobson Beach, is a massive **war canoe▶▶▶**, also built for the centenary in 1940. Called *Ngatokimatawhaorua*, this 35m (115ft)-long canoe is one of the largest in the world, carrying 80 paddlers.

▶ Whangarei   66C2

New Zealand's northernmost city, Whangarei (pronounced 'Fa-nga-ray') has a huge deep-water harbour with three separate port areas: Whangarei means 'cherished harbour' in Maori.

The harbourside of the Town Basin has been redeveloped into an attractively landscaped complex with shops and outdoor cafés, as well as the new **Museum of Fishes▶** (tel: 09 438 5681. *Open* daily 10–4. *Admission: inexpensive*), which has a small saltwater aquarium and a rock pool. **Clapham's Clock Museum** (tel: 09 438 3993; www.claphamsclocks.co.nz. *Open* daily, winter 9–5; summer 9–8. *Admission: inexpensive*) has thousands of different timepieces.

Other attractions nearby include **Whangarei Falls▶▶**, which cascade into a bush-fringed pool 25m (82ft) below (on Ngunguru Road, 6km/4 miles northeast of the main city). In the same area, there are good bush walks at Parakahi Scenic Reserve, and walks through kauri at AH Reed Memorial Park. In the opposite direction (8km/5 miles west of the city, on SH14 to Dargaville), the parklands of **Whangarei Museum and Kiwi House▶** (tel: 09 438 9630; www.northland-museums.co.nz. *Open* daily 10–4. *Admission: inexpensive*) contain displays that include a kiwi house, a pioneer homestead, vintage machinery and a good range of Maori objects, among them a rare burial chest (see panel).

Whangarei Falls, a popular picnic spot

BURIAL CHESTS
In the Northland region in pre-European times, the dead bodies of chiefs or other high-ranking Maori were exposed on *atamira* (platforms) until the flesh had rotted. Then certain bones were removed, cleaned, painted with red ochre and put in a *waka-túpápaku* (burial chest) before being placed in a cave or other sacred site. The burial chests often bore the likeness of Hine Nui Te Po, goddess of the underworld. Whangarei Museum contains a rare example, unusually sculpted as a bird, perhaps to resemble the bird-god Hukerunui, and thought to be 400–500 years old.

The magnificent kauri is one of the world's mightiest trees, often reaching heights of 50m (165ft) or more, with a trunk girth of up to 23m (75ft). Two hundred years ago kauri forests covered much of the warmer north half of the North Island, but today just four per cent of this forest remains. The felling and transporting of kauri timber, and the digging of the gum the trees produce, shaped the development of the Coromandel Peninsula, Northland and the Auckland region for well over 100 years.

The growing tree The New Zealand species, *Agathis australis*, is just one of 13 species in the kauri family, a form of pine that bears male and female flowers each spring. Kauri seedlings grow to maturity in two stages: for the first century or so, they push upward at the rate of around 28–30cm (11–12in) a year, sprouting numerous side branches and developing a distinctive conical crown. Then they start to shed the lower branches and develop a clean trunk with a crown of upper branches, although it may be another 200 to 300 years before a tree reaches full maturity. Some kauri in New Zealand are thought to be around 2,000 years old.

Ship-builders and millers Early sailors were quick to realize that young kauri trunks made excellent ships' masts and spars, and from the 1790s British naval supply vessels called in at the Firth of Thames for timber—often after unloading convicts in Australia.

Ship-building began at Hokianga Harbour in 1826, and ship-builders and timber-millers were among the first to settle many of the coastal regions where kauri grows. They also discovered that kauri yielded sawn timber of high quality, with the huge trunks producing clean lengths of timber that were easily worked. Each tree could provide enough to build three or four houses, and many of these distinctive cottages are still sound today.

Tane Mahuta, a kauri giant

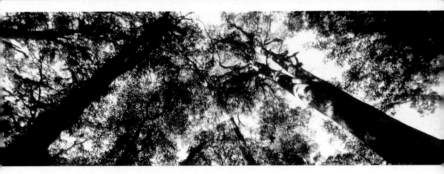

Working in the forests

Moving the kauri logs out of the forest was a major operation. Massive logs were 'sniped' out of the bush and then dragged ('snigged') by bullock teams to the nearest mill. Bullocks were still in use until the 1920s, when they were succeeded by crawler tractors and trucks; bush tramways were also built into areas where there was enough kauri to justify laying the track. In really rugged areas kauri dams were built: Logs were piled up behind the dam, shooting downstream by the hundred when the dam was tripped. At the river mouth the logs that had not been broken up on the way were held in giant 'booms', a floating mass of timber which could then be towed to the mills or waiting ships.

In the early days kauri logs were sawn into planks using a pit saw, with one man standing above the log and the other pulling the saw downward from underneath. In the 1840s, steam-driven saws and water-powered mills took over; mechanization greatly increased the rate of exploitation, with output reaching its peak in 1906.

Kauri gum Kauri gum, the solidified resin from the tree, was used by Maori for chewing (when it was fresh and soft) and, because it burns easily, as a firelighter or torch, impregnated on a stick of flax. The kauri ash was then mixed with shark oil to make a pigment for tattooing.

The settlers soon discovered that this high-quality gum was ideal for making varnishes, and gum-diggers made up a second wave of settlers in the northern regions. In the second half of the 19th century, exports of kauri gum from Auckland were greater than those of wool, gold or kauri timber itself. In the 1930s, synthetics took over in the manufacture of varnish, but the lower-quality gums started to be used for making linoleum and false teeth.

Amber-coloured kauri gum, dug from the petrified remains of prehistoric forests

THE GUM-DIGGERS

At the peak of the kauri gum industry there were some 20,000 gum-diggers in the north, including Chinese, Malay and Maori workers. A gum-digger was generally equipped with a spear (to poke around in the bogs), a hurdy-gurdy (a cross between a washing machine and a sifter, to clean the gum), a spade and an axe. Gum was also bled from live trees, but this damaging process was banned in 1905.

Bubbling mud pools, geysers and other seething sulphurous features are all part of the volcanic activity around Rotorua

The Chinese gooseberry was renamed the kiwifruit when New Zealand began to export it commercially in the 1960s

THE COROMANDEL Across the Hauraki Gulf from Auckland, the Coromandel is a popular weekend retreat, just a couple of hours' drive from the city. The rugged ranges that run down the middle of the peninsula provide a scenic backdrop to the deep blue sea—and great trekking. Once heavily exploited for kauri timber and gold, the peninsula's bush forests are now slowly regenerating and are fiercely protected by local residents. Many artists and craftspeople have settled here, and browsing in craft workshops is a popular option; more energetic activities include bush-walking, sailing, 'rock hounding' (looking for minerals) and horseback-riding, or you can simply take it easy on one of the many sheltered east-coast beaches.

THE BAY OF PLENTY Aptly named by Cook, the Bay of Plenty is a fertile agricultural region where fruit (particularly kiwi and citrus fruit) flourishes in the rolling countryside. A busy holiday area, it has excellent beaches

Mount Ruapehu burst into action in 1995, spreading debris up to 70km (44 miles) away

(especially for surfing), plenty of adventure activities and a smattering of historical attractions. The biggest urban area in the bay is **Tauranga**, a commercial harbour that is also quickly developing as a resort hub. Across the harbour bridge, **Mount Maunganui** is home to an ancient Maori *pā* site, hot salt-water pools and good beaches for swimming and surfing.

The main service point for the eastern part of the Bay of Plenty is **Whakatane**, which lies at the mouth of the river of the same name. Here, too, there are superb beaches. The most famous is **Ohope Beach**, 18km (11 miles) long, to the west of the town. Inland, vast areas of forest supply timber for the many board and paper mills around Whakatane.

White Island, one of the world's most accessible continuously active volcanoes, lies 50km (31 miles) offshore from Whakatane. Another volcanic creation, Whale Island (Motuhora), is just 8km (5 miles) to the north.

CENTRAL NORTH ISLAND Bisected by a major fault in the earth's crust, the heart of the North Island is the most active volcanic area in the country. Volcanic lakes, geysers, mud pools and hot springs are just some of the manifestations of this turmoil beneath the volcanic plateau. Visitors have been drawn to this region since Victorian times, and Rotorua in particular caters for every type of activity, from helicopter flights over volcanic craters to jet-boating, guided fishing, back-country horse-riding, tramping and much more besides.

Between the volcanic plateau and the Tasman Sea is the **Waikato**, one of the richest farming districts in the country thanks to its fertile volcanic topsoil and high rainfall. Winding through the heart of this evergreen countryside is the Waikato River, at 425km (264 miles) the longest river in New Zealand. The river gave its name (which means 'flowing waters') to this region and has been an important trading route from Maori times onwards. Today it is extensively exploited for hydroelectric power and has numerous dams and artificial lakes.

MAORI COUNTRY
Both the Waikato and the volcanic plateau were heavily populated by Maori almost from the time of the first migrations. The Waikato was the scene of many bitterly fought battles during the New Zealand Wars, and was one of the last areas in the North Island to be opened up to settlers.

▶▶▶ REGION HIGHLIGHTS

Cathedral Cove *page 84*
Mercury Bay *page 84*
Rotorua area
pages 87–91, 96–97
Waitomo Caves
pages 104–105

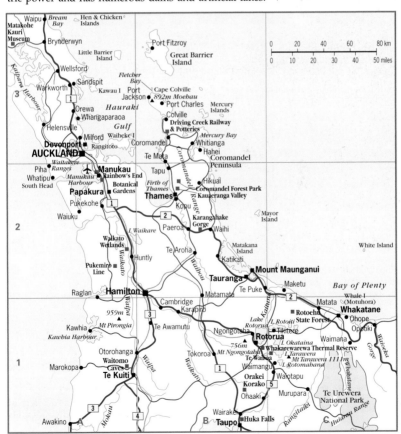

The small community of Colville is the last chance to stock up before heading north along the dramatic Port Jackson Road

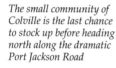

ROCK HOUNDING
The Kauaeranga Valley is well known for its gemstones and rare rocks, and 'rock hounding' (fossicking) in and around the valley's streams is a popular pastime. Agates, jaspers, rhodonite and petrified wood of various kinds can all be found here by those with a keen eye. Geological hammers are allowed, but digging below the surface is not. Permits for fossicking are obtainable from the DoC office. Beaches along the west coast (particularly Te Mata Beach) are also good places for fossicking.

Coromandel

▶▶ Colville and the Cape Road   81B3

From Coromandel township the coast road wends its way up the west side of the peninsula past many scenic bays and inlets. **Colville**, 27km (17 miles) north of Coromandel, is a small rural village with just a general shop/café and a petrol station—the last one before the Cape. After Colville, the rugged interior is dominated by the bulk of **Moehau** (892m/2,925ft), with the views along the coast opening out towards a succession of sandy beaches and campsites such as those at **Fantail Bay** and **Port Jackson**. Finally, after 35km (22 miles) of hair-raising road from Colville, you reach **Fletcher Bay▶▶**, the most northerly bay on the peninsula.

▶▶ Coromandel Forest Park   81B2

Coromandel Forest Park covers 740sq km (286sq miles) of bush-clad hills and valleys in the Coromandel Range, with one of the most popular and easily accessible areas being the **Kauaeranga Valley▶▶** east of Thames. Heavily logged for kauri at the end of the 19th century, this is now regenerating bushland, with a few surviving patches of kauri. Between 1870 and 1924 some 70 dams were built in the valley, and the remains of about a quarter of them form part of the historical attraction of Kauaeranga; there are also over 20 walking tracks (and two overnight huts) in this scenic valley. The DoC visitor centre, 15km (9 miles) from Thames at the lower end of the valley, has information on logging, the dams and many walks (tel: 07 867 9080. *Open* daily, summer 8–4; winter Mon–Fri 8–4). Close by (20 minutes round trip) is a one-third scale working replica of Tarawaere Dam.

▶▶ Coromandel Township 81B3

The township of Coromandel is 56km (35 miles) north of Thames on the west coast of the peninsula. Named after HMS *Coromandel*, which called here in 1820 to collect kauri spars for the British Navy, it was founded on the timber trade, but later boomed with the discovery of gold at nearby Driving Creek in 1852 (the first payable gold strike in New Zealand, see page 218). During the peak gold-rush years of the 1860s and 1870s the township's population reached 10,000. Today its inhabitants only number around 1,000 people and it has a carefully nurtured 'village' atmosphere.

Most of Coromandel's cafés and shops, as well as the visitor centre (tel: 07 866 8598; www.coromandeltown.co.nz. *Open* summer, Mon–Sat 9–4; winter, Mon–Fri 10–3), are on Kapanga Road, which runs at right angles to the harbour. Further along is the **Coromandel School of Mines and Historical Museum** (*Open* summer, 10–4. *Admission: inexpensive*), housed in the original School of Mines (1897), which includes mineralogical displays and, at the back, New Zealand's first jailhouse.

A short drive north of the town is the **Driving Creek Railway and Potteries▶▶**, one of the most popular attractions on the peninsula. Local artist and railway enthusiast Barry Brickell set up a pottery at Driving Creek in 1974 and built the railway to bring clay and pinewood fuel for his kilns down from the hills. The 2.5km (1.5-mile) line passes five viaducts, two spirals, a double switchback and two tunnels. As well as bringing materials downhill, the railway also carries visitors up and back again, and the one-hour round trip makes for an enjoyable excursion through regenerating bushland (tel: 07 866 8703; www. drivingcreekrailway.co.nz. Trips daily at 10AM and 2PM; also noon and 4PM in summer. *Admission: moderate*).

OYSTERS AND MUSSELS

The sheltered waters of the Firth of Thames and the high rate of water exchange between the Pacific Ocean and the Hauraki Gulf create perfect conditions for delicious shellfish. In the intertidal area, Pacific oysters are farmed on sticks held on racks, with around 6 million oysters harvested annually. The New Zealand green-lipped mussel is grown on long lines in deeper water, with around 12,000 tonnes produced annually. You may see the barges (there are 17 for the mussels and two for the oysters) working the aquaculture beds along the coast.

83

The Driving Creek Railway snakes up the hillside

▶▶▶ Mercury Bay   81B3

Mercury Bay is one of the most delightful coastal areas in the Coromandel, and with its superb beaches sheltered by bush-clad headlands it makes a pleasant base for visiting the peninsula. The explorer Kupe landed here some time between AD 800 and 950, and Cook anchored in the bay in November 1769 to make observations on the transit of Mercury, naming the bay after the planet.

The main settlement in Mercury Bay is **Whitianga▶**, one of the most accessible anchorages on the coast thanks to the absence of a harbour bar (the name comes from *Te Whitianga a Kupe*, 'the crossing place of Kupe'). The port is a popular base for boating and deep-sea fishing, and the commercial fleet also hauls in catches of crayfish and scallops. A good choice of accommodation, restaurants and other facilities attracts around 20,000 visitors during the summer season, who come for the sea-kayaking, swimming with dolphins, horse-riding, fishing, boat trips and windsurfing.

The main beach in Whitianga is Buffalo Beach, 4km (2.5 miles) long, named after the convict ship HMS *Buffalo*, which was wrecked here in 1840. The town adjoins the harbour on the south side of the bay and the visitor centre is on the main street (66 Albert Street, tel: 07 866 5555; www.whitianga.co.nz. *Open* Mon–Fri 9–5, Sat–Sun 9–1).

On the harbour front, the **Mercury Bay Museum▶** (tel: 07 866 0730; www.mercurybaymuseum.co.nz. *Open* summer, daily 10–4; winter, Tue, Thu, Sun 11–2. *Admission: inexpensive*) has exhibits from the kauri milling days and remnants of old shipwrecks.

Across from the museum is the main wharf, with a passenger ferry (frequent services daily, tel: 07 866 5925; www.whitianga.co.nz/ferry.html) that shuttles across to **Ferry Landing▶▶** on the other side of the narrows. This was the original site of the township, and the stone wharf (built in 1837) is said to be the oldest in the country. An enjoyable walk leads to a *pā* site at the top of the hill above the wharf, and you can rent bicycles or walk to a string of excellent beaches.

Cathedral Cove▶▶▶ is a superb beach with sand tinted pink by crushed seashells and framed by a massive rock arch at its southern end. The offshore islands sheltering the beach form part of Cathedral Cove Marine Reserve and are popular spots for diving and snorkelling. Cathedral Cove can be reached by boat (see panel) or via a walking track (two hours round trip) from **Hahei**.

South of Hahei, at **Hot Water Beach▶**, watching the hot springs welling up through the sands is a wonderful way to spend an afternoon.

▶ Thames   81B2

Lying at the base of the peninsula on the Firth of Thames, this sizeable town is the main gateway to the Coromandel. It gained its name indirectly when Captain Cook, visiting in 1769, named the Waihou River (which disgorges just south of the town) the Thames because he felt it bore 'some resemblance to the River Thames in England'.

Dig your own thermal pool at Hot Water Beach (right), where thermal activity heats the sand

84

OFFSHORE TRIPS
Trips to Cathedral Cove and Hot Water Beach operate from both Whitianga and Hahei. From the wharf at Ferry Landing, Hot Water Beach Connection (tel: 07 866 2478) run daily excursions by road lasting 4–5 hours. From Hahei, the Hahei Explorer (tel: 07 866 3910; www.hahei explorer.co.nz) also incorporates snorkelling in the Cathedral Cove Marine Reserve. Dolphin swimming is organized by Dolphin Quest at Whitianga (book through Whitianga visitor centre, tel: 07 866 5555).

A massive gold strike was made on the nearby Kuranui Stream in 1867, and by the following year the population of Thames had increased to 18,000, with 40 stamper batteries pounding away day and night to crush quartz for gold. Relics from that era include a stamper battery at the **Goldmine Experience** (tel: 07 868 8514; www.goldmine-experience.co.nz. *Open* daily, summer 10–4; winter 11–2. *Admission: inexpensive*) on the northern outskirts of town, and the **Thames School of Mines and Mineralogical Museum** at the corner of Cochrane and Brown streets (tel: 07 868 6227. *Open* summer, daily 11–4; winter, Tue–Sun 11–3. *Admission: inexpensive*).

Thames also has a handful of attractive buildings, which are described in an *Urban Heritage Trail* leaflet available from the visitor centre (206 Pollen Street, tel: 07 868 7284; www.thames-info.co.nz. *Open* Mon–Fri 9–5, Sat–Sun 9–4).

RANGE ROADS
The two coasts of the Coromandel are linked by four roads crossing the Coromandel Range. The longest (50km/31 miles) is SH25, which crosses from Coromandel township to Whitianga via the beach at Kuaotunu; No. 309 Road from Coromandel to Whitianga (33km/20 miles) passes a Scenic Reserve; the newest crossing (also 33km/20 miles) is SH25A between Kopu and Hikuai road. Perhaps the most scenic route is the rugged Tapu–Coroglen road (29km/18 miles), which passes the delightful Rapaura Water Gardens (tel: 07 868 4821; www.rapaurawatergardens.co.nz. *Open* daily 9–5).

85

Wave action has created a rock arch at Cathedral Cove

HAUHAU MOVEMENT
This was a revivalist religion of the 1860s, whose supporters believed themselves to be immune to British bullets. The Opotiki area was subject to repeated attacks by Hauhau, who would then retreat to the impenetrable wilderness of Te Urewera to seek sanctuary. Hauhauism finally fizzled out at the beginning of the 1870s.

Lady Knox geyser erupting in Rotorua

Bay of Plenty

▶ Opotiki   81C1

At the eastern end of the Bay of Plenty, Opotiki is set on a harbour inlet formed by the junction of the Otara and Waioeka rivers, with over 25km (15 miles) of sandy beaches. Opotiki is the main gateway to the wilderness of the Raukumara Range and the Motu River, and the beginning of the East Cape Road to Gisborne, which is 343km (213 miles) long.

In the township, the **Church of St. Stephen the Martyr▶** (Church Street) was the scene of the bloody murder in 1865 of a Lutheran missionary, the Rev. Carl Volkner, by followers of the Hauhau movement (see panel).

Outside Opotiki, the **Hukutaia Domain▶** (6km/4 miles, signposted after turning south beyond Waioeka Bridge) is a lovely 5ha (12-acre) native plant reserve that includes one of New Zealand's most ancient trees, a massive puriri estimated to be around 2,000 years old.

▶▶▶ Rotorua   81B1

ROTORUA INFORMATION
Downtown is the custom-built Tourism Rotorua complex (1167 Fenton Street, tel: 07 348 5179; www.rotorunanz.com. *Open* daily, summer 8–6; winter 8–5:30). It houses not only the information office but also a DoC office, an excellent map shop, toilet and shower facilities and a restaurant.

Rotorua, at the heart of the volcanic plateau, is one of the country's most popular and commercialized tourist resorts, with a range of large-scale attractions geared towards the incoming busloads. The city is built around (and on top of) a series of spouting geysers, hissing fumaroles and bubbling pools of mud and sulphur; these geothermal phenomena are more accessible here than almost anywhere else in New Zealand. The emissions of hydrogen sulphide from thermal areas have earned it the nickname 'sulphur city', and the pungent odour is highly noticeable when you first arrive: strangely, you soon get used to it.

Rotorua is on the shores of the lake of the same name, and there are numerous other scenic lakes near by to visit. The area is an active base for Maori culture, and traditional concerts are on offer in many hotels and outlying *marae* (see panel page 88). The city was first developed as a spa town at the end of the last century, and the bathhouse (built in 1908) still exists, although today it is a museum. Other popular attractions and activities include soaking in hot pools, sheep shows, trout and wildlife parks and scenic flights or cruises on the lake.

The mock-Tudor Tourism Rotorua complex

The main thermal area within the city boundaries is **Whakarewarewa▶▶▶**, which has boiling mud pools, silica terraces, steam vents and a host of other facinating phenomena. The main part of the reserve is Geyser Flat, which has at least seven active geysers, including two that perform remarkably reliably: the Prince of Wales Feathers, which shoots up as high as 12m (39ft), and mighty Pohuto (Maori for 'splashing'), a spectacular sight that can reach as high as 30m (98ft) and spouts 10–20 times a day. Access to the reserve is through **New Zealand Maori Arts and Crafts Institute▶▶**, which trains young craftspeople in the old tradtions. Visitors can watch them at work and there is a gallery with carvings on display. There is also a replica Maori village with a daily show at 12:15 (tel: 07 348 9047; www.nzmaori.co.nz. *Open* daily, summer 8–6; winter 8–5).

Next to the geyser reserve is the living Maori **Whakarewarewa Thermal Village** (tel: 07 349 3463; www.whakarewarewa.com. *Open* daily 8:30–5, guided tours approximately half-hourly; cultural performances at 11:15 and 2. *Admission: moderate.*

Also near Rotorua city is the thermal zone called **Hell's Gate▶▶▶**, east of Lake Rotorua (tel: 07 345 3151; www. hellsgaterotorua.co.nz), while other major areas of thermal activity such as Waimangu, Wai-o-tapu and Orakei Korako are some distance away to the south.

*The exterior of
Bath House*

MAORI CONCERTS
Rotorua is one of the
best places in New
Zealand to experience a
traditional Maori concert
and *hangi*. Maori-owned
operators for these
evening events include
Rotoiti Tours (tel: 07 348
8969) and Tamaki Tours
(tel: 07 346 2823;
www.maoriculture.co.nz).

On the lakeshore, the **Government Gardens** are an extensive park-like area issuing steam incongruously from the manicured croquet lawns and rose beds. At the middle of the gardens is the **Bath House**, a mock-Tudor structure whose orange half-timbering is either vulgar or charming, depending on your point of view. Built in 1908, it was once an actual bathhouse and was a deliberate attempt to emulate the elegance of a European spa. It had all the latest balneological equipment, as well as thermal pools, massage cubicles and a foyer graced by 13 classical marble sculptures. By the 1920s faith in spa treatment was waning and the building was neglected. Rotorua City Council took it on in 1963 and it now houses the **Rotorua Museum of Art and History▶▶** (tel: 07 349 4350; www.rotoruamuseum.co.nz. *Open* daily, summer 9:30–6; winter 9:30–5. *Admission: inexpensive*), with some excellent exhibits displayed in rather cramped conditions. Permanent exhibitions include 'In the Shadow of the Volcano', which traces the story of the effects of the 1886 eruption on the people of the area; 'The Legacy of Houmaitawhiti', which deals with the history and *taonga* (treasures) of the Te Arawa Maori, and 'The Way We Were', which gives some idea about the beginnings of Rotorua as a spa town.

Near the Bath House, the **Polynesian Spa▶** (tel: 07 348 1328; www.polynesianspa.co.nz. *Open* daily 6:30AM–11PM. *Admission: varies*) contains a number of different mineral pools and hot springs to suit your ailment or state of fatigue, with total relaxation practically guaranteed by means of 'Aix massage' (administered under jets of hot water). Also within the grounds of Government Gardens, the **Orchid Gardens** (*Open* daily 8:30–5:30. *Admission: moderate*) have year-round displays of orchids, ferns and other exotic plants, and there is also a water organ (on the hour 9–5) with synchronized lighting and music.

Several major attractions lie just a few minutes' drive along the west shore of the lake. At the **Skyline Skyrides▶** (tel: 07 347 0027; www.skylineskyrides.co.nz. *Open* daily 9–late. *Admission: moderate*), a gondola whisks you 200m (650ft) up the side of Mount Ngongotaha to a café/restaurant complex at the top. The young-at-heart can whizz back down again for part of the way on a luge (a sledge running down a track) or a flying fox (an aerial cableway).

Just past the gondola base is **Rainbow Springs▶▶▶** (tel: 07 350 0440; www.rainbownz.co.nz. *Open* daily 8–5. *Admission: moderate*), the largest and best-known of the trout springs in the area. The big tourist complex here includes a gift shop, photo processing facilities and a restaurant. Just inside the park entrance, the Rainbow Spring itself flows at a rate of 4.5 million litres (1 million gallons) a day, welling up into a series of crystal-clear pools where hundreds of trout come to feed and spawn (the trout are free to swim back to the lake via a small stream at any time). Spawning usually occurs in July, when pairs of trout can be seen laying and fertilizing their eggs in the shingle bed of the stream. There is a large underwater viewing window for close-up views of the rainbow, brown and tiger trout in the pools. Beside the springs is a small zoo-type area that specializes in animals introduced to the country (such as deer and wild pigs), as well as native and introduced birds. It also has a nocturnal aviary housing kiwi and morepork.

Across the road (and linked by a tunnel) is the **Rainbow Farm▶▶**, part of the same complex. Here a huge barn is the setting for regular shows (at 10:30, 11:45, 1, 2:30 and 4. *Admission: moderate*) of sheep-shearing, sheepdog mustering, a staged sheep auction and plenty of other educational agricultural entertainment. There is also a shop incorporating displays on pioneers and farming.

Continue along the highway to the **Agrodome▶▶**, which has another show barn with regular demonstrations and sheep/cattle shows (tel: 07 357 1050; www.agrodome.co.nz. *Open* daily at 9:30, 11 and 2:30. *Admission: moderate*). The Rainbow Farm setting is perhaps better, because the barn is open-ended and overlooks fields where the sheep are mustered, but otherwise the jokes and patter are remarkably similar in both shows.

Looping behind Mount Ngongotaha, Paradise Valley Road leads to **Paradise Valley Springs▶▶** (tel: 07 348 9667; www.paradisev.co.nz. *Open* daily 9–5. *Admission: moderate*). This is another trout-viewing area, with a dozen spring-fed pools strung out alongside the Ngongotaha stream; the 6ha (15-acre) park is home to a range of native New Zealand wildlife and a pride of African lions; there is also a wetlands area with native birds.

THE LEGEND OF THE LAKE
Mokoia Island, in the middle of Lake Rotorua, is central to the romantic story of Hinemoa and Tutanekai. Hinemoa was a young girl living on the shore who fell in love with an illegitimate young chief, Tutanekai, who lived on the island. Her family opposed the union, and in despair she lashed together calabash gourds and began the long swim over to Mokoia. The lovers' union was later accepted by their families, and their descendants still live in Rotorua today.

Top sheep-shearers demonstrate their art at Rotorua Agrodome

When Mount Tarawera erupted in 1886, volcanic ash buried the Maori village at Te Wairoa, preserving the huts and their contents

Rotorua environs

Rotorua's other outlying attractions are scattered over a wider area to the southeast of the lake and the city. One of the most fascinating is **Te Wairoa Buried Village**▶▶▶ (tel: 07 362 8287; www.buriedvillage. co.nz. *Open* daily 9–5. *Admission: moderate*), 15km (9 miles) along Tarawera Road. The village was the main resort for trips to the Pink and White Terraces before the Tarewera eruption (see panel) and had two hotels, a shop and numerous *whare* (Maori houses), all of which were buried beneath volcanic ash in 1886. Excavations began in 1936, and in this village the Maori huts, preserved beneath the ash, are the genuine article—unlike those you are likely to see almost everywhere else, which have been built specifically for tourists. A path tours the excavated huts and other interesting relics (including a storehouse with rare stone-carvings), culminating in a short bush walk alongside Te Wairoa Falls. There is also a small gallery displaying old photographs and objects.

About 20 minutes' drive from the city, the **Waimangu Volcanic Valley** (tel: 07 366 6137; www.waimangu.co.nz. *Open* daily 8:30–5. *Admission: moderate*) is an extensive thermal area leading down to Lake Rotomahana, with many different geothermal phenomena visible on the one-hour downhill walk to the lakeshore; a bus carries you back up again, or you can combine it with a boat trip on the lake past the site of the former Pink and White Terraces. Hot springs and fumaroles, steaming cliffs and a boiling lake are among the attractions here.

Further south still, the **Wai-o-tapu Thermal Wonderland**▶ (tel: 07 366 6333; www.geyserland.co.nz. *Open* daily 8:30–5:30. *Admission: moderate*) is another major thermal zone, with pathways between the blowholes and boiling mud

THE TARAWERA ERUPTION
The celebrated Pink and White Terraces beneath Mount Tarawera were one of the country's most famous natural attractions during the 19th century. Previously thought to be extinct, Mount Tarawera erupted without warning in the early hours of 10 June 1886, with Lake Rotomahana beneath it, exploding with a roar heard hundreds of kilometres away. Rescuers arriving from Rotorua the next day were met with scenes of 'utter distress and unimaginable desolation', with three Maori villages (including Te Wairoa) completely devastated and 153 people dead. Ash, lava and mud were scattered over an area of 16,000sq km (6,175sq miles), and the Pink and White Terraces were totally destroyed.

pools. Highlights include bright mineral deposits around the Champagne Pool and Artist's Palette, vast sulphurous craters and the Lady Knox Geyser (primed with soap to foam daily at 10:15AM).

Tucked away in a 'hidden valley' between Taupo (32km/20 miles) and Rotorua (72km/45 miles), **Orakei Korako**▶▶ is a fine thermal area well worth visiting for its silica terraces, which—since the destruction of the famous Pink and White Terraces by the Tarawera eruption in 1886—are considered to be the best remaining example of this geothermal phenomenon in the country.

Orakei Korako's hot springs bubble out from the north side of the valley on the other side of Lake Ohakuri, created in the 1960s by damming the Waikato. Entrance to Orakei Korako (tel: 07 378 3131; www.orakeikorako.co.nz. *Open* daily 8:30–4, extended hours in summer. *Admission: expensive*) includes the short boat trip across the lake, from where you first see the Emerald Terrace. The largest in New Zealand, this silica terrace is around 20m (65ft) thick and continues for 35m (115ft) beneath the waters of the lake.

From the jetty next to the Emerald Terrace, walking tracks continue up through the thermal zones, which include a number of geysers, mud pools and further silica terraces. A bush walk leads to Ruatapu Cave ('sacred cave'), which has an entrance framed by tree ferns leading down to a 'pool of mirrors', where Maori women are said to have groomed themselves—the valley takes its name from this custom, and *orakei korako* means 'the place of adorning'. Passing one last gusher, the Soda Fountain, the track leads back to the boat jetty. Amid the fernery on the track, look out for the silver fern, the national emblem of New Zealand.

MURAL TOWN
The small town of Katikati (40km/25 miles north-west of Tauranga on SH2) was in economic decline until someone had the bright idea of painting murals all over the place and turning the whole town into an outdoor art gallery. As the idea mushroomed, more and more murals appeared—so did the tourists. This friendly town prospered once more. The high-quality murals are described in detail in a leaflet available from the visitor centre (36 Main Road, tel: 07 549 1658. *Open* Mon–Fri 9:30–4:30; Sat 10–1).

The Rainbow Terrace, one of the unusual thermal formations at Orakei Korako

Rainbow Terrace

MAYOR ISLAND

During the main holiday period (25 December to the end of January), there are regular ferry trips (crossing time 2.5 hours) to Mayor Island from Tauranga and Mount Maunganui. At other times private charters and fishing excursions can be arranged through Tauranga visitor centre (tel: 07 578 8103 for details and bookings).

▶▶ Tauranga   81B2

The principal city in the Bay of Plenty, prosperous Tauranga is protected from the ocean by Mount Maunganui and Matakana Island, and its harbour has provided shelter for mariners for centuries (the name means 'safe anchorage'). Today it is the busiest export port in New Zealand, while the surrounding region produces an abundance of subtropical fruit.

Within the waterfront area (a large chunk of which is being transformed into an imaginatively conceived pedestrian area) there are several historic sites, including the second-oldest mission station in the country, the **Elms Mission House**▶▶ (Mission Street, tel: 07 577 9772; www.theelms.co.nz. *Open* house Sun 2–4, gardens daily 2–6. *Admission: inexpensive*). Completed in 1847, it has a tiny chapel, a fascinating library and a superb garden.

Near by on Cliff Road the **Monmouth Redoubt** was once a fortified encampment (only the earthworks remain) built by British troops during the New Zealand Wars. Below Cliff Street, at the top of The Strand, is a fine war canoe, *Te Awanui*, carved from kauri wood in 1973.

A few minutes' drive from the middle of the city, the **Compass Community Village**▶ (155 17th Avenue West, tel: 07 571 3700. *Open* daily 8:30–4. *Admission: free*) has a period Main Street, a Maori village and other attractions, including craft shops and bases for community groups.

Attractive parks within the city include Robbins Park, Tauranga Domain and, 4km (2.5 miles) outside the town, Yatton Park. Also outside town is the lakeside **McLaren**

92

Mount Maunganui, an important pā site, marks the eastern entrance to Tauranga harbour

Historic Elms Mission House in its lovely garden, one of the oldest mission stations in New Zealand

Falls Park (20 minutes along SH29, 11km/7 miles westwards), popular for picnics and trout fishing; next door to it is **Marshalls Animal Park** (tel: 07 543 1099. *Open* Oct–May, Wed–Sun 10–4:15; Jun–Sep, Sat–Sun 10–4:15. *Admission: inexpensive*), where you can see some unusual animals, such as Tibetan yaks.

Mount Maunganui▶▶, linked to Tauranga by the harbour bridge, is an attractive resort area with a long surfing beach. The mount itself, at the tip of the peninsula, marks the eastern entrance to Tauranga harbour and is a fine viewpoint. An important Maori defensive site, it still has many remains of fortifications. Several walking tracks wind their way up to the 232m (761ft) summit; the entrance is on Adams Avenue, and you should allow at least two hours for the round trip. At the bottom you can soothe aching muscles in the **Hot Salt Pools**▶ (Adams Avenue. *Open* daily 8AM–10PM. *Admission: inexpensive*).

Mayor Island (Tuhua), 35km (19 miles) offshore from Tauranga, is a famous big-game fishing base (see panel opposite). It has an underwater marine reserve and some *pā* sites. Extinct craters hold two lakes.

▶ Te Puke
81B2

The largest inland town in the Bay of Plenty area (southeast of Tauranga), Te Puke claims to have launched New Zealand's kiwifruit industry, amply documented in **Kiwifruit Country**▶ (tel: 07 573 6340; www.kiwifruit country.co.nz. *Open* daily 9–5. *Admission: inexpensive*), 5km (3 miles) east of the town on SH2. In May and June, when the trees are in fruit, there is a tour of the orchards and packing sheds. There is also a children's playground. Next door at the **Vintage Auto Barn**▶ (tel: 07 573 6547; www.vintagecars.nzhere.com. *Open* hourly 9:15–3:45. *Admission: moderate*) there are over 90 classic and vintage vehicles (*Open* daily 8:30–5. *Admission: moderate*).

On the shore 15km (9 miles) east of Te Puke is **Maketu**, where the Arawa canoe first landed over 600 years ago; a **cairn** by the river mouth commemorates this event.

RIVER RAFTING
Opotiki is the main base for rafting expeditions on the Motu River. The rapids are mostly grades three and four, and several adventure options (lasting from one to four days) are operated by the Wet 'n' Wild Rafting Company (tel: 0800 462 723; www.wetnwildrafting.co.nz). Rafting on the Motu is also available through Motu River Expeditions (tel: 07 308 7760).

A replica of the canoe Mataatua, in front of the sacred rock arch Pohaturoa. According to legend, Mataatua brought the first kumara (sweet potato) to Aotearoa

► **Whakatane**   81C1

Whakatane gained its name with the arrival of the *Mataatua* canoe from Hawaiki in the 14th century: as the menfolk stepped ashore to test the lie of the land, the canoe started drifting out to sea with all the women aboard. Although it was *tapu* (forbidden) for women to handle the paddles, the captain's daughter Wairaka grabbed a paddle and cried '*Kia Whakatane au i ahau*' (I will be bold and act as a man) and the others followed suit, bringing the canoe back to shore. The settlement was thus named Whakatane ('to be manly').

The main street of Whakatane is The Strand. Bisecting it is Boon Street, where you will find the visitor centre (*Open* daily 9–5) and the small **Whakatane Museum and Gallery►** (tel: 07 306 0505; www.whakatanemuseum.org. nz. *Open* Tue–Fri 10–4:30, Sat 11–1:30, Sun 2–4:30. *Admission: donation*), which has displays on the eastern Bay of Plenty and its people, as well as a gallery showing changing exhibitions of arts, crafts and history.

In the heart of the town, Whakatane's origins are commemorated by a model of the canoe *Mataatua* next to an old rock arch known as **Pohaturoa**; this once stood on the foreshore, and was a sacred place where *tohunga* performed tattooing and other ceremonies. Now it is the focus of a small park (corner of The Strand and Commerce Streets), a memorial to the dead of World War I. Next to it stands a statue of Te Hurinui Apanui, a local Mataatua chief.

A statue of Wairaka stands on the Whakatane Heads at the mouth of the river, while a nearby plaque marks the landing place of the canoe.

► **Whale Island (Motuhora)**   81C1

Slightly smaller than White Island, Whale Island or Motuhora is also volcanic and has numerous fumaroles (particularly in the aptly named Sulphur Bay); the island is a major bird-nesting site, with one colony of grey-faced petrels numbering some 10,000 birds. Occupied in pre-European times by Maori, it was also the site of a whaling station in the 1830s. The English name, however, refers not to this but to its shape, which resembles a humpback whale (the Maori name also refers to this likeness). The island is privately owned and is now a wildlife refuge.

▶▶ White Island   81C2

Lying at the northern end of the Taupo–Rotorua volcanic zone, White Island usually emits a visible plume of steam and often spurts clouds of ash that can be seen for some distance around. Its Maori name is Whakaari ('to make visible') and Cook gave the volcano its English name in 1769, inspired by the dense clouds of smoke.

At the end of the 19th century there was a huge demand for sulphur to fertilize farmlands, and the first sulphur was mined on White Island in the 1880s. An eruption in September 1914 caused a mudflow that swept the mining settlement out to sea, leaving no trace of the 12 people who worked there. Parts of the abandoned workings can still be seen on the southeast side of the island. The bankrupt White Island Sulphur Company gave the island to the father of John Buttle, who owns it today. In 1953 it was declared a Private Scenic Reserve, now administered by the Department of Conservation.

Organized boat trips run to the island; the journey takes about an hour each way, with half an hour on shore to gaze at steaming fumaroles and peer into the crater itself. Scenic flights over the island are also popular (see panel).

ISLAND TRIPS
Tours to White Island from Whakatane can be made with White Island Tours (tel: 07 308 9588; www.whiteisland.co.nz). For scenic flights contact Vulcan Helicopters (tel: 0800 804 354; www.vulcanheli.co.nz) or East Bay Flight Centre (tel: 07 308 8446). Trips to Motuhora (Whale Island) operate only in high summer; details from Whakatane DoC (236 The Strand, tel: 07 308 7213).

95

White Island looking north. The sulphur workings were at Te Awapuia Bay (foreground), and the bare patch is the gannet colony at Otaketake

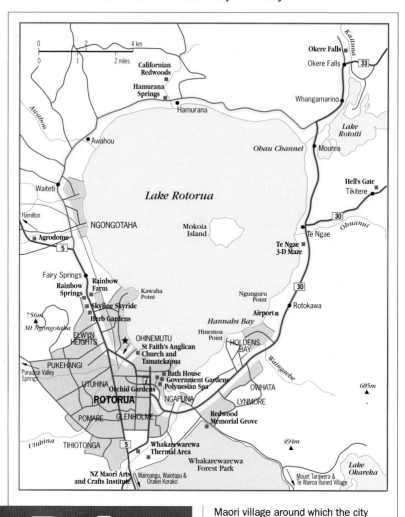

0   2   4 km
0   1   2 miles

Okere Falls
Okere Falls
33
Kaituna
Californian Redwoods
Hamurana Springs
Hamurana
Whangamarino
Awahou
Lake Rotoiti
Aratoha
Obau Channel
Mourea
Waiteti
Hell's Gate
Tikitere
Lake Rotorua
NGONGOTAHA
Mokoia Island
30
Obuanui
Te Ngae
Hamilton
Agrodome
5
Fairy Springs
Rainbow Springs
Rainbow Farm
Kawaha Point
Te Ngae 3-D Maze
Ngunguru Point
30
Skyline Skyride
Herb Gardens
756m
Mt Ngongotaha
ELWYN HEIGHTS
OHINEMUTU
St Faith's Anglican Church and Tamatekapua
Hannahs Bay
Hinemoa Point
Airport
Rotokawa
PUKEHANGI
HOLDENS BAY
Paradise Valley Springs
UTUHINA
Orchid Gardens
Bath House
Government Gardens
Polynesian Spa
Waingaehe
OWHATA
685m
ROTORUA
NGAPUNA
LYNMORE
POMARE
GLENHOLME
Redwood Memorial Grove
Utuhina
TIHIOTONGA
5
Whakarewarewa Thermal Area
494m
Lake Okareka
NZ Maori Arts and Crafts Institute
Waimangu, Waiotapu & Orakei Korako
Whakarewarewa Forest Park
Mount Tarawera & Te Wairoa Buried Village

Drive

Around Lake Rotorua

This pleasant drive along the shores of Lake Rotorua affords several possible stops to see the original Maori village of the lake, trout springs, volcanic activity, waterfalls and a wildlife park. It is about 60km (37 miles), so allow the best part of a day.

Starting from the lakeside jetty, turn right into **Ohinemutu▶▶**, the original Maori village around which the city eventually developed. Here is **Tamatekapua▶▶**, an elaborately carved meeting house (built in 1873, rebuilt 1941), with **St. Faith's Anglican Church▶▶** opposite (*Open* 8:30–5). Constructed in Tudor style in 1910, it has an unusual window depicting Christ as if walking on the lake draped in a *korowai* (chief's cloak), and has some particularly rich carvings and lattice panel work.

Head down Lake Road and turn right onto SH5 to Hamilton; after 2km (1 mile) you will see the turning on your left for the **Skyline Skyrides▶** (see page 89) up the slopes of Mount Ngongotaha, from which there is a fabulous panorama of the lake.

Past the Skyline is **Rainbow Springs** with **Rainbow Farm** opposite (see page 89). At the roundabout where the Hamilton road turns left, carry straight on towards Ngongotaha. After passing through the village, the road diverts inland before rejoining the lakeshore at Hamurana; from here there are lovely views back across to Mokoia Island with Mount Tarawera dominating the far lakeside. There is a small wildlife refuge on the shoreline, with the 80ha (198-acre) **Hamurana Springs**▶▶ on the left of the road (in Hamurana Gardens). Pull over into the parking area and walk across the bridge that spans the springs.

Follow the path upstream to a mighty and unusual glade of Californian redwood trees planted in the 1920s. Rejoin the road, which now winds through a scenic part of the lakeshore (with the roadside verges shaded by numerous tree ferns) before turning left onto SH33 just before the Ohau Channel. On the right-hand side are the pretty bays and inlets of the western reaches of **Lake Rotoiti**▶▶, once used as a link by canoe between the lakes to the east and Lake Rotorua.

Continue on around Lake Rotoiti, turning left immediately after the Okere Falls Garage down Trout Pool Road before the next bridge. **Okere Falls**▶▶ can be reached by walking

from the parking area here: these spectacular falls drop some 100m (330ft) over a series of cascades and rapids in a relatively short distance; this is where the combined outflow from lakes Rotorua and Rotoiti starts its journey to the sea. Steps lead down the rock to a cave at the foot of one of the main falls where, according to legend, Maori women and children would hide when the *pā* site on top of the hill was under attack.

Return down the same road, continuing on through Mourea towards Rotorua. At the junction with SH30, make a detour to the left for 4km (2.5 miles) to **Hell's Gate**▶▶▶ (*Open daily 9–5. Admission: moderate*). Also known as 'Tikitere', this reserve covers some 10ha (25 acres), with a 2.5km (1.5-mile) walking track around and between the bubbling mud pools, crystal formations, gas vents and other seething sulphurous features. Part of the track includes a bush walk that passes beside the Kakahi Falls; fed by hot lakes higher up, these falls are said to be the only hot thermal waterfalls in the southern hemisphere.

Follow the SH30 back around the lakeshore to Rotorua city.

St. Faith's Anglican Church has a window where Christ appears to walk on the lake

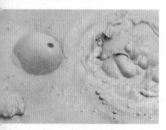

New Zealand is famed for its beautiful scenery, and in particular for its serenely spectacular mountains and lakes. Yet these panoramas mask enormous pressures underground (indeed they were created by them), and the country is still geologically highly active. In fact the country's history is punctuated with natural disasters.

98

THE RING OF FIRE

The earth's surface is divided into vast, moving sheets known as tectonic plates. At places where these meet, 'fault lines' develop through which molten magma can force its way. In the Pacific Ocean, continental blocks press against the plate which holds the sea, and the volatile fault line that surrounds the ocean is known as the 'Pacific Ring of Fire'. The islands of New Zealand were thrust up from the ocean bed at the southern extremity of the Ring of Fire.

A fumarole in the crater of volcanic White Island

Shaping the landscape Many of the country's natural features have been created by volcanic activity, and in the South Island the main mountain range, the Southern Alps, is still undergoing tectonic uplift. Hot springs bubble through fissures in the earth at Hanmer and on the Lewis Pass. The harbours of Otago (Dunedin) and Lyttelton (Christchurch) have been created in the drowned craters of ancient volcanoes. In the North Island a major fault runs from the still active volcano of White Island in the Bay of Plenty down through Rotorua, where boiling mud pools and steaming vents have been an attraction for well over a century. Farther south, the crater in which Lake Taupo lies was created by several massive explosions.

The Taupo eruptions Some 250,000 years ago a huge eruption from Taupo spread rock debris and ash across 2,500sq km (965sq miles) of countryside, and material from the eruption has been found in the waters of Antarctica, near South America. This explosion is the largest known in the southern hemisphere. About 26,500 years ago another vast blast spread ash over most of the country, and in the most recent eruption, 1,800 years ago, pumice and ash buried everything in the surrounding region.

Earthquake zone The same forces that produce volcanic activity also cause earthquakes, as tectonic plates grind against each other. The first known earthquake in New Zealand occurred in the Wellington region in 1460, and is thought to have been of about magnitude 8 on the Richter scale. The first earthquake recorded by Europeans was in Queen Charlotte Sound in 1773.

The fledgling settlement of Wellington was awakened at 1:40AM on 16 October 1848 by a big earthquake, which was followed by three more over the next eight days. The town was virtually destroyed, but amazingly only three people died. Seven years later another massive earthquake (8.1 on the Richter scale) rocked Wellington and the Wairarapa, raising the shoreline by up to 3m (10ft) in places. Over the next 90 years there were a further ten severe earthquakes in the region.

The worst disaster in the 19th century in terms of lives lost was the Tarawera eruption of 10 June 1886, which killed 153 people. With no warning the entire side of the volcano blew out, shattering its base and in the process destroying the famous Pink and White Terraces (see page 90).

More recently One of the country's most powerful earthquakes of the 20th century struck the west coast of the South Island on 16 June 1929. Measuring 7.8 on the Richter scale, the Murchison earthquake was so strong that earth movements were noticed over 483km (300 miles) away in Auckland. Huge tracts of land were uplifted, and 17 people lost their lives. But the worst disaster of all was the Napier earthquake in 1931, when in just two and a half minutes the towns of Napier and Hastings were reduced to rubble, and 256 people died. During the two weeks that followed, 525 aftershocks were recorded.

On 24 June 1942 the Wellington and Wairarapa area was hit by two earthquakes, the second one (of magnitude 7 on the Richter scale) damaging some 8,000 homes. Two more severe earthquakes followed in August. The biggest recent earthquake was in the Bay of Plenty on 2 March 1987, when a magnitude 6.1 earthquake rocked the whole region. Miraculously, no one died.

Emerson Street in Napier immediately after the devastating earthquake of February 1931

THE EARTHQUAKE COMMISSION
During the 1942 Wellington and Wairarapa earthquakes hundreds of buildings collapsed, and most people found they had inadequate insurance to cover their rebuilding costs. Realizing that something needed to be done, the government set up the Earthquake and War Damage Commission, levying a premium on fire insurance to assist in rebuilding after earthquakes. In 1993, this became the Earthquake Commission (EQC) and cover was extended to other natural disasters. In 1994, the EQC successfully intervened for the first time to prevent a disaster before it happened, by stabilizing a massive landslip that was threatening to engulf homes at Akaroa on Banks Peninsula.

Hamilton, commercial hub for the rich agricultural district around the Waikato River

The Waikato

▶ Cambridge

81B1

On the Waikato River 24km (15 miles) southeast of Hamilton, Cambridge was first a *pā* site and then a military base, chosen because it was as far upstream as the British gunboats could navigate in 1864. A large redoubt was built in Fort Street behind the present police station, but the town's military phase lasted less than a decade, and it soon developed into a flourishing market town.

The town has a charming atmosphere, with fine parks and gardens, stately trees, old churches and a village green. One of these churches (dating from 1898) has been converted into the acclaimed **Cambridge Country Store** (92 Victoria Street, tel: 07 827 8715; www. cambridgecountrystore.co.nz. *Open* daily 8:30–5), which claims to be New Zealand's largest retail complex for crafts. There are also several antiques shops and galleries, and craft workshops that you can visit. The visitor centre is on the corner of Queen and Victoria streets (tel: 07 823 3456. *Open* Mon–Fri 9–5, Sat, Sun 10–4).

▶▶ Hamilton

81B2

The commercial and industrial hub of the Waikato region, Hamilton is the largest inland city in New Zealand. With a population of over 158,000, it has prospered through the dairy industry, forestry and manufacturing; since the beginning of the 1990s much of the heart of the city has been renovated to include extensive shopping malls, 'boulevard-style' streets, chic hotels and trendy cafés and restaurants. Its many attractions and a busy calendar of events make it an attractive city for a stop-over.

The Waikato River winds through the middle of the city, with several peaceful parks and gardens laid out on both banks and linked by footpaths and bridges. The city centre is on the west side of the river. Its heart lies halfway down the main thoroughfare, **Victoria Street**, in **Garden Place**, a popular venue for street theatre, buskers and outdoor markets, and also where you will find the visitor centre (Municipal Building, tel: 07 839 3580. *Open* Mon–Fri 9–4:45, Sat–Sun 10–2).

PADDLE-STEAMER TRIPS
Moored at Memorial Park, directly across Victoria Bridge from the middle of Hamilton, the MV *Waipa Delta* is modelled on the old paddle-steamers and has a fully licensed restaurant. There are three scenic cruises upriver daily, including a luncheon cruise and a moonlight dinner cruise. For reservations, tel: 07 854 7813; www.waipadelta.co.nz.

A couple of minutes' walk away is the **Waikato Museum of Art and History**▶▶ (corner of Victoria and Grantham streets, tel: 07 838 6606; www.waikatomuseum.org.nz. *Open* daily 10–4:30. *Admission: donation*), with galleries (and a good café) overlooking the Waikato. Permanent exhibits include the 150-year-old war canoe *Te Winika*, and contemporary Tainui carvings and Tukutuku weavings commissioned for the opening of the museum in 1987. Most of the display space is devoted to changing exhibitions, fine arts, Tainui cultural history, crafts, film and video and music performances.

Hamilton Gardens▶ (Cobham Drive, tel: 07 856 3200; www.hamitongardens.co.nz. *Open* 10–4. *Admission: free*) cover 58ha (143 acres), with numerous themed gardens, including Chinese, English, Japanese and herb gardens. They are also home to the Waikato Institute of Technology Horticulture Education Centre, and there is a café/restaurant overlooking Turtle Lake.

Outside the main city, **Hamilton Zoo**▶▶ (Brymer Road, signposted from Avalon Drive on SH1, tel: 07 838 6720; www.hamiltonzoo.co.nz. *Open* daily 9–5, last admission 3:30. *Admission: moderate*) covers 14ha (35 acres) and has a strong conservation theme. Its modern free-flight, walk-through aviary is the largest in New Zealand, and other displays include a rain forest exhibit and a Waikato Wetlands area.

The **National Agricultural Heritage**▶, 10km (6 miles) to the south of the city on Mystery Creek Road (*Open* daily 9:30–4:30. *Admission: inexpensive*), has an agricultural museum, dairy museum, Clydesdale horses and a 'Down on the Farm' area where children can touch the animals. There are also farm animal demonstrations (daily at 11:30 and 1:30).

HERITAGE WALK
Among its gleaming malls and modern blocks, Hamilton also has a number of historic buildings. Although many are privately owned and not open to the public, some fascinating hidden corners are described in the *Architrek Heritage Trail*, an excellent illustrated booklet available free from the visitor centre.

101

The massive New Zealand Fieldays, the biggest agricultural exposition in the southern hemisphere, is held at the Mystery Creek Events Centre in June

102

Washing the bow carving before a waka *(war canoe) race*

▶▶ Marokopa   81A1

The road from Waitomo westwards towards Marakopa and the coast passes a number of scenic attractions, and the three- to four-hour round trip makes a pleasant excursion from Waitomo. The first stop is at the remarkable **Mangapohue Natural Bridge▶**, 26km (16 miles) from Waitomo; this massive limestone arch above the Mangapohue stream is the remnant of a collapsed cave. The bridge is a 15-minute walk from the main road. Near by is the **Marokopa Tunnel**, another limestone formation; it has a 50m (165ft)-high roof and runs for 270m (295 yards) through the hillside (guided tours daily 10:30. *Admission: expensive*; contact King Country Tours, tel: 07 871 0324; www.kingcountry.co.nz). Farther on, the **Marokopa Falls▶▶** drop 36m (118ft) over a fault in the limestone. There are tracks leading to impressive viewpoints.

▶ Otorohanga   81A1

Set on the fertile flats surrounding the Waipa River, Otorohanga was once the northern stronghold of the great Ngati Maniapoto tribe. Its name (which means 'place of food spun out to last a long journey') refers to the story of a chief who set out from here to Taupo, and who made a small amount of food last the whole journey by means of a magic chant.

Since 1887, tourists have used Otorohanga as a base for visiting the Waitomo Caves (16km/10 miles to the south-

west), a role it has retained to this day. The town has several good-quality motels, tea rooms, craft shops and other facilities. There is a small **Historical Museum** (Kakamutu Road. *Open* Sun 2–4. *Admission: donation*), but the main attraction in the town itself is the **Kiwi House and Native Bird Park**►► (Alex Telfer Drive, tel: 07 873 7391; www.kiwihouse.org.nz. *Open* daily, Sep–May 9–4:30; Jun–Aug 9–4. *Admission: moderate*). Guides are on hand to show you the kiwi, and there is also a breeding colony of tuatara. Outside is one of the largest walk-through aviaries in the country, containing 300 species of native birds, including tui, saddleback, kakariki and bellbird. Native waterfowl include the endangered blue duck, New Zealand shoveller, brown and grey teal duck and Auckland Island teal. There is also a Raptor Walk, with harriers and owls.

► Waikato Wetlands   81A2

Hidden from casual view is a network of wetlands along the valley of the Waikato River. Between Te Awamutu and Hamilton, peat lakes were formed when river sand and gravel blocked valleys, and between Hamilton and Huntly the internationally recognized Whangamarino Wetland, Lake Waikare, Lake Whangape, Lake Waahi and other ox-bow lakes provide havens for wildlife. Full details about the wetlands are available from the DoC in Hamilton (tel: 07 838 3363).

BLACK-WATER RAFTING
This exciting adventure, which started in the 1980s, is now one of the most popular activities at the Waitomo Caves. Up to 20,000 people annually explore the caves (see pages 104–105) this way. Equipped with wetsuit and caver's helmet, you set off on a magical journey through the cave (part of the way beneath twinkling glow-worms), floating placidly along on an inflated inner tube. This highly recommended soft adventure is open to anyone. Tours take three hours (90 minutes in the cave) and depart several times daily; booking advised. Contact Black Water Rafting (PO Box 13, Waitomo Caves, tel: 0800 228 464; www.blackwaterrafting. co.nz), or Waitomo Down Under (PO Box 24, Waitomo Caves, tel: 07 878 6577).

BUSH TRAMWAYS
New Zealand used to be covered in native forest (commonly called 'native bush'). When felled, trees had to be transported to the sawmill and many loggers used tramways laid through the bush, powered by strange assortments of steam locomotives. Fortunately, nearly all logging of native timber has ceased, and working bush tramways are no longer needed. However, the Bush Tramway Club at Rotowaro, near Huntly, has preserved 'lokeys' operating on the Pukemiro Line on the first Sunday of each month from April to December (tel: 07 828 4851; www.bushtramwayclub.com)

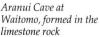

CROWDED CAVES
Time your visit to see the main attraction, the Glow-worm Cave at its best. Tourist buses from Auckland and Rotorua arrive between 10:30 and 3, during which time the site is jam-packed. Some sections (such as the Organ Loft) may also be shut off during this time in order to prevent a build-up of carbon dioxide. To enjoy the caves to the full, go early or late.

Aranui Cave at Waitomo, formed in the limestone rock

▶▶▶ Waitomo Caves   81A1

The limestone features and glow-worms of Waitomo Caves have been the main visitor attraction in the Waihuto since Europeans became aware of them over 100 years ago. The rugged hill country around Waitomo (*wai* = water, *tomo* = hole) is characterized by karst formations, with numerous caves, underground rivers, sink holes and other limestone features. The caves at Waitomo are simply the best known of these wonderful natural phenomena.

The village at Waitomo Caves developed as a visitor base for the caves at the turn of the 20th century, when the magnificent old Waitomo Caves Hotel was built. Today the activities on offer include various caving adventures, horse-trekking, mountain-biking and canoeing.

Maori knew of the existence of the Waitomo Caves long ago, but they were first explored by Europeans when an English surveyor, Fred Mace, persuaded a local chief, Tane Tinorau, to take him inside in 1887. As the caves were mapped by the government, visitors started arriving, and Tane and his wife Huti began the first tour business. But damage to the caves prompted the government to take them over, and it was not until 1989 that they were returned to the descendants of the original owners.

First stop in Waitomo should be the exceptional **Museum of Caves▶▶** (tel: 07 878 7640; www.waitomo-museum.co.nz. *Open* daily 8:30–5:30. *Admission: inexpensive*), with displays on all aspects of limestone caves, including their formation, flora and fauna and exploration, illustrated with videos on glow-worms and the Waitomo area, and an audiovisual presentation on caving. The museum also functions as an information and booking centre for all the nearby activities.

The most famous cave is the outstanding **Glow-worm Cave▶▶▶** (tel: 07 878 8227; www.waitomocaves.co.nz. Tours depart every half-hour 9–4:30. *Admission: expensive*). Outside the entrance (500m/545 yards past the museum) a huge carving, *Te Poupou a Tane Mahuta*, commemorates the centenary of its first exploration. The 45-minute tour of the three-level cave starts off in the Banquet Chamber (where early tourists used to stop for a meal), before leading back up to the Organ Loft where there is a large stalactite forma-

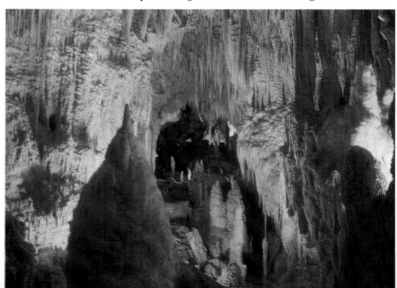

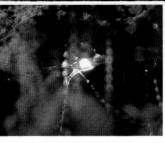

tion. From here it descends to the Cathedral, a dramatic cave with incredible acoustics. Finally, a small boat carries you through the most awesome part of the tour, a silent journey along an underground river with millions of glow-worms sparkling on the walls and ceiling.

The second most-visited cave is **Aranui**▶▶ (tours at 10, 11, 1, 2 and 3. *Admission: expensive*), 3km (2 miles) from the main village. Discovered in 1910 by a young Maori, Ruruku Aranui, it has vast caverns up to 20m (65ft) high, stalactites 6m (20ft) tall and many thousands of delicate straw stalactites. There are no glow-worms, but the limestone formations are possibly more spectacular than those in the main cave.

The third cave is **Ruakuri**▶ (tours hourly 9–4. *Admission: expensive*), opened to the public more recently owing to a long-running land dispute. It has plenty of limestone formations and patches of glow-worms; the river that runs through it is one of the main locations for black-water rafting (see panel page 103).

Only experienced cavers are advised to descend into the 100m (328ft)-deep *tomo* (limestone shaft), dubbed the **Lost World** (see panel), which leads down into a cave system (Mangapu Cave) alive with mosses and ferns and thousands of glow-worms, with underground waterfalls, fossils and astonishing stalactites.

Outside Waitomo, about 2km (1 mile) along SH37, the **Ohaki Maori Cultural Centre**▶▶ (*Open* daily 10–4:30. *Admission: inexpensive*) is well worth a visit, offering the opportunity to see works made using traditional tools by two of the country's best-known weavers—Diggeress Te Kanawa and her mother, the late Dame Rangimarie Hetet. There is also a contemporary art gallery with woodcarvings, paintings, prints and ceramics of high quality. On the hillside above the centre is a replica Maori village.

The nearby **Rabbit World** (tours daily 9:30–5. *Admission: inexpensive*) has fluffy angora rabbits.

*Sparks of light in the Glow-worm Cave are produced by the New Zealand glow-worm (*Arachnocampa luminosa*), luminous at all stages in its life*

THE LOST WORLD
There are several options available for abseiling into the Lost World, the easiest of which is a tandem abseil tethered to a guide (four hours). A one-and-a-half-day option includes complete abseil training and an underground river journey. Contact Waitomo Adventures (tel: 07 878 7788; www.waitomo.co.nz).

A dramatic sunset from Te Mata peak at Hastings (above); a monument to Captain Cook at Kaiti Hill, Gisborne (far right)

Grapes flourish in the Hawke's Bay region, home of some of New Zealand's most prestigious vineyards

EASTLAND Beyond Whakatane, at the southern edge of the Bay of Plenty, stretch the vast wilderness areas, bush-clad mountains and long deserted beaches of Eastland, a remote corner of the North Island that bulges out into the Pacific half-way down the eastern coastline.

Captain (then Lieutenant) Cook made his first landings here, astutely (if unimaginatively) naming the eastern-most promontory East Cape, even though he had yet to complete his circumnavigation of the island. But the rugged hinterland (in particular the Raukumara Range, running along the spine of Eastland) discouraged early settlers, who flocked instead to the fertile lands and warm climate of the Hawke Bay hinterland. This pattern of settlement by newcomers meant that Maori were left more or less in peace. Much of Eastland is still Maori-owned, with Maori culture much in evidence in the many small communities that dot the area. The principal tribe is the Ngati Porou, centred mostly on Tikitiki and Ruatoria.

Running through the Raukumara Range is the **Motu River**, which rushes through a spectacular 100km

The East Coast

(62-mile) gorge bordered by virgin native forest. *Motu* means 'isolated', and it is an apt description for this mysterious river. The Motu remained unexplored by Europeans until 1919, when four local lads set off in two wooden boats for what they thought was a three-day adventure downriver. Ten harrowing days later they arrived at the Pacific Ocean, after battling rapids and negotiating precipitous gorges. In 1970, a special Act of Parliament designated the river and a large part of the Raukumura as a Wilderness Zone.

The northern gateway to Eastland is **Opotiki** in the Bay of Plenty. From here there are two routes across Eastland. SH2 goes inland directly to **Gisborne** (148km/92 miles), passing through fern-lined **Waioeka Gorge** and **Raukumara Forest Park**, while a more compelling but longer option is to take SH35, the coastal route along the **East Cape Road** (see page 111). Gisborne, on the southern

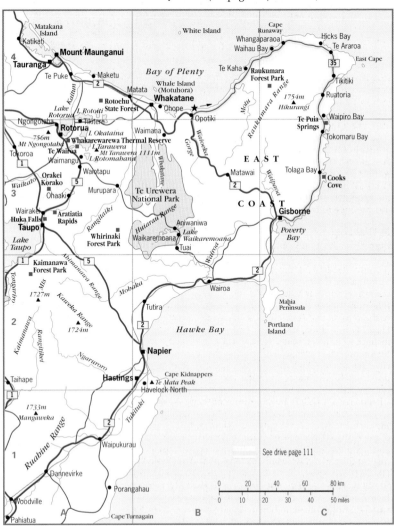

See drive page 111

side of the Eastland promontory, is the region's capital and a major wine-producing area. Thanks to its position towards the International Date Line, it is also the first city in the world to witness the sunrise every day.

HAWKE'S BAY One of the country's prime wine regions, the fertile Hawke's Bay region lies around Hawke Bay itself. The largest city and resort in the area is Napier, an unusual and interesting base for visiting the region. Flattened by a massive earthquake in 1931, it was rebuilt almost entirely in art deco style, and has an impressive unity of design throughout the city. The 'bay city', as locals know it, has smartened itself up in recent years to capitalize on its architectural heritage, and is now reaping the rewards in the form of a tourist boom.

At the heart of a thriving horticultural district, Hastings lies inland, 19km (12 miles) southwest of Napier in the middle of the Heretaunga Plains. While perhaps not as attractive as its sister city, it is the main departure point for visits to the gannet colony at nearby Cape Kidnappers.

Art deco architecture in Napier, at the heart of the Hawke's Bay wine-growing region

► **Gisborne** 108C3

Cook made his first landfall here in 1769, an event that is commemorated in the **Cook Landing Site National Historic Reserve** at the end of Kaiti Beach, across the Turanganui River just east of central Gisborne. Above the reserve, a statue of Cook gazes out from the top of **Kaiti Hill**, from where there is a terrific view of the city and harbour to the northwest, and southwest to Young Nick's Head. Other landmarks celebrating this historic landing include a statue of **Young Nick** (the surgeon's boy on the *Endeavour* who first spotted land) on the north side of the rivermouth at Waikanae Beach, and a **totem pole** presented by Canada to mark the bicentenary of the landings (in Alfred Cox Park, just off Grey Street).

Beneath Kaiti Hill, **Te Poho-o-Rawiri Meeting House►** on Queens Drive is one of the largest and most decorative in the country, with elaborately carved gable boards inside (*Open* daily; ask permission before entering). Maori objects and exhibits on the natural history of the area are displayed in the **Tairawhiti Museum and Arts Centre►** (18–20 Stout Street, tel: 06 867 3832. *Open* Mon–Fri 10–4, Sat–Sun 1:30–4. *Admission: free*). The grounds contain historic cottages and other buildings; on the riverbank is a small maritime museum housed inside the remains of the *Star of Canada*, wrecked on a reef offshore in 1912.

HAWKE'S BAY WINES
Hawke's Bay is the oldest established wine-growing region in New Zealand and has an unusually warm and balmy climate. Since its vineyards are planted on a range of soil types, there is scope for all the classic grape varieties. The growing season continues right through to April, which is ideal for late-maturing varieties such as Cabernet Sauvignon and Riesling. The region's Chardonnay and Cabernet Sauvignon blends are often considered the best in New Zealand, with its Sauvignon Blanc and Riesling also commanding recognition.

GANNET TRIPS

Most tours to the gannet colony at Cape Kidnappers depart from Te Awanga, 20 minutes south of Hastings. The long-established Gannet Beach Adventures (tel: 06 875 0898; www.gannet.com) has been running tours by tractor-trailer (four hours) for over 50 years. Gannet Safaris (tel: 06 875 0888; www.gannet safaris.co.nz) runs a three-hour trip in 4WD vehicles. Another option is a tour in a 4x4 FunBus, which has the advantage of much higher seats; contact Gannet Coastline Tours (tel: 06 844 4538; www.gannets.co.nz). All tour times are dependent on tide tables.

Up to 15,000 gannets crowd the rocks at Cape Kidnappers during the nesting season

▶ Hastings   108B2

Maori knew this area as *Heretaunga Haukunui Ararua*, poetically translated as 'resting place for canoes with life-giving dews and arcadian pathways'. Today, there are rows of fruit trees and vines, and fruit-processing and winemaking are the major industries.

Like Napier, Hastings was devastated by the 1931 earthquake (see page 112); more buildings survived here, but many lost their masonry façades, so the rebuilt town looked almost completely new. The middle of town has numerous interesting architectural embellishments, shopfronts and other Spanish mission-style features to discover described in *Take a Walk through Historic Hastings*, available from the visitor centre (Russell Street North, tel: 06 878 0510. *Open* Mon–Fri 8:30–5; Sat–Sun 10–3).

Mission Estate Vineyards (Church Road, Taradale, tel: 06 845 9350; www.missionestate.co.nz), **Te Mata Estate** (Te Mata Road, Havelock North, tel: 06 877 4399; www.temata.co.nz) and **Vidal Winery** (913 St. Aubyn Street East, tel: 06 876 8105; www.vidal.co.nz) are all good places to see (and taste) local viticulture in action.

As well as the town's fine parks, children will also enjoy a visit to **Splash Planet▶** (Grove Road, tel: 0508 SPLASH; www.splashplanet.co.nz. *Open* summer, daily 10–6; winter, weekends and school holidays 10–5. *Admission: moderate*), with its rides, boat trips and other amusements.

Hastings is also the main access point for the **Cape Kidnappers Gannet Sanctuary▶▶▶** (*Closed* Jul–Oct), on a dramatic promontory at the southern end of Hawke Bay. In Maori legend the cape was the hook with which Maui fished the North Island from the sea, but it was renamed by Captain Cook after local Maori tried to kidnap a Tahitian boy from the *Endeavour*.

The gannets flock here in their thousands from July onwards, making this one of their biggest and most spectacular mainland nesting sites in the world. The best time to visit is between November and late February.

Drive

The wharf at Tolaga Bay behind a crimson-flowered pohutukawa tree

See map on page 108.

East Cape Road (SH35)

This magnificent drive, starting in Opotiki and finishing in Gisborne to the southeast, follows the East Cape Road (the SH35) past rocky coves and sandy beaches backed by jagged bush-clad ranges. The 343km (213-mile) road is at its most spectacular in summer, when flowering pohutukawa trees add vivid splashes of crimson to the seashore.

From Opotiki, the road passes several small beaches and bays and crosses the Motu River before leading to **Te Kaha▶**, set in a picturesque cove. A whaling town until the 1930s, it is now a popular holiday resort. The **Tukaki Meeting House▶** on the *marae* has an elaborately carved lintel, said to be the finest example of Maori carving in the region.

Beyond, the Bay of Plenty ends at **Cape Runaway**. The beach at **Whangaparaoa** played a prominent part in Maori history as the arrival point for the first great canoes from Hawaiki. **Hicks Bay** (153km/95 miles from Opotiki) is the site of the **Tuwhakairiora Meeting House▶▶▶**, one of the grandest in Eastland, with carvings dating from the 1870s.

Te Araroa has a 600-year-old pohutukawa tree; turn off here to the **East Cape Lighthouse▶**, the most easterly in New Zealand, with fine views to East Island off the coast.

From Te Araroa the road passes inland to reach **Tikitiki**, which has an elaborately carved Anglican church, **St. Mary's▶**, built in 1924 as a memorial to local Maori who died in World War I. Farther south, overlooked by the sacred mountain of Hikurangi, is **Ruatoria**, the main settlement of the Ngati Porou. **Waipiro Bay▶** and **Tokomaru Bay▶** are the next two beaches, with the hot springs of **Te Puia** between the two. Tokomaru Bay is a stronghold of Maori culture with four active *marae*. **Tolaga Bay** boasts the longest wharf in New Zealand and a good surfing beach; to the south is **Cooks Cove▶▶▶**, which is reached via a 4km (2.5-mile) walkway across private land.

The coast road ends at **Gisborne**.

The East Coast

▶▶▶ Napier

Napier—named after the British General Sir Charles Napier—developed from a whaling and trading station established in the 1840s. Maori had for many years grown kumara crops on the flatlands in the bay, and gradually the settlers extended the area under cultivation; soon Napier was a thriving commercial hub with a busy port servicing a wide area.

But at 10:47AM on 3 February 1931, the town's neat, orderly streets of brick buildings were reduced to a heap of rubble by a massive earthquake measuring 7.8 on the Richter scale. There was also widespread damage in nearby Hastings and as far afield as Wairoa and the northern Wairarapa, but Napier was a scene of devastation, as fires destroyed those buildings that had managed to survive the tremor. On that day, 256 people died. Rescue work was hampered by subsequent tremors and by the destruction of road and rail links.

The town was completely rebuilt in the art deco style, then at the height of its popularity, a wholehearted choice which symbolized the burying of the tragedies of the past and the anticipation of a new age of optimism. An impressive example of a planned townscape in a single, coherent style, Napier possesses one of the most significant collection of art deco buildings in the world.

A good starting point for exploring this rich architectural heritage is the **Art Deco Shop** at the headquarters of the Art Deco Trust (Desco Centre, 163 Tennyson Street, tel: 06 835 0022; www.artdeconapier.com. *Open* daily 9–5). As well as showing a half-hour video (*Open* on

Napier's splendid A&B (formerly T&G) building on Marine Parade dates from 1936

The devastation after the earthquake (below and inset)

demand. *Admission: free*) on the city's well-preserved buildings, they also conduct **guided walks** (at 2PM Oct–Jun, daily; Jul–Sep, Wed, Sat, Sun. *Admission: moderate*). If you want to wander on your own, pick up a copy of their *Art Deco Walk* booklet. Numerous events designed to relive the 1920s and 1930s are staged during Napier's annual Art Deco Weekend, held in February (details from the Art Deco Trust).

The story of the earthquake and its aftermath is told in the superb **Hawke's Bay Museum**▶▶▶ (Marine Parade, tel: 06 835 7781; www.hawkesbaymuseum.co.nz. *Open* daily, Dec–Apr 9–6; May–Nov 10–4:30. *Admission: inexpensive*), with additional displays on art deco around the world and 20th-century interior design. The first gallery you pass through, however, entitled *Nga Tukemata* ('the awakening'), focuses on Maori history, presenting a visually exciting display of the art, carvings and other treasures of the Ngati Kahungunu people who dominated much of the eastern North Island.

The museum's newest section is part of the recently established New Zealand Dinosaur Centre, and includes the country's first robotic, animated dinosaur, as well as a display featuring the ground-breaking discoveries of local amateur palaeontologist Joan Wiffen.

Farther along Marine Parade is **Marineland**▶▶ (tel: 06 834 4027; www.marineland.co.nz. *Open* daily 10–4:30. *Admission: moderate*) with seals, penguins, sea lions and dolphins. Dolphin shows (daily at 10:30 and 2) may be frowned upon nowadays, but Marineland has tried to keep abreast of the times with 'Behind the Scenes' tours

WINE AND FOOD EXTRAVAGANZA

The Hawke's Bay wine and food extravaganza is a two-day event held each February, with food and wine tastings, art exhibitions, live music, banquets and even a barrel race through the vineyards. There are gourmet dinners, followed by an auction of wine by the barrel to raise funds for a local hospice—the only wine auction of its kind in New Zealand. Details from Harvest Hawke's Bay Weekend, 0800 442 946; www.harvesthawkesbay. co.nz.

WINE TRAILS AND RESTAURANTS

A Guide to Hawke's Bay Wineries (available in either Napier or Hastings) lists around two dozen wineries that you can visit for tastings and purchases direct from the producer. Wineries in the Hawke's Bay area now sometimes have restaurants attached to them, where you can enjoy good food while sampling the often extensive range of wines from the vineyard. Those recommended for winery lunches include Brookfields Vineyards (tel: 06 834 4615; www.brookfieldsvineyards. co.nz), Clearview Estate (tel: 06 875 0150; www. clearviewestate.co.nz), Sacred Hill Winery (tel: 06 844 0138; www.sacred hill.com) and Vidal Winery (tel: 06 876 8105; www.vidal.co.nz). Organized tours are also offered by Town & Country Tours (tel: 06 843 9971; www.townandcountrytours. co.nz/tours) and Bay Tours and Charters (tel: 06 843 6953; www.baytours.co.nz).

TE MATA PEAK

From the top of Te Mata Peak there are superb views of the Heretaunga Plains and Hawke Bay, with Hastings laid out neatly in the foreground and Napier sparkling in the middle distance. Beyond, the panorama extends as far as the Mahia Peninsula and the Kaimanawa Ranges, with even Mount Ruapehu in Tongariro National Park said to be visible on an exceptionally clear day. The 399m (1,309ft) peak is popular for hang-gliding and paragliding, and there is a road all the way to the top (11km/7 miles from Hastings via Havelock North).

(daily 9AM. *Admission: moderate*) and swimming with the dolphins (daily at noon. *Admission: expensive*; advanced booking required, tel: 06 834 4027).

Farther down still, the **National Aquarium of New Zealand▶** (tel: 06 834 1404; www.nationalaquarium.co.nz. *Open* daily, summer 9–7; winter 9–5. *Admission: moderate*) is centred around a giant fish tank, which holds up to 30 different species (including some massive rays and a seven-gill shark). Again, there are 'Behind the Scenes' tours (daily 2:30. *Admission: moderate*), and experienced divers can even swim in the main tank (by arrangement only, tel: 06 834 1404 for bookings. *Admission: expensive*).

The National Aquarim has a nocturnal house, with two kiwi, Rimu and Ruakiwi, on loan from Napier's Westshore Wildlife Reserve, examples of the very successful breeding programme.

Another fascinating creature you can see here is the tuatara. These lizard-like creatures have been described as living fossils, as they have survived other beak-headed reptiles by about 100 million years. They grow very slowly. The ones here were born in 1980, and are only just reaching maturity. Males grow up to 60cm (24in) long, with a weight of 1kg (2lb)—but that won't be for another 40 years.

On the other side of Marine Parade is **Opossum World▶▶▶** (157 Marine Parade, tel: 06 835 7697; www. opossumworld.co.nz. *Open* daily 9:30–4:30. *Admission: inexpensive*). Though relatively small, it is the only one of its kind in New Zealand and is very imaginatively presented. Part of a working tannery for possum hides, it includes an extremely graphic display on the possum's life cycle.

Just outside Napier itself, **Otatara Pā Historic Reserve▶▶** (Springfield Road, signposted after the Taradale Shopping Centre 10km/6 miles from the city. Open site. *Admission: free*), is well worth a detour, not only because of its impressive size (about 33ha/82 acres), but also because a large number of the original earthworks are still visible. They have been greatly enhanced by a conservation project, completed in 1993, which included re-creating the palisades and the ancestral figures (*powhenua*) surrounding the *pā*, in order to create an impression of the true appearance of a fortified encampment all those hundreds of years ago. There are two separate *pā* (Otatara and, above it, Hikurangi), and a one-hour loop track around the site is dotted with panels indicating the various defensive systems, *rua* (food pits), gardens and *whare* (houses).

Fishing in the fast-flowing streams of Te Urewera National Park, to the north of Hawke's Bay

▶▶ Te Urewera National Park   108B3

Te Urewera National Park is popular for trekking and has numerous walks, ranging from short strolls to the Lake Track, which is 52km (32 miles) long, plus canoeing, bird-watching, fishing and hunting (red deer and wild pig are widespread, and it is considered one of the best hunting grounds in the North Island).

Covering 55sq km (21sq miles) at the southern edge of the park is **Lake Waikaremoana▶▶**, fed by waterfalls and streams from the dense forests that surround it.

According to mythology a local chief, Mahu, asked his daughter to fetch water from a well. She refused, and in his anger he drowned her. She turned into a *taniwha* (water monster), and in her desperate attempts to escape, filled the nearby valleys with water and created the lake. It is her spirit which is said still to agitate the lake—Waikaremoana means 'sea of rippling waters'. Later, Mahu also threw his other children into the lake, and they turned into stone and became the islands known today as Te Whanau-a-Mahu ('Mahu's children').

At **Aniwaniwa**, on the eastern shore of the lake, is the main DoC visitor centre (tel: 06 837 3900. *Open* daily 8–noon, 1–5), which has a number of informative displays on the park's natural and human history. As well as providing information on trekking, huts, fishing licences and so on, it produces a booklet, *Local Tracks*, which describes 23 short walks within the park. There is a motor camping ground here, and this is also a busy boating and fishing area.

The Lake Track has superb views of the lake from the surrounding beech forests, and you can go swimming at isolated beaches, fishing and bird-watching; one of the most popular walks in the North Island, the extensive track takes between three and four days to complete.

115

Sprawling over two hilltops, Otatara Pā Historic Reserve has carved ancestral figures around the palisades

Otatara Pa
Historic Reserve

Captain James Cook rediscovered New Zealand in 1769. In his journals, published after his return, he described a land rich in resources and populated by a people who were 'well built, intelligent, highly skilled, courageous and artistic'. But his first encounters with Maori were not auspicious.

The explorer Captain James Cook

First landfall Cook had promised a reward to the first crew member to spot land, and it was at 2PM on 6 October 1769 that a ship's boy, Nicholas Young, sighted the east coast of the North Island. As promised, the headland (off Gisborne) was named Young Nick's Head. Two days later Cook led a landing party ashore, hoping to establish friendly relations with the Maori, but their visit ended badly when they killed a Maori whom they believed to be attacking one of the ship's boats. The next day five more Maori were killed in a canoe that might (or might not) have been about to attack the ship.

Cook left the bay on 11 October, naming it Poverty Bay because 'it afforded us no one thing which we wanted'. He sailed north to Tolaga Bay (56km/35 miles north of Gisborne), where the crew rested for six days, collecting wood, water and plant specimens, and trading with local Maori. At one end of the cove a natural rock arch (which still stands today) caught the eye of the naturalist Joseph Banks, who claimed it was 'certainly the most magnificent surprise I have ever met with'.

From Tolaga Bay, Cook then turned south again towards Hawke Bay, anchoring off the cape at its southern end. Here, while bartering with Cook from their canoes, local Maori seized a Tahitian boy and dragged him overboard. The crew opened fire, killing several Maori in the canoe. Cook named the promontory Cape Kidnappers, then continued on as far south as Cape Turnagain before doubling back around the East Cape.

His Majesty's name
Crossing the Bay of Plenty, he then anchored off Whitianga in what is now the Coromandel. Here he stayed for 11 days, during which time

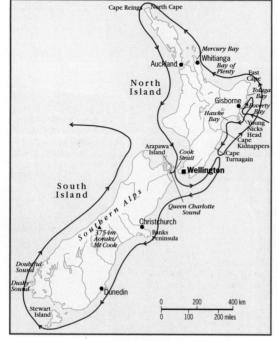

he observed the transit of the planet Mercury, after which he named the bay. Cook made friendly contact with the local tribes, then raised the Union Jack, and 'took formal possession of the place in the name of His Majesty'.

From Mercury Bay, Cook sailed around North Cape following the western coastline of the North Island and then anchored off the South Island, having previously entered 'a very deep and broad inlet' which he named Queen Charlotte Sound. He spent three weeks here in an anchorage he named Ship Cove, while the ship's naturalists, Joseph Banks and Daniel Solander, made detailed studies of the local flora and fauna. Cook also climbed a hill on Arapawa Island and spotted open sea to the east, thus discovering the strait now named after him. He was to return to Ship Cove five times on this and subsequent voyages. On his second voyage, in 1773, he let loose the first sheep in New Zealand here and witnessed his first cannibal feast. 'There was not one of us but had the least doubt but what this people were Canabals' he wrote. Cook then sailed north to Cape Turnagain to prove to his sceptical officers that the North Island was indeed an island.

The South Island As he circumnavigated the South Island, Cook was blown out of sight of land four times—which explains his major errors in mapping Banks Peninsula and Stewart Island. Cook thought it too risky to enter Doubtful Sound, much to the disappointment of the naturalists on board. On his second voyage he spent several weeks in Dusky Sound, resting his crew, setting up workshops on shore and brewing spruce beer to counter scurvy.

Cook's expeditions collected plants, birds and insects previously unknown to Europeans

A NEAR MISS
At the same time as Cook was making his first land-fall in New Zealand, the French explorer de Surville was somewhere off the North Island on board the *Saint Jean Baptiste*, desperately seeking an anchorage in order to rest his sick crew, but prevented from doing so by a storm. As Cook travelled anticlockwise around the North Island, he sailed around Cape Reinga in the same storm. The ships passed each other unawares—thus being ignorant of a remarkable coincidence in the history of exploration.

Lake Taupo, in the middle of the North Island south of Rotorua, is the largest inland lake in New Zealand and feeds the Waikato River. Famous for its trout fishing, the township of **Taupo** also has its own thermal attractions and a host of other activities geared towards tourism.

Active volcanic craters, lava flows, hot springs, lakes, forest and alpine herb fields are just a few of the natural attractions in **Tongariro National Park**, at the heart of the North Island. As well as its three active volcanoes—Tongariro (1,967m/6,454ft), Ngauruhoe (2,287m/7,504ft) and Ruapehu (2,797m/9,177ft)—it also has the only permanent snow and commercial ski fields in the North Island, and so draws skiers from the cities throughout the winter. Summertime activities include day walks, trekking, rock- and ice-climbing, mountain-biking and flightseeing. Around a million people visit the park annually.

Pages 118–119 (top): You can bungee-jump from a huge cantilever projecting from a cliff face above the Waikato River
Page 118 (bottom): A jet-boat cruises the Waikato River at Wairakei, below Huka Falls

Open tussock lands around Mount Taranaki

Mount Taranaki/Mount Egmont, a classically symmetrical volcanic cone, is the most striking feature of the west coast—when it's not covered in cloud! Captain Cook spotted it on 10 January 1770, noting that it resembled 'the peak of Teneriffe'. He named it Egmont in honour of the Earl of Egmont, then First Lord of the Admiralty, but Maori continued to know it as Taranaki. The matter was settled in 1986, when the government ruled that both Mount Egmont and Mount Taranaki may officially be used. The surrounding 33,000ha (81,543 acres) of parkland is still called **Egmont National Park** (the second-oldest national park in the country, created in 1900).

The mountain slopes are popular for skiing in winter, and in summer the numerous tracks are busy with day walkers and trekkers. It is also possible to climb the summit in a day.

Overshadowed by Mount Taranaki's bulk is **New Plymouth**, a touring base on the coast that is well known for its parks and gardens and nearby surfing beaches.

WANGANUI AND THE WHANGANUI RIVER To the south-east of Taranaki, at the mouth of the **Whanganui River** is **Wanganui** (it has not regained its lost 'h'), one of the oldest towns in New Zealand. Legend has it that a Taranaki chief spent several days here waiting for transport to cross the river mouth, and the river became known as Whanganui (*whanga* = to wait, *nui* = long).

The first missionaries ventured up the river valley in 1840, collecting signatures for the Treaty of Waitangi. As settlers followed, the river developed into a major artery, and by the mid-1860s the first steamer service had reached **Pipiriki**. By 1891, this had become a regular service between Wanganui and Taumarunui, a journey which took three days, with overnight stops at Pipiriki and a houseboat moored at Maraekowhai.

The wonders of the scenery soon attracted a thriving tourist trade, and by 1905 no fewer than 12,000 visitors had made the journey. The houseboat *Makere* was a model of elegance, with its own dining-room complete with chandeliers (it even had electricity) and silverware. A hotel was built at Pipiriki in 1899, but burned down in 1909. Rebuilt as one of the most luxurious hotels in the country, it was again destroyed by fire in 1959.

Today a network of tracks throughout **Whanganui National Park** gives access to large tracts of wilderness. The Whanganui is the most canoed river in the country and, despite some 239 rapids between Taumarunui and the sea, it is classed as a beginner's river. It can also be explored by a trip on a paddle-steamer or jet-boat, and there is an excellent scenic drive (see pages 138–139) along the valley.

▶▶▶ REGION HIGHLIGHTS

Egmont National Park
pages 130–131

Lake Taupo *page 122*

Pukeiti Rhododendron Trust *page 132*

Tongariro National Park
pages 126–127

121

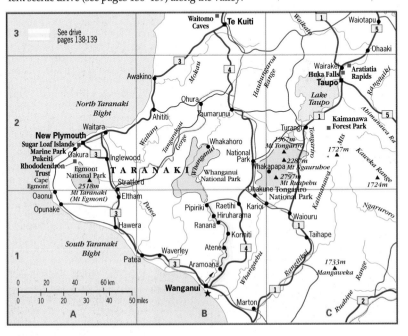

WALKS AROUND TAUPO

There are a number of enjoyable short walks in the environs of Taupo that are suitable for the whole family; it takes around an hour, for instance, to walk along the riverbank to Huka Falls, or you could walk from Huka Falls to the Aratiatia Rapids (two hours one way). There are also walks around the lakeshore to Acacia Bay, through nearby forests or to historic sites. Around 30 walks (including longer tramps) are listed in the *Walking Trails* booklet available from the information centre.

Central North Island

▶▶▶ Lake Taupo   *121C2*

This famous trout-fishing mecca covers 606sq km (234sq miles) and lies 359m (1,178ft) above sea-level. The lake is fed by a dozen or more streams and rivers flowing down into the ancient volcanic crater in which it lies; its only outlet is the Waikato River, which runs alongside Taupo through a series of rapids before beginning its long journey to the sea just south of Auckland.

The surrounding streams and river estuaries, and the lake itself, present almost unlimited opportunities for anglers. The fishery is tightly controlled, but there is always good fishing to be had somewhere: trout from the lake average over 1.4kg (3lb), although catches of twice this size are not unusual. The Department of Conservation operates an acoustic monitoring system to estimate the numbers of fish in the lake, and in the 1995 fishing season there were thought to be around 200,000 of these monsters out there waiting to be caught—about twice the number that were there when monitoring first started in the late 1980s. Nearly 900 tonnes of trout are caught in the lake each year but you won't find it on restaurant menus, as commercial fishing is not permitted.

Apart from fishing, Taupo has a number of family-orientated attractions and a wide range of adventure activities, including river-rafting, mountain-biking, helicopter sightseeing and tandem skydiving from 2,713m (8,900ft). There are also several rides which you might not find elsewhere, such as driving racing cars on the Taupo Raceway Circuit, setting off on a four-wheel motorbike into the bush or going for a drive on the back of a Harley Davidson.

The township of Taupo is on Tapuaeharuru Bay, at the northeastern corner of the lake. Laid out in a hard-to-get-lost grid pattern, it has the usual selection of resort shops, restaurants and takeaways. The Taupo Information Centre (Tongariro Street, tel: 07 376 0027. *Open* daily 8:30–5), at the front of the Great Lake Centre, can book any activity as well as supply information on fishing guides, licences and so on.

Take to the water to see Maori rock carvings

Across from the Great Lake Centre is the small **Taupo Museum** (tel: 07 378 4167. *Open* Mon–Sat 10:30–4:30. *Admission: free*), with colonial and natural history exhibits.

Most of Taupo's attractions (apart from those which are lake-based) are spread out along the west bank of the Waikato River down as far as the Aratiatia Rapids: you can easily make a loop, setting off north along SH1 (towards Auckland), returning via Huka Falls Road, which will encompass all the sightseeing spots in a day, including a river trip or jet-boat ride.

Drive

Wairakei and Taupo

Wairakei Park

Spread across a vast area of the west bank of the Waikato River, this route combines rolling farmland with forests, geothermal areas (including power stations), and recreation facilities.

Following SH1, turn down Huka Falls Road to reach the **Huka Falls Viewpoint▶**; known as *hukanui* ('great body of spray') to Maori, the falls plunge nearly 10m (33ft), with the water flowing through at peak times at the rate of 282,000L (62,000gal) a second. A footbridge across the top leads to another viewpoint on the east bank. A short distance farther on is the Helistar Centre, with a café and helipad, and then comes the **Honey Hive▶** (tel: 0508 BZZZZZ; www.honey.co.nz. *Open* daily 9–5. *Admission: free*), which has glass hives that enable visitors to see the bees busily at work, as well as videos about bees and honey for tasting and for sale.

Next is the **Volcanic Activity Centre▶▶** (tel: 07 374 8375; www.volcanoes.co.nz. *Open* Mon–Fri 9–5, Sat–Sun 10–4. *Admission: free*), in which the Taupo Volcanic Zone can be explored through a series of audio-visual shows, active models and other displays. The building is part of Wairakei Research Centre, run by the Institute of Geological and Nuclear Sciences, which studies and monitors the volcanoes and geothermal fields in this volatile zone.

At the end of the road is a jetty where the Huka Jet and *African Queen* riverboat share a berth: the *African Queen* (originally the MV *Waireka*, built in 1908) has leisurely sightseeing tours along this section of the river (*Tours* daily 10 and 2. *Admission: expensive*), or you can opt for a somewhat faster pace on board the Huka Jet (Tour every half-hour. *Admission: expensive*). Both vessels visit exactly the same section of river, since neither can go farther than the Huka Falls at one end or the Aratiatia Rapids at the other.

Beside the dock is the **Prawn Park▶** (tel: 07 374 8474; www.prawnpark.co.nz. Tours on the hour 11–4. *Admission: inexpensive*), the world's only geothermally heated facility devoted to raising prawns; the 20-minute tour covers the complete life cycle of the giant Malaysian river prawns bred here. You can then buy the raw prawns or sample them cooked in a dozen different ways at their Prawn Works Bar and Grill (*Open* daily 9–5, later in high summer; reservations recommended).

Heading back up to the main road, double back briefly towards the **Craters of the Moon▶** thermal area (*Open* dawn–dusk. *Admission: free*) administered by the DoC, which has walkways between the steam vents, mud pools and other geothermal phenomena.

Farther down the main road are the unmistakable stainless-steel pipes, wreathed in steam, of **Wairakei Geothermal Power Station▶▶**. Along with the nearby Ohaaki station, this produces around eight per cent of the country's electricity. The visitor centre (tel: 07 378 0913. *Open* daily 9–4:30. *Admission: free*) has displays and videos on all aspects of geothermal power, and it is also possible to follow the massive pipes down through the steamfield itself to a lookout point (*Open* 24 hours. *Admission: free*).

Just past the road-bridge over the steam pipes, a sign points to **Wairakei Natural Thermal Valley** (tel: 07 374 8004. *Open* summer 9–7:30; winter 9–5:30. *Admission: moderate*), where there are tea rooms and walks through the bush either side of the Wairakei Stream; the geysers and mud pools are no longer as interesting as they once

were, since the neighbouring power project has taken the heat (literally) out of the ground.

Finally, driving along SH5 and turning right down Aratiatia Road you will reach **Aratiatia Rapids►**. These rapids were once a continuous attraction, but since the building of a dam and Aratiatia Power Station the spectacle can only be enjoyed at set times of day (summer 10, noon, 2 and 4; winter 10, noon and 2. *Admission: free*). A warning siren sounds just before the radial dam gates open, with the water thundering down the rapids for about half an hour before subsiding once more.

Heading out from the town centre on the south side of the Waikato River, Cherry Island is not far. Small children might enjoy **Cherry Island Park** (tel: 07 378 9427. *Open* daily 9–5. *Admission: moderate*), a small island roamed by peacocks, goats, ducks, angora rabbits and a few other tame animals, but they will probably be more thrilled by the **Spa Dinosaur Valley►►** (tel: 07 378 4120. *Open* daily 10–4. *Admission: inexpensive*), which is much better value. It has a dozen or so life-size dinosaur models that are given added credibility by the hissing steam vents surrounding them. If you have not watched the madness of bungee-jumping before, stop off at **Taupo Bungy** (tel: 07 377 1135; www.taupobungy.co.nz. *Open* daily 9–5) to see people hurling themselves off the huge cantilever projecting out from the cliff face 47m (154ft) above the Waikato.

The **AC Thermal Baths** (tel: 07 377 3600; www.taupovenues.co.nz/ acbaths. *Open* daily 8–9. *Admission: inexpensive*) contain a number of private hot mineral pools, a sauna house and a giant swimming pool complete with water slide.

Cruises around the north shore of Lake Taupo are popular, with several sailings daily on several different kinds of boat. Most visit Mine Bay, where there is a contemporary Maori rock carving depicting the arrival of the Tuwharetoa tribe in the Taupo area (on private land, it can be viewed only from the lake). Options for cruises include the steamboat *Alice*, the oldest commercial vessel in New Zealand (tel: 07 378 6389), or sailing on the *Barbary*, a 15m (49ft) yacht once owned by the actor Errol Flynn; or on a replica 1920s steamboat, the *Ernest Kemp* (tel: 07 378 3444).

Walkways lead through the steaming fumaroles at the Craters of the Moon thermal area

121C2

AN HISTORIC GIFT

Most of the land around Tongariro belonged to the Tuwharetoa, to whom the peaks were *tapu* (sacred), but this did not stop early Europeans attempting to climb them. Concerned about the fate of their sacred mountains, the paramount chief of the Tuwharetoa, Te Heuheu Tukino, took a visionary step and gifted the mountains to all of New Zealand's inhabitants on 23 September 1887. It was the first national park in the country, and only the fourth in the world. The original area of 2,648ha (6,543 acres) has since been expanded to 76,000ha (187,796 acres); in 1991 it was declared a World Heritage Site.

▶▶▶ Tongariro National Park

Dominating Tongariro National Park is **Mount Ruapehu**, the highest peak in the North Island, with a beautiful crater lake at its summit. Mount Ruapehu is still active. In 1945 it erupted over a nine-month period, showering fine volcanic ash over much of the central North Island; in 1953 a *lahar* (volcanic mudflow) caused the Tangiwai disaster (see page 128); in 1969 and 1975 eruptions of ash and water caused *lahars* that damaged ski facilities and led to the installation of a *lahar* warning system in the park. In 1995 a giant mushroom cloud signalled its biggest eruption for 50 years. These continued in 1996, disrupting air traffic in the region and shooting boulders as large as cars into the air, but the mountain has been quiet since then. **Mount Ngauruhoe** is the youngest of the volcanoes, and still occasionally bubbles and spits lava and ash in a menacing fashion. **Mount Tongariro** last erupted in 1926 and its truncated peaks conceal some spectacular craters and lakes.

The Park Headquarters is in **Whakapapa Village**, which has a population of 200 and, at 1,127m (3,697ft), is the highest settlement in the country with permanent residents. The DoC visitor centre (tel: 07 892 3729. *Open* daily 8–5) has interesting displays on volcanoes and the natural history of the park, as well as information on trekking (there is a fine range of walks from here), huts, skiing and weather conditions. At the entrance stands a bust of Te Heuheu Tukino (see panel). Just below the visitor centre is the **Grand Château** (tel: 07 892 3809; www.chateau. co.nz), a splendid hotel (built in 1929), which is worth a visit for tea.

Above Whakapapa, ski lifts rise from Iwikau Village to the Whakapapa ski fields, the biggest ski area within the park. These lifts are open all year round to give sightseers and trekkers easier access to the upper mountains.

Back down at the junction of SH47 and SH4, **National Park** is a small settlement with summer activities, as well as skiing in winter. It has a railway station, and shuttle buses that run to either end of the Tongariro Crossing (see panel opposite) and up to the Whakapapa ski fields.

On the southern side of the mountain is **Ohakune**, the biggest resort in the area, and the Turoa Skifield, which was opened in 1978 to relieve pressure on Whakapapa; the Ohakune visitor centre has details of the many activities available (54 Clyde Street,

Bust of Te Heuheu Tukino, Tongariro National Park

tel: 06 385 8427. *Open* Jun–Oct, Mon–Fri 8–5:30, Sat 9–4, Sun 9–2; Nov–May, Mon–Fri 9–4:30, Sat 9–noon, Sun 9–11).

From Ohakune, an excellent scenic drive leads up the **Ohakune Mountain Road** to the Turoa Skifield. The road winds gradually up through majestic stands of rimu, matai and miro and then traverses the higher altitude beech forest, tussock and alpine fields before emerging onto the bare volcanic reaches farther up Mount Ruapehu. From the ski station (1,600m/5,250ft) there are fabulous views back across to Egmont National Park. The 17km (10.5-mile) drive takes about one hour, and there are several walking tracks off the road if you have more time.

▶ **Turangi** 121C2

On the south side of Lake Taupo, the town of Turangi was developed in the 1960s to meet the needs of the nearby Tongariro hydroelectric project and has since expanded into a resort—principally for fishing, but it also makes a good base for exploring Tongariro National Park or the adjacent Kaimanawa Forest Park.

Turangi is on the banks of the Tongariro River—world renowned for its rainbow and brown trout fishing. The visitor centre (Ngawaka Place, PO Box 865, Turangi, tel: 07 386 8999. *Open* daily 8:30–5) can provide details on fly-fishing guides, licences and other fishing services. To find out more about trout, visit the nearby **Tongariro National Trout Centre▶** (www.troutcentre.org.nz. *Open* daily 10–3. *Admission: free/donation*), 4km (2.5 miles) south along SH1.

Around 270,000 visitors a year flock to the Whakapapa ski fields

THE TONGARIRO CROSSING
The Tongariro Crossing is a seven- to eight-hour trek that skirts several of the crater lakes around the summit of Mount Tongariro, with fabulous views across the central North Island. Considered to be one of the finest one-day tracks (albeit an exhausting one) in the country, it is walked by around 40,000 people every year. In summer, DoC staff run guided walks along the track, taking up to 80 people at a time.

Drive

Tongariro circuit

Allow a full day for this 170km (106-mile) round trip circling the volcanoes of Tongariro National Park, with its forest and desert scenery, Army Museum and historic *pā* site.

Starting in **Ohakune**, head east along SH49. The road passes the Rangataua and Karioi forests and the Karioi pulp mill before reaching a **memorial** (on the left) in front of the Whangaehu River Bridge at Tangiwai: this was the site of the country's worst-ever rail disaster, on Christmas Eve 1953, when a volcanic mudflow (*lahar*) from Mount Ruapehu swept an express train into the river; 151 people died.

Continue to **Waiouru**, turning right at the junction to reach the **Queen Elizabeth II Army Memorial Museum**▶▶ (tel: 06 387 6911; www.armymuseum.co.nz. *Open* daily 9–4:30. *Admission: moderate*). Mock-ups of the NZ Army in action, from the New Zealand Wars through to Vietnam, are accompanied by a 23-minute audiovisual presentation (9:15, then every 45 minutes from 9:45 to 3:45) on its history. A new pavilion houses a massive greenstone sculpture, *Tears on Greenstone*, which commemorates soldiers killed overseas in active service.

Return to the junction and continue north on SH1 along the **Desert Road**▶▶. The volcanic gravel fields and tussock plateaux create an eerie, empty landscape with an unearthly appeal, punctuated by tank tracks and notices warning you to keep out of the enormous army training area, which has its own herd of wild horses. To the west rise the snow-clad peaks of Mount Ruapehu, with the North Island's only glaciers visible during summer.

After passing the summit (2,797m/3,544ft, signposted), the Desert Road cuts through a series of eroded banks of richly coloured desert ash, twisting and dipping over several streams. The

Tussock lands on the aptly named Desert Road to the east of Mount Ruapehu

regenerating bushlands of **Kaimanawa Forest Park** now take over from the desert landscapes. As the road emerges from Poutu Forest, the rounded form of the extinct volcano **Pihanga** (1,325m/4,347ft) is straight ahead.

Turn left at **Rangipo** along SH46 to National Park, cutting behind Pihanga and passing along the shore of **Lake Rotoaira**▶▶; beyond, steam rises from the Ketetahi Hot Springs beneath the cone of **Mount Tongariro's** north crater.

At the junction, turn left onto SH47. Another 1.6km (1 mile) farther on, a signpost marks the parking area for **Te Porere Historic Place**▶▶. The two sets of earthworks here are the remains of fortified *pā* built by the Maori warrior and prophet Te Kooti Rikiranga te Turuki. This was the site of one of the last battles of the New Zealand Wars, in October 1869, when Te Kooti and his people made a determined stand against government troops; 37 of Te Kooti's men were killed but he escaped through the bush with his remaining forces.

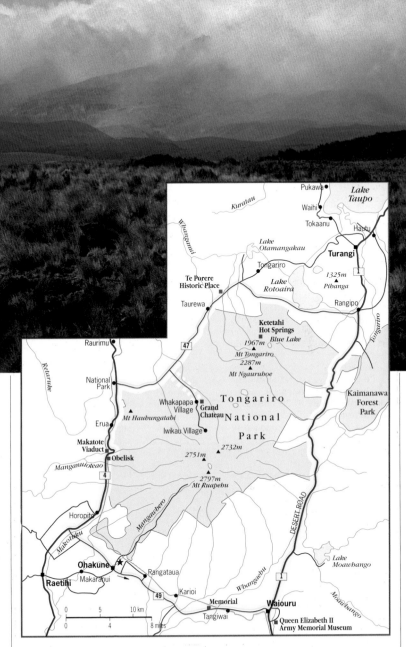

Continue on SH47, skirting **Mount Ngauruhoe** before reaching the turning for SH48 to **Whakapapa**. Make a detour up here or continue on to **National Park** and turn left onto SH4. On your left is the bulky mass of **Mount Hauhungatahi** (1,520m/4,990ft), now a nature reserve. Running alongside the road is the last section of the North

Island Main Trunk railway to be completed: after the impressive **Makatote Viaduct▶**, an **obelisk** on the left-hand side of the road marks where the north and south railheads met in 1908, completing the railway between Wellington and Auckland.

Just past Horopito turn left on SH49 to return to Ohakune.

EARLY TROUBLES
The Plymouth Company sent six ships from Devon, the first of which arrived in March 1841. As the local Te Atiawa peoples had been driven away by the Waikato tribes, the early settlers snapped up large tracts of land—only to find themselves involved in a war lasting a decade or more when Te Atiawa returned from exile on Kapiti Island. Despite this unpromising start, a new wave of immigrants in the 1870s led to the establishment of New Plymouth's major source of wealth, the dairy industry.

Charming Pukekura Park is in the heart of New Plymouth

The West Coast

▶▶▶ Egmont National Park   *121A2*

The 2,518m (8,262ft)-high volcano at the heart of this national park dominates the lush farmlands of the surrounding Taranaki district. Maori settlements on the lower slopes of Taranaki and the coastline were among the first in New Zealand. Maori considered higher slopes *tapu* (sacred), although they ventured up the valleys to collect red ochre for pigment, and to take the bones of their chiefs and *tohunga* to secret caves on the mountain.

According to one version of one of the most enduring legends, at one time Taranaki lived with the other volcanoes in the middle of the island. Once, however, when Tongariro was away, Taranaki seduced his beautiful wife Pihanga. When Tongariro returned he exploded (literally) with jealousy. Taranaki beat a hasty retreat, gouging out the Whanganui River as he withdrew towards the coast, where he still weeps for his lost love.

Taranaki is part of a chain of three volcanoes running southwards from New Plymouth. The two other volcanoes (Pouakai and Kaitake) are older; Taranaki probably appeared approximately 70,000 years ago and last erupted in about 1755. Just to the south of the main crater is a secondary cone called Fanthams Peak, named after the first woman to climb it, Frances Fantham, in 1885.

The first climbers to reach the summit of Taranaki, in December 1839, were Ernst Dieffenbach, a naturalist with the New Zealand Company, and James Heberly. Summertime ascents were popular in the 1860s and 1870s, and today it is the most climbed mountain in New Zealand.

There are fabulous views from the summit, from the peaks of the South Island across to Tongariro National

Park, and northwards to Pirongia in the Waikato—if it's not cloudy or raining, that is. Taranaki has one of the highest rainfall records in the country, with an average 698cm (272in) annually. Despite the relatively small size of the park there are some 140km (87 miles) of tracks, and if you do not feel like tackling the summit or the 55km (34-mile) round-the-mountain track, there are plenty of shorter walks. In winter skiing is popular—the ski field is at the end of Pembroke Road, above Stratford Mountain House.

The main point of access to the park is at **North Egmont**, 27km (17 miles) from New Plymouth, where there is an excellent DoC visitor centre (tel: 06 756 0990. *Open* Nov–Easter, daily 9–5; Easter–Oct, Sat–Thu 9:30–4:30). On the south side of the mountain there is another DoC visitor centre at **Dawson Falls** (tel: 027 443 0248. *Open* Thu–Mon 9–5:30). It is imperative to check with one of these centres before setting off up the mountain, since weather conditions can change rapidly.

▶▶ **Hawera**   *121A1*

When passing through this small town 74km (46 miles) south of New Plymouth, it is worth making a detour 4km (2.5 miles) to the north to visit the **Tawhiti Museum▶** (47 Ohangai Road, tel: 06 278 6837; www.tawhitimuseum. co.nz. *Open* Sep–Dec, Feb–May, Fri–Mon 10–4; Jun–Aug, Sun 10–4; Jan, daily 10–4. *Admission: moderate*), which has an extensive collection of life-size displays and dioramas depicting the heritage of south Taranaki. In addition, a bush railway runs through logging areas to an interpretation centre set in an old sawmill.

▶▶ **New Plymouth**   *121A2*

Dominated by the towering peak of Mount Taranaki to the south, New Plymouth is the main focus of a rich dairy region, thanks in part to the fertile volcanic soil bequeathed by Taranaki's past explosions. It is also a major energy production area, with oil and gas flowing from several offshore fields.

The early settlement was named after Plymouth in England, the home town of many of the first colonists. One of the few remaining buildings from the earliest days is **Richmond Cottage▶** (corner of Ariki and Brougham streets. *Open* Nov–May, Mon, Wed, Fri 2–4, Sat–Sun 1–4; Jun–Oct, Fri 2–4, Sat–Sun 1–4. *Admission: inexpensive*). Built in 1853 from beach stones, the cottage was moved to its present site in the 1960s, and has been furnished in period style with items from the neighbouring Taranaki Museum.

Similarly built from beach stones is **St. Mary's Church▶** (Vivian Street, tel: 06 758 3111; www.stmarys.org.nz), completed in 1846 and New Zealand's oldest surviving

Surf's up! Taranaki's consistent but varied surf makes it the area for the serious surfer

HERITAGE TRAIL
The 150km (93-mile) Stratford–Taumarunui Heritage Trail leads north-eastwards from Stratford to the north of Whanganui National Park. This interesting back-country road passes through the scenic Tangarakau Gorge and touches the upper reaches of the Whanganui River; along the way, over 30 points of interest (from *pā* sites to historic graves) are marked by Heritage Trail plaques. A free booklet on the Heritage Trail is available from DoC offices in New Plymouth, Stratford and Taumarunui.

THE ENERGY PROVINCE
Taranaki is the hub of New Zealand's energy business, based on local oil and gas fields. The main gas fields are Maui (offshore, piped to Oaonui, 8km/5 miles northwest of Opunake) and Kapuni (30km/15 miles east of Opunake). Apart from being piped around the North Island, natural gas is an important industrial raw material. At Kapuni, it is used as a feedstock to make urea; at Waitara, it is turned into methanol; and near Waitara is the Motunui gas-to-gasoline plant, with an information centre on SH3. Also near Waitara, at Otaraoa Road there is an observation platform at the McKee oilfield.

The volcanic cone of Mount Taranaki (right)

stone church. During the Taranaki wars it was used as an ammunition dump and military post, and the graveyard contains the tombstones of soldiers who died in the wars as well as those of early settlers.

Also worth visiting is the **Puke Ariki▶** (Ariki Street, tel: 06 759 6060; www.pukeariki.com. *Open* Mon–Fri 9–6 (Wed 9–9), Sat–Sun 9–5. *Admission: free*), dubbed Taranaki's information and heritage centre. It has an extensive collection of Maori items (including Te Atiawa woodcarvings) as well as displays on natural history and the colonial era.

In the heart of the city, the **Govett-Brewster Art Gallery▶** (Queen Street, tel: 06 759 6060; www.govettbrewster.com. *Open* daily 10:30–5. *Admission: free*) enjoys a good reputation for innovative contemporary art exhibitions.

The city is famous for its parks and gardens, most notably **Pukekura Park▶▶** (main entrance on Fillis Street, three blocks south of the visitor centre. *Open* daily 9–5. *Admission free*), 20ha (50 acres) of woodland, lawns and gardens and two lakes; the tea kiosk next to the main lake affords a lovely view of Taranaki framed by trees.

Separated from Pukekura by the TSB Bowl of Brooklands (tel: 06 759 6080; www.bowl.co.nz) sound shell and amphitheatre is **Brooklands Park▶▶** with a rhododendron dell, English-style gardens and woodlands. Within the grounds is **The Gables** (*Open* Sat–Tue 1–5, Wed and Fri 10:30–5, Thu 10:30–4), once a cottage hospital and now a medical museum and art gallery.

New Plymouth is something of a mecca for surfers, with good surfing and windsurfing at nearby beaches such as Fitzroy, Strandon, Back Beach and Oakura. The small rocky islets of Whareumu (Lion Rock) and Moturoa, just past the western end of New Plymouth's port, are part of the **Sugar Loaf Islands Marine Park** (see panel page 131), and are home to a variety of marine life, including fur seals.

New Plymouth environs

Following Carrington Road south from New Plymouth, it is a short drive (8km/5 miles) to **Hurworth Cottage▶▶** (906 Carrington Road, tel: 06 753 6545. *Open* Wed–Sun 10–4. *Admission: inexpensive*), one of the earliest homesteads in the region. It is the sole survivor of six pioneer cottages built in a cluster here in the mid-1850s by members of two families from Devon, England. It was built by Harry Atkinson, later four times premier of New Zealand.

Further down the same road is the **Pukeiti Rhododendron Trust▶▶▶** (tel: 06 752 4141; www.pukeiti.org.nz. *Open* daily Sep–Mar 9–5; Apr–Aug 10–3. *Admission: moderate*). Arguably the country's top garden, and at its best between September and November. It has superb rhododendron and azalea displays in 400ha (988 acres) of native bushland.

▶ Stratford   *121A2*

The access point for the eastern slopes of Mount Taranaki, this market town was named in honour of Shakespeare's birthplace. The Patea River runs through the town, which was originally named Stratford-upon-Patea. The town hosts an annual Shakespeare Festival.

Just south of the town (1km/0.5 miles along SH3) is the **Taranaki Pioneer Village▶**, an outdoor museum with displays of local and provincial history (tel: 06 765 5399. *Open* daily 10–4. *Admission: moderate*).

Wanganui's main street, Victoria Avenue

▶▶ Wanganui

One of the oldest towns in the country, Wanganui was settled in the 1840s when the New Zealand Company found itself running out of land at Wellington and had to relocate the constant flow of immigrants somewhere else. Wanganui was an obvious choice (as Maori had earlier discovered) thanks to its rich arable lands and the broad, navigable river. Colonel William Wakefield conducted dubious and hurried negotiations over the land in 1840, handing over blankets, tobacco and trinkets on the site of present-day Moutoa Gardens in return for the 'sale' of 16,000ha (39,500 acres) of land. Several years of strife followed, but in 1848 an agreement was finally reached (again in Moutoa Gardens), and during the New Zealand Wars the Wanganui Maori even helped to prevent the destruction of the settlement by the Taranaki tribes.

To get an overview of the city and the broad mouth of the Whanganui River, head first for the **Durie Hill Elevator▶** (*Open* Mon–Fri 7:30–6, Sat 9–5, Sun 10–5. *Admission: inexpensive*) on the other side of the Wanganui City Bridge. This unusual elevator was built in 1919 to provide a commuter service to the city for residents of the suburbs of Durie Hill: A 213m (700ft) tunnel leads into the hillside, from where the elevator rises 66m (217ft) to the summit. Visitors can walk up a further 176 steps to the top of the **Durie Hill Memorial Tower▶** (*Open* daily 8–6. *Admission: free*); the excellent view encompasses Mount Taranaki, Mount Ruapehu and the South Island coast.

Durie Hill residents can commute by the tunnel and elevator inside the hill

The central thoroughfare of the city is Victoria Avenue, a semi-pedestrianized shopping street that in summer is ablaze with flowers that cascade down from over 600 hanging baskets. Half-way down Victoria Avenue and one block east is **Queen's Park**. To the right of the broad steps is the **Memorial Hall**, and to the left is the modern **Whanganui Regional Museum▶▶** (tel: 06 345 7443; www.wanganui-museum. org.nz. *Open* Mon–Sat 10–4:30, Sun 1–4:30. *Admission: inexpensive*). It is renowned for its

Maori collection, which includes the impressive 23m (75ft) war canoe *Te Mata o Hoturoa*.

The domed building at the top of the steps houses a library and the **Sarjeant Gallery▶** (tel: 06 349 0543; www.sarjeant.org.nz. *Open* Mon–Fri 10:30–4:30, Sat–Sun 1–4:30. *Admission: free/donation*), which regularly hosts touring exhibitions as well as mounting displays from its permanent collection of British and New Zealand paintings.

Behind Queen's Park lie the small and rather formal **Moutoa Gardens▶**, which have played a pivotal role in Wanganui's history. Originally a market where Maori from upriver traded fruit and vegetables, they became the site of controversial negotiations over land sales in 1840 and 1848. In 1995, they were again in the spotlight as Maori and *Pakeha* supporters from all over the country converged here to protest the government's current offer to settle outstanding land claims (see page 21).

Across from Moutoa Gardens on the quayside at Taupo Quay is the **Whanganui Riverboat Centre▶** (tel: 06 347 1863; www.riverboat.co.nz), with the old paddle-steamer *Waimarie* moored alongside. Built in 1900, this 34m (112ft) steamer plied the river until 1952, when she sank. Salvaged in 1993, she is now fully restored and offers daily cruises up the river.

RIVER TRIPS
The Whanganui River has been called New Zealand's Rhine and was a major thoroughfare until the arrival of the railway early in the 20th century. Get a taste of those days with a trip on the *Waimarie*, or go upriver on a jet-boat with River City Jet Boat Tours (tel: 06 342 1718; www.riverspirit.co.nz).

A Maori carving in Whanganui Regional Museum

135

The longest navigable waterway in New Zealand, the Whanganui River flows from Taumarunui 239km (148 miles) down to the sea and is steeped in legend and history. It lies at the heart of Whanganui National Park, whose magnificent scenery was attracting tourists over a century ago.

TREKKING IN WHANGANUI NATIONAL PARK

The two main tracks in Whanganui National Park (the Maungapurua and the Matemateonga) are accessible only by canoe or jet-boat. For more details contact the DoC visitor centres at Wanganui, 101 Guyton Street, Wanganui, tel: 06 345 2402, or Taumarunui, Cherry Grove, Taumarunui, tel: 07 895 8201.

136

A forested gorge on the Whanganui

The environment The Whanganui River has its origins as an alpine stream on Mount Tongariro, winding its way down through the central volcanic plateau and sweeping in a huge arc north towards Taumarunui before turning south towards Wanganui and the Tasman Sea. In the central and lower reaches it wends its way through large tracts of lowland forest.

The landforms in the valley are only about a million years old: sandstone and mudstone (*papa*) from the ocean bed have been eroded by the water into deep gorges, sharp ridges and sheer *papa* cliffs. Cloaking this distinctive landscape is a broad-leaf podocarp forest consisting of species such as northern rata, rewarewa, rimu, tawa, kamahi and kowhai, with black beech dotted along the ridge tops. Distinctive tree ferns, sedges and herbaceous plants thrive on the steep riverbanks and in the gorges. This is one of the largest areas of untouched broadleaf forest in the North Island, and it forms the heart of Whanganui National Park.

Birdlife commonly seen includes native pigeons, fantails, tui, grey warblers, North Island robins and long-tailed and shining cuckoos. The distinctive call of the brown kiwi can often be heard at night.

The river legend When the mighty mountains of Taranaki and Tongariro came into conflict over Pihanga (see page 130), the defeated Taranaki tore himself free from his homeland. Wild with grief and anger, he ripped a deep gash through the earth as he left on his journey to the coast. Soon a clear stream sprang from the side of Tongariro, nourishing green forests throughout the valley, which filled and healed this wound. Thus was the Whanganui River born.

Maori habitation The legendary explorer Kupe is said to have sailed 22km (13 miles) up the Whanganui on his voyage to New Zealand in about AD 950. By 1100 Maori had begun to settle the river valley, and the river became an important canoe route linking the interior with the coast. Food was abundant within the forest, and *kāinga* (villages) sprang up on almost every bend of the river. The inhabitants cultivated the sheltered terraces and built elaborate weirs to trap eels and lamprey in the river channels; the sheer bluffs and sharp ridges along the river valley provided ideal *pā* sites to retreat to when war threatened. By about 1700 there were three *hapū* (sub-tribes) along the river: Hinengakau occupied the upper sections, Tamaupoko the middle reaches of the river and Tupoho the area stretching downstream to the sea. Collectively these tribes were known as Te Atihau Nui a Papa Rangi.

Unpromising farmlands From the beginning of the 20th century settlers had cleared sections of the riverbank for farming, principally from Pipiriki downstream. Wheat was grown on the undulating lands around Pipiriki.

After World War I tracts of the rugged terrain above Pipiriki were offered to the returning servicemen as rehabilitation settlements, but the problems of access, erosion and fighting an unequal battle against the ever-encroaching bush meant that most of these farms were eventually abandoned.

Once an important canoe route, the Whanganui is New Zealand's longest navigable river

137

CANOEING THE WHANGANUI
The 145km (90-mile) journey from Taumarunui to Pipiriki takes five to six days; a three- to four-day journey from Whakahoro to Pipiriki is also feasible, or you can take a one-day 'picnic trip'. Independent canoeists should consult the *Guide to the Whanganui River* (New Zealand Recreational Canoeing Association; www.rivers.org.nz), available from local DoC offices. Adventure operators include: Adrift Guided Outdoor Adventures, tel: 07 892 2751; www.adriftnz.co.nz; Wades Landing Outdoors, RD2, Owhango, tel: 07 895 5995; www.whanganui. co.nz; Yeti Tours, PO Box 140 Ohakune, tel: 06 385 8197; fax: 06 385 8492; www.canoe.co.nz.

Drive

See map on page 121.

The Whanganui River

This drive follows the Whanganui River for nearly 80km (50 miles), passing many historic sites along the way. Black posts with red tops mark places of interest. Fill up with petrol as there is none en route. The Whanganui River Road is unsealed and can be difficult, particularly after rain. To check road conditions, contact Wanganui visitor centre (101 Guyton Street, tel: 06 349 0508).

Up the Whanganui River from Durie Hill

Leave Wanganui on SH4 to Raetihi, passing through Upokongaro and then turning left along River Road. The road climbs steeply up to the summit of **Aramoana**, where a view of the lower reaches of the river unfolds in front of you; on a clear day you can even see Mount Ruapehu.

Descending to the valley floor, you pass the settlement of Parikino before reaching **Oyster Shell Bluffs**. These white cliffs, embedded with clearly visible giant oyster shell deposits, are a reminder that this area once lay beneath the sea.

One of the curiosities of this route is the number of place-names of classical or biblical origin, adapted to Maori pronunciation. With the arrival of the missionaries in the 1840s, warfare between the tribes along the river ceased, and many villages moved from the *pā* sites down to the valley,

where farming was easier. The mission stations suggested new names, which were then transcribed into Maori equivalents: Atene for Athens, Koriniti (Corinth), Hiruharama (Jerusalem), and so on.

Some 8km (5 miles) past Oyster Shell Bluff you reach the first of these settlements, **Atene**; the meeting house here is notable for its curved roof, a peculiarity of the region.

The next stop is at **Koriniti**, where you should turn left down a track to visit Otukopiri Marae (tel: 06 342 8288), which has two well-maintained traditional *wharenui* **(meeting houses)**▶▶. The right-hand one, *Te Waiherehere*, is the original building, while *Poutama* was brought here from the old village of Karatia and was built in 1888. In front of the *marae* is the bow-piece of a large canoe, *Te Aomarua*, which once plied the river. To the south stands a small **Mission Church**, built in the 1920s; a memorial cairn of river stones in front of it was erected in memory of Sister Elsie Smith, a missionary who travelled the length of the river ministering to the local communities; honoured by the state with the MBE decoration for her work, she died in 1968.

Just outside the village on the left-hand side of the road is **Operiki Pā**▶; though it witnessed many attacks and skirmishes, it was never taken in battle. Now obscured by trees and vegetation, its earthworks are nevertheless in good condition.

The next stopping point is the old **Kawana Flour Mill**▶▶, the longest-operating and most successful of many flour mills that existed in the valley at the turn of the century. Walk down a short track to peer through the windows of a reconstructed two-room **Miller's Cottage** and enter the **Mill** (Open site. *Admission: free*), where displays amid the restored machinery on the second floor trace the history of the mill.

After passing through **Ranana** (London), you will see the picturesque settlement of **Hiruharama** on a bend in the river. This is still home to the Sisters of Compassion Roman Catholic convent (www.hoc.org.nz), with steepled **St. Joseph's Church**▶, a distinctive landmark; built in the

The millstone at Kawana Flour Mill

1890s, it has an elaborately carved Maori altar.

After Ranana there are several good viewpoints. The best are at the **River View Picnic Site**, the highest point on the river road, where you can look down on the Whanganui rushing through the, bush-clad gorges below, and at **Omoehu Waterfall Lookout**, with the waterfall on the opposite bank.

Finally you reach **Pipiriki**: the end of the road and the beginning of the wilderness. Near the riverbank is the **Colonial House Information Centre and Museum**▶▶ (tel: 06 385 5022. *Open* Nov–Apr, daily 11–4. *Admission: inexpensive*), in a building dating from the 1880s. It has some interesting displays on early tourism on the river, the ecology of Whanganui National Park and the early inhabitants of the house.

Take the road to Raetihi and either return to Wanganui on SH4 or continue on to Tongariro National Park.

CABLE CA

141

Lower North Island

THE FIRST SHEEP STATIONS

Although Cook had landed sheep in the South Island in 1773, none survived. The first flocks in the country date from 1843 when a certain Charles Bidwill brought 1,600 sheep with him from Sydney to Nelson, and then on to Wellington. He then drove them around the coast to the Wairarapa. Together with several partners, Bidwill leased grazing land from Maori, and although his partners eventually gave up, he persisted in his efforts and the country's first true sheep station was thus established near Martinborough in 1844.

LOWER NORTH ISLAND The southernmost part of the North Island consists of the Manawatu to the west, Wellington to the south and the Wairarapa to the east. Lying to the south of the rugged Ruahine range and divided down the middle by the equally rugged Tararuas, the area encompasses rolling farmlands and bush-clad hills. Large urban areas include Palmerston North and Wellington, with its suburbs sprawling over the southern end of the island, where it meets the turbulent waters of Cook Strait.

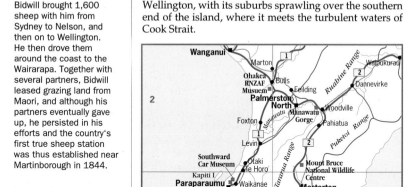

SOUTH TO WELLINGTON The Manawatu, lying on the western side of the ranges that divide the lower North Island, consists mostly of flat, tree-studded plains devoted to sheep and cattle farming. The main commercial hub is Palmerston North, a university town well known for its agricultural and biochemical research.

Cutting through between the Ruahine and Tararua ranges, the Manawatu Gorge is one of the few road routes through the mountains and a gateway to the Wairarapa. Reaching down to the rugged Pacific coastline, the Wairarapa was one of the first sheep-grazing regions in the country (see panel). International sheep-shearing competitions are an annual fixture in the main town, Masterton. Some of New Zealand's rarest birds are bred and studied at the Mount Bruce National Wildlife Centre to the north of Masterton; a major feature of the Centre is that many of the species you can see here are otherwise found only in inaccessible or remote parts of the mainland or on offshore islands.

GREATER WELLINGTON The Kapiti Coast stretches northwards from the suburbs of Wellington to the fruit-growing areas around Otaki, 35km (22 miles) along the coastline. A popular weekend retreat for Wellingtonians, with many sandy beaches, seaside attractions and water sports, it is easily accessible for day-trips from the capital.

Pages 140–141: Looking across Kelburn Park from the city to Oriental Bay and Mount Victoria

▶▶ Kapiti Coast

The Kapiti Coast starts at **Paekakariki**. Here the **Engine Shed** (tel: 0800 783 264; www.steaminc.org.nz. *Open* Sat only 10–4:30. *Admission: inexpensive*) has old steam locomotives on display, and the Wellington **Tramway Museum** (www.wellingtontramwaymuseum.fr.fm. *Open* weekends and holidays 11–4:30. *Admission: inexpensive*) in Queen Elizabeth Park, 5km (3 miles) north of the town, offers rides down to the beach.

Paraparaumu, 50km (30 miles) north of the capital, is the biggest resort along the coast, with an amusement park and a wide sandy beach. Just to the north is **Lindale**▶ (tel: 04 297 0916. *Open* daily 9–5), a farm park with craft and souvenir shops and farm shows (Sat and Sun at 2PM. *Admission: inexpensive*). Offshore is Kapiti Island, once a Maori stonghold and now a nature reserve (see panel).

Farther down the road, **Southward Car Museum**▶▶▶ (tel: 04 297 1221; www.southward.org.nz. *Open* daily 9–4:30. *Admission; inexpensive*) is the largest and most varied collection of its kind in the southern hemisphere.

The next stop is at Te Horo, where the grandly named **Hyde Park Museum**▶ (tel: 04 298 4515. *Open* Tue–Sun 10–5. *Admission: free*) has an enjoyable and quirky collection of Kiwiana, including a grocery store with over 3,000 items (complete with their 1937 price tags), as well as craft shops, a garden centre and a café.

Otaki, marking the end of the Kapiti Coast, has a sizeable Maori community. They used to be able to claim one of the grandest Maori churches in the country, the **Rangiatea Maori Church**. Known as the Maori cathedral, this elaborately decorated wooden building is a faithful reconstruction of the 1850 original that was burned to the ground by arsonists in 1995.

A copper car is one of the many unusual exhibits in the Southward Car Museum

KAPITI ISLAND

Offshore from Paraparaumu looms the bulk of Kapiti Island—forested on the shore facing the mainland and with dramatic cliffs on the far side. It has a long history as the power base of one of the great Maori leaders, Te Rauparaha, and later as the site of seven whaling stations and a farming community. Almost a century ago the 1,760ha (4,350-acre) island was declared a nature reserve, and access is now strictly limited. Of the several tracks on the island, two lead to the summit of Tuteremoana (520m/1,709ft). Permits to visit Kapiti can be obtained from DoC (Government Buildings, Lambton Quay, Wellington, tel: 04 472 7356).

Lower North Island

RARE BIRDS

Mount Bruce National Wildlife Centre had its beginnings in 1958 when a captive rearing programme was set up for four takahe chicks brought here from the South Island: this rare bird, once thought to be extinct, had been rediscovered in Fiordland in 1948. Today the Centre plays an important role in ensuring the survival of some of the country's most vulnerable species. Work is currently focused on takahe, tui, kereru (New Zealand pigeon), kaka, hihi (stitchbird), kokako, scaup, Campbell Island teal and shore plover. Don't miss the spectacular kaka feeding (daily 3PM).

▶▶▶ Mount Bruce National Wildlife Centre   142B2

30km (19 miles) north of Masterton, tel: 06 375 8004
www.mtbruce.doc.govt.nz
Open: daily 9–4:30. Admission: moderate
Well worth a stop if you are travelling on SH2 between Wellington and Hawke Bay, the National Wildlife Centre (see panel) lies by the side of the main road. As most of the birds here are strongly territorial, only a few can be held in each aviary, so you need some patience in order to spot them in their bush surroundings. There is a large nocturnal house for watching kiwi and tuatara.

▶ Ohakea Wing RNZAF Museum   142A2

Ohakea RNZAF base, 3km (1.8 miles) south of Bulls,
tel: 06 351 5020; www.airforcemuseum.co.nz
Open: daily 9:30–4:30. Admission: inexpensive
This small but interesting museum has a number of hands-on displays (such as flight simulators), and tells the story of the people and planes of Ohakea from the time of its establishment during World War II. There's a good café overlooking the runway, giving a tremendous view of aircraft taking off and landing.

▶ Palmerston North   142B2

On the banks of the Manawatu River, this provincial city is a major junction for road and rail links in the North Island and the main focal point of the Manawatu district.

Gardens in The Square, at the heart of Palmerston North

Palmerston North styles itself the 'Knowledge City', a tag which is justified by the presence of Massey University (the second-largest university in the country), a polytechnic, a college of education and the private International Pacific College. Knowledge industries (including a number of agricultural research companies) contribute NZ$500 million annually to the local economy, and it is estimated that at least 40 per cent of the population either attends or teaches at one of the 70 local educational establishments. With all these schools and colleges, it is not surprising that it has a high proportion of young people, with around a quarter of the population aged 15 to 24.

The original settlers (who bought the land from the Rangitane in 1866) destroyed the surrounding bushland to create pastures, but set aside a vast green space in the middle of their township, and the tree-lined **Square** is still the focal point of the city. Today, it is surrounded by shops, and contains the civic centre and visitor centre (tel: 06 354 6593. *Open* Mon–Fri 8:30–5, Sat 10–2). It is a pleasant place to stroll.

A short distance from the Square is the excellent **Te Manawa▶▶** (396 Main Street, tel: 06 355 5000; www.temanawa.co.nz. *Open* daily 10–5. *Admission: free, excluding Mind section*). Opened in 1994, the complex has brought the Science Centre (Mind), the Manawatu Museum (Life) and the Manawatu Art Gallery (Art) together under one roof, providing a huge amount of space for the museum's extensive collections.

In the Life section, the Maori galleries are outstanding, with skilfully lit and well-presented exhibits from the Manawatu, Rangitikei and Horowhenua areas, including elaborate carvings and rare *taonga* (treasures). The historic Totaranui Settlers' Cottage and Awahou South Schoolhouse have been rebuilt here.

The Mind section (*Admission: moderate*) has interactive exhibits and displays geared towards young people.

The Art section has five galleries with an ever-changing programme of touring exhibitions and others from the permanent collection.

Back at the Square, the **Square Edge Creative Centre▶** is the local community arts centre, housing around 17 craft shops under one roof (tel: 06 353 2806. *Open* Mon–Fri 9:30–5:30, Sat 9:30–4, Sun 10–3).

Claiming to have the most comprehensive collection of rugby memorabilia anywhere in the world, the **Rugby Museum of New Zealand▶** (87 Cuba Street, tel: 06 358 6947; www.rugbymuseum.co.nz. *Open* Mon–Sat 10–noon, 1:30–4:30, Sun 1:30–4. *Admission: inexpensive*) houses displays on New Zealand international rugby, with videos of the famous All Blacks' games.

A LOAD OF BULLS
The small farming community of Bulls (at the junction of SH3 and SH1 about 31km/19 miles west of Palmerston North) has put itself on the map by erecting signs outside almost every shop and business in town (about 50 altogether) with word plays on their names such as 'const-a-bull' (police station), 'indispens-a-bull' (pharmacy), 'bank-a-bull' (bank) and 'relieve-a-bull' (public toilets).

New Zealanders' addiction to sport is legendary, with over a third of the population belonging to a sporting club of some kind. In a land where sport is almost a religion, sports heroes are probably better known than many elected politicians.

SPORTING HEROINES
Although perhaps not as well known internationally as some of the great sportsmen, sportswomen in New Zealand have shown a vast improvement in international competitions within the last decade. Some of those who have excelled include Sandra Edge in netball, Susan Devoy in squash, Brenda Lawson and Philippa Baker in rowing, Lynette Brooky in golf, Barbara Kendall in windsurfing, Annelise Coberger in skiing, Alison Rose, Lorraine Moller and Anne Audain in athletics, Madonna Harris in cycling, Tinks Pottinger in equestrian events and Sarah Harrow and Erin Baker in triathlons.

Mountaineering Sir Edmund Hillary, one of the most internationally famous New Zealanders, was born in Auckland on 20 July 1919. As a member of Sir John Hunt's Everest Expedition he attained the summit of Everest with Sherpa Tenzing Norgay in 1953, an achievement for which he was knighted. Not content with that, he then completed a journey to the South Pole as leader of the New Zealand Transantarctic Expedition in 1958, and then in the 1960s took up jet-boating, leading several expeditions up Himalayan rivers (which included the first ascent of the 290km/180-mile Sun Kosi River by jet-boat in 1968). A prolific writer and lecturer, Sir Edmund has been showered with awards from around the world, and founded a charity to provide hospitals and schools for Sherpas as well as the Hillary Commission, which promotes sports in New Zealand.

Cricket Cricket is one of New Zealand's sporting obsessions, and one man responsible for putting Kiwi cricketers on the map is **Sir Richard Hadlee**, who was born in Christchurch and started his career with Canterbury in the early 1970s. In 1973 he made his Test (international) debut, and over the following 17 years, before his retirement in 1990, went on to break several Test records. A great all-rounder, he was an aggressive left-hand batsman and right-arm fast bowler; he also played for Nottinghamshire and Tasmania. In 1985 he became the first New Zealand player to complete the 2,000 runs/200 wickets Test double during a match-saving innings against the West Indies; in 1988 he took his 374th Test wicket (against India at Bangalore), surpassing the previous Test record held by England's Ian Botham. On his 80th Test appearance at Lancaster Park in Christchurch he bowled out Indian Sanjay Manjrekar to become the first player from any country to take 400 Test wickets. At 38 years old he was knighted for his services to cricket. Since his retirement, New Zealand cricket has not been the same.

Yachting New Zealanders have always loved boats, and keen competition in offshore waters (particularly around the northern half of the North Island) combined with a burgeoning yacht-building industry was bound to produce results. In 1990 *Steinlager II* came first in the prestigious Whitbread Round-the-World race, an achievement repeated by *New Zealand Endeavour* in 1994. But it was not until 1995 that the ultimate prize, the America's Cup, fell to the Kiwis. The legendary **Sir Peter Blake** and skipper **Russell Coutts** in New Zealand's *Black Magic I* trounced Dennis Conner's *Young America* in the first five races of a best-of-nine series. With his famous lucky red socks, Blake had played a canny game, even spreading rumours in Auckland water-front bars that their boat was no good. The day they won was proclaimed 'New Zealand's proudest day since Everest' by Dame Catherine Tizard, the then Governor-General of New Zealand. This success was repeated in 2000, but in 2003, the team was thrashed 5–0 by the Swiss Alinghi team, skippered by their own Russell Coutts.

Plain sailing for Team New Zealand's yacht in the 2000 America's Cup

Rugby The game that excites the most passion and commitment among New Zealanders is rugby, and the nation's self-esteem seems to rise and fall with the fortunes of the **All Blacks**, the national team. In 1995 they came within reach of winning the World Cup, when their hero was undoubtedly Auckland-born Tongan **Jonah Lomu**. Against Japan, New Zealand broke all records by scoring 145 points, including 21 tries, but it was against more evenly matched teams that the myth of Lomu escalated: he may well have weighed 114kg (252lb) and stood 2m (6ft 5in) tall, but for all the fear his massive bulk engendered he could have been bigger still. In the semi-final, Lomu got the credit for the All Blacks' demolition of England, and although the Kiwis were favourites for the Johannesburg final, the Cup eventually went to the South Africans. In the 1999 and 2003 World Cups the All Blacks went out of both touraments at the semi-final stage, losing to France and Australia, respectively.

Jonah Lomu (below) has joined the ranks of New Zealand's sporting heroes, which include cricketer Sir Richard Hadlee (left)

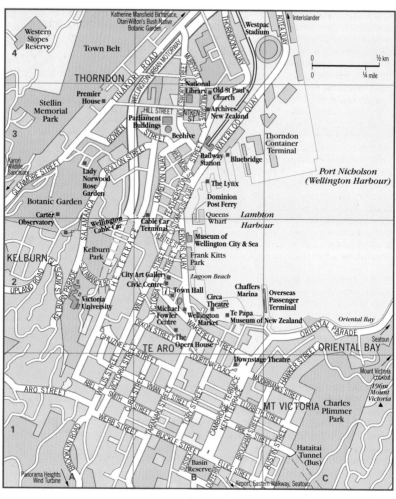

Wellington

A huge harbour, steep hills and ferocious winds are the three defining physical characteristics of the nation's capital. It was probably its strategic position in relation to the South Island that prompted the New Zealand Company to choose Wellington harbour as the site of its first settlement in 1840. In so doing, it successfully anticipated the colonial administration—which 25 years later moved the capital from Auckland to Wellington for that very reason, fearful that the inhabitants of the South Island might try to form a separate colony. Previously, the land had been occupied by the Ngati Tara tribe, and the New Zealand Company's dubious and premature 'purchase' of land blocks later led to bitter fighting. However, this was the most successful of their settlements, and with the arrival of the diplomats and government officials in 1865 the future of the city was assured.

Today the harbour city lies partly on reclaimed land, with the original waterfront streets (such as Thorndon

WINDY CITY

The Venturi effect caused by the channelling of air flows through Cook Strait can produce winds of over 100kph (62mph) whistling through the capital—not for nothing is it known as 'Windy Wellington'. Most prevalent in the spring and autumn, these ferocious winds are further funnelled by high-rise buildings in the downtown area to create some distinctly bracing conditions.

Quay and Lambton Quay) now high and dry in the middle of the central business district. Most of the compact downtown area is flat, but the rest of the city climbs across the surrounding hillsides, with old houses and high-rise developments clinging to their steep slopes. Many central buildings are being rebuilt or renovated to meet stricter earthquake resistance laws.

In addition to being a major transport hub and the departure point for ferries to the South Island, Wellington has plenty of attractions in its own right, and is well worth exploring for a day or two—preferably on a weekend, since many of the best hotels offer weekend deals to compensate for the massive outflow of their city clientele on Fridays. There is always plenty going on, with a lively schedule of performances, festivals and entertainment right through the year. Wellington is home to the Royal New Zealand Ballet and the New Zealand Symphony Orchestra, as well as four professional theatre groups. This cultural vibrancy is complemented by excellent shopping and a cosmopolitan range of cafés, bars and restaurants.

▶ Archives New Zealand   148B3

10 Mulgrave Street, tel: 04 499 5595; www.archives.govt.nz
Open: Mon–Fri 9–5, Sat 9–1 (exhibitions only). Admission: free
Archives do not usually feature highly on sightseeing tours, but it is certainly worth looking in here to see the original Treaty of Waitangi. Other displays include the 1893 Women's Suffrage petition and many other interesting, if less well-known, documents.

▶▶ Botanic Garden   148A3

Tel: 04 499 4444
Sprawling down the hillside behind Wellington's commercial district, this extensive garden is the city's green heart. It has a range of native and exotic plantings with separate areas for succulents, herbs, ferns, rhododendrons, threatened and Australian species, begonias, fuchsias and roses.

DOCKSIDE DEVELOPMENTS
Wellington's wonderful setting on Lambton Harbour has seen some development—a shopping mall on Queens Wharf (now converted to offices), a new marina, events centre, dockside seafood restaurants and wine bars and recreation areas (such as Frank Kitts Park, opposite Civic Square) are just some of them. But a lively debate is taking place over whether the waterfront is losing its unique character as a result. For most visitors the highlight is undoubtedly Te Papa, the imaginative Museum of New Zealand, opened in 1998.

149

The lights of Wellington sparkle across Lambton Harbour

EARTHQUAKE-PROOF
Experts have expressed surprise that Te Papa, the massive Museum of New Zealand, was being built in what is effectively an earthquake zone. In fact, the new museum is one of the safest public buildings in the country: It sits on a series of base isolators, huge shock absorbers that are designed to minimize the effects of any tremors.

Many of Katherine Mansfield's stories are set in Wellington

The top entrance to the garden is just next to the cable-car terminal (see map), and once you have wandered downhill through the garden you can leave either through the exit on the north side, to explore around Tinakori Road and visit Katherine Mansfield's birthplace, or through the rose gardens to walk back to the Parliament Buildings.

Also at the top end of the garden is the **Carter Observatory►** (tel: 04 472 8167; www.carterobs.ac.nz. *Open* Mon–Fri 10–5, Sat, Sun 12–5; also Tue, Thu Sat evenings 6:30–10. *Admission: inexpensive*), the national observatory of New Zealand, which has astronomy displays, video shows, hands-on computer programmes and a planetarium (continuous shows 10:15–4:15 on weekends and public holidays. *Admission: inexpensive*).

► Cable car 148A2
Lambton Quay, tel: 04 472 2199
Open: Mon–Fri 7AM–10PM, Sat 9AM–10PM, Sun 10:30–10. Admission: inexpensive
A good start to any visit to Wellington is to jump on the cable car for the five-minute ride from Lambton Quay up to the Botanic Garden's entrance, where there are good views of the city and harbour. Built in 1902 to link the suburb of Kelburn with the central city, it still carries commuters along with tourists, although the historic wooden cable cars were replaced in 1979 by modern Swiss-built carriages.

►► City Art Gallery 148B2
Civic Square, tel: 04 801 3021; www.city-gallery.org.nz
Open: summer 10–6; winter 11–5 (every Thu until 8PM). Admission: donation
The City Art Gallery, housed in the former public library building, covers a broad spectrum of art, architecture, design and the moving image, with several first-rate exhibitions at any one time. There are also free guided tours of the exhibitions (Tue 12:30 and 1:30, Sat–Sun 1 and 2).

►►► Katherine Mansfield Birthplace 148, off B4
25 Tinakori Road, tel: 04 473 7268
Open: daily 10–4. Admission: inexpensive
The birthplace and childhood home of Katherine Mansfield (1888–1923), New Zealand's most famous author, was built in 1888 for her father Harold Beauchamp, a merchant who later became a successful businessman. Although the young writer left for Europe at the age of 19, she drew directly on her memories and experiences of this house in some of her best-known short stories (including *Prelude*, *The Aloe* and *A Birthday*).

The house has been lovingly restored, with permanent and changing exhibitions, including photographs and excerpts from Mansfield's writings, an exhibition on the restoration itself and a biographical video. The garden has also been faithfully restored to its 1880–1900 appearance.

►► Karori Wildlife Sanctuary 148, off A3
Waiapu Road, Karori, tel: 04 920 2222; www.sanctuary.org.nz
Open: Nov–Feb, Mon–Fri 12–8, Sat, Sun and public holidays 10–8; Mar–Oct, Mon–Fri 12–5, Sat, Sun and public holidays 10–5. Admission: moderate

Karori Wildlife Sanctuary is 252ha (623 acres) of protected land, where the biodiversity of the forest is being restored—a 500-year project. The 8.6km (5.3-mile) perimeter is surrounded by a predator-proof fence, specifically designed to exclude 14 species of non-native mammals, ranging from possums to mice. Over 50 species of threatened native wildlife will be reintroduced, and already visitors and local residents can hear the little spotted kiwi, the most threatened kiwi, calling at night. Evening guided tours (booking essential) are particularly recommended.

▶ Mount Victoria Lookout   148C1

The wind whistles around the top of Mount Victoria (196m/643ft), but the trip up here is worth it for the panoramic views of the city, the harbour and the surrounding hills. Early Maori appreciated the strategic advantage of this spot, which they called Matai-rangi ('to watch the sky'). The road to the lookout is signposted from Oriental Bay and Courtenay Place, or you can take a bus (No. 20 from the railway station).

▶▶▶ Te Papa, Museum of New Zealand   148B2

Cable Street, tel: 04 381 7000; www.tepapa.govt.nz
Open: daily 10–6 (Thu 10–9). Admission: free
Te Papa reflects the country's bicultural heritage and identity, setting out to celebrate the diversity of the *Tangata Whenua* ('those who belong to the land by right of discovery') and the *Tangata Tiriti* ('those who belong by right of treaty') within the context of the natural environment.

Covering the area of three soccer pitches, it is one of the largest new museums in the world. The innovative design makes full use of the harbour setting, with a landscaped outdoor area with exhibitions and performance space.

On entering the building you encounter a dramatic 20m (65ft)-high lobby with stairs and bridges passing through its upper levels, which give views outwards to the city and inwards to the exhibitions. Exhibition spaces include one devoted to the natural environment, a children's learning centre, a canoe gallery (with windows overlooking the harbour), a human cultures gallery, a gallery of the future and many other attractions.

The museum was expected to attract over 700,000 visitors in its first year, becoming Wellington's top attraction, but it achieved that figure in just three months. With all that there is to see, one visit is not enough to do it justice.

WELLINGTON WALKS
The harbourside is one of the city's most pleasant places to stroll; other good walks include the Red Rocks Coastal Walk on the south coast (where fur seals 'haul out' between April and September) and the Eastern Walkway (see pages 154–155). The information centre can also provide leaflets on longer walks, and the Historic Places Trust produces a booklet, *Historic Wellington*, which describes a walk encompassing 30 historic buildings. The information centre is on Civic Square (tel: 04 802 4860. *Open daily 9–5*).

151

This sealife exhibit is one of the main attractions of Te Papa, the Museum of New Zealand

CITY TOURS

The main operator of minibus tours of the city's highlights is Wally Hammond's Tours (tel: 04 472 0869; www.wellingtonsight seeingtours.com).

The glowing interior of Old St. Paul's and (inset) the exterior from Mulgrave Street

▶ **Museum of Wellington City and Sea**   *148B2*

Queen's Wharf, tel: 04 472 8904
www.museumofwellington.co.nz
Open: summer, daily 10–6; winter, Mon–Fri 10–5, Sat, Sun and public holidays 10–5:30. Admission: moderate

Wellington's long association with seafarers and its history as a harbour are well documented in this museum, housed in the Harbour Board building on the quayside. Its collection includes over 80 ship models as well as figureheads, ships' paraphernalia, video displays, an oil-spill computer game—the aim is to save the coastline—and a beautiful old teak cabin from an 1879 steamship. There is also a display on the tragedy of the *Wahine*, an inter-island ferry that was blown off course and sank in the harbour in 1968 with the loss of 51 lives—one of New Zealand's worst maritime disasters.

▶▶▶ Old St. Paul's   148B3

Mulgrave Street, tel: 04 473 6722
Open: daily 10–5. Admission: free
Consecrated on 6 June 1866, this lovely church has a wonderful interior designed in Early English Gothic revival style and was built exclusively with native timbers: rimu for the framing and trusses, matai and totara for the flooring and rimu and kauri for the pews. The subtly lit roof vaults and dark timbers combine with the brilliance of the stained-glass windows to create a warm, peaceful atmosphere. The church served as the city's cathedral for 98 years until the new St. Paul's Cathedral was built; the old building was purchased for the nation and extensively renovated. Weddings, funerals and other services are still held here, and it is also used for musical and cultural events.

▶▶▶ Otari-Wilton's Bush Native Botanic Garden   148, off B4

Wilton Road, Wilton, tel: 04 499 4444.
Admission: free. (No. 14 bus from centre)
Otari is the only garden devoted to New Zealand plants and, with 12,000 species, it is the largest single collection. There are 10km (6 miles) of attractive walks through a variety of habitats, and it is well worth visiting.

▶ Panorama Heights Wind Turbine   148, off A1

Signposted from Brooklyn Road
Open: daily, summer 8–8; winter 8–5.
Admission: free
If you have your own transport, it is worth driving up to this aptly named viewpoint, with its comprehensive vista of Wellington and its surroundings. Towering 30m (98ft) above the hilltop site is a Danish wind turbine, commissioned by the Electricity Corporation (ECNZ) as part of a continuing study into the feasibility of wind power in New Zealand. The wind averages 32kph (20mph), generating a maximum output from the turbine's slender blades of 225 kilowatts; display boards show how much energy is being generated.

Designed by British architect Sir Basil Spence, the Beehive contains ministerial offices and the Cabinet Room

▶▶▶ Parliament Buildings   148B3

Lambton Quay/Molesworth Street, tel: 04 471 9999;
www.parliament.govt.nz
Open: tours hourly Mon–Fri 10–4, Sat 10–3, Sun 12–3; closed 6 Feb. Admission: free
In the middle of the Parliamentary Complex is Parliament House. It was built in 1922 and has been restored with extensive earthquake-proofing. To the right is the oldest building in the complex—the Gothic-style Parliamentary Library, completed in 1897.

On the left is the unmistakable, circular Beehive, designed by British architect Sir Basil Spence. This site was the home of the New Zealand Company's first Resident, Col. William Wakefield, and later of the first Government House. It now houses New Zealand's executive offices.

On the opposite side of Lambton Quay is old Government Buildings, one of the largest wooden structures in the world, built in 1876.

BEACHES
No one expects beach life in Wellington, but surfers and windsurfers will find plenty of good locations (such as Lyall Bay and Houghton Bay) within easy reach of the city. The nearest resort beaches are on the Kapiti Coast. One of the best swimming beaches is Days Bay, on the east side of the harbour; behind it, the native bush of Williams Park is a popular picnic area, and Eastbourne village has restaurants, cafés, crafts and antiques shops. The Dominion Post Ferry (tel: 04 499 1282; www.eastbywest.co.nz) runs from Queens Wharf, with up to nine departures daily for the 30 to 40-minute crossing, some calling at Matiu/Somes Island reserve en route.

Walk

Eastern Walkway

This pleasant coastal walk makes a welcome change from the city streets. Starting from Tarakena Bay, it follows 4.5km (2.75 miles) of the eastern coast of the Miramar Peninsula, and can easily be walked in 90 minutes.

To reach the starting point, follow SH1 south from the city centre, turning left at the airport roundabout. In Seatoun, turn right at Inglis Street, just past the shops, continue around the coastal bays and park in Tarakena Bay.

The Eastern Walkway is clearly signposted up the hill, a brief ascent that brings you to Palmer Head, the site of the **Kemal Ataturk Memorial**. Erected in 1990, this monument to the founder of the modern Turkish state also honours the New Zealand troops who died at the battle of Gallipoli in World War I; a container of soil from Anzac Cove, Gallipoli, is buried within it.

Out in Cook Strait the inter-island ferries ply back and forth, and on a clear day you can see the Kaikoura Ranges on the South Island. To the right is a small headland on which lies Wellington's only untouched *pā* site: Although they are not discernible, there are traces of terraces and ditches dating back to the earliest Maori occupation, when this area was known as Te Whanganui a Tara ('the great harbour of Tara'). Later, in the 17th century, it became the stronghold of Tutere Moana, chief of Ngati Tara.

The track now traverses the saddle below Palmer Head, with views of the Wellington harbour heads to the right. Below, the small inlets of Palmer Bay, Reef Bay and Eve Bay lead round to the sweeping beach at Breaker Bay. Directly offshore is the notorious **Barrett Reef**, the site of many shipwrecks since the

The Kemal Ataturk Memorial

154

19th century (including the ill-fated *Wahine*: see page 152). Canoeists now paddle happily around these treacherous rocks, while yachts returning through the heads give them a wide berth.

Passing beside a residential district, the track dips up and down through an area of typical coastal vegetation; although gorse and other introduced plants dominate the eastern hills, some native plants (such as flax, cabbage tree and *kanuka*) are being reintroduced here.

Make a brief detour at the sign that reads 'Exit to Beacon Hill Road' to reach the **Beacon Hill** lookout, from where there is virtually a 360-degree panorama of the eastern suburbs and the airport, Cook Strait, and Baring and Pencarrow heads.

Return to the track to pass beneath Beacon Hill Signal Station, which has been in operation since 1864 and maintains a round-the-clock, 365-day-a-year lookout for shipping at the heads.

The track continues, winding gently round the hillside

The entrance to Wellington Harbour, as seen from the Eastern Walkway

until it starts to descend through a pine forest. Opening out to the right are views of Point Dorset, with an observation point and gun battery (manned in both world wars) visible on the top of the headland.

To complete the walk, leave the track at the Pass of Branda and head back around the coast to Tarakena Bay, passing many unusual and interesting little seaside dwellings on the way: note the 'Slow Down! Penguins Crossing' signs in Maori and English.

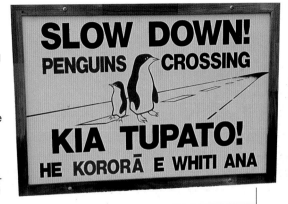

UPPER SOUTH ISLAND Straddling the northernmost section of the island, the provinces of Marlborough on the east and Nelson on the west embrace a diversity of attractions, ranging from wine tours to whale-watching, and craft trails to country hiking. Glorious beaches and a sunny, warm climate contribute to the region's popularity as a holiday destination.

MARLBOROUGH The small port of Picton is where visitors arrive by ferry from the North Island, and it is also the gateway to the extensive **Marlborough Sounds**, a fascinating maze of inlets, beautiful islands, bays and peninsulas with plenty of opportunities for walking, fishing, camping, yachting, kayaking or simply enjoying the scenery. The islands and inlets are mostly thick with vegetation and largely unspoilt—roads are unsealed and often tortuous, and boats are the principal means of transport. The two main sounds are Queen Charlotte and Pelorus, and a hundred or so scenic and nature reserves make up the Marlborough Sounds Maritime and Historic Park.

The province of Marlborough is protected to the south by the Kaikoura Ranges and to the west by the Richmond Ranges, with the Wairau Plain stretching between them. The sheltered climate has led to the establishment of numerous vineyards, most of them dotted around the region's main town, **Blenheim**.

▶▶▶ **REGION HIGHLIGHTS**

Abel Tasman National Park *page 160*

The *Edwin Fox* *page 173*

Farewell Spit *page 163*

Kaikoura *pages 164–165*

Marlborough and Nelson

*Pages 156–157:
Marlborough Sounds
(top); sperm whales
(bottom)*

*Waves crash over
dramatic rock formations
at the entrance to
Marlborough Sounds*

To the east of the Kaikoura Ranges the coastal highway hugs the coast for 60km (37 miles) on the way to **Kaikoura**, 130km (81 miles) south of Blenheim. This small seaside town is riding on the crest of an ecotourism wave, with up to 50,000 visitors coming here annually for just one main activity—whale-watching. Since its beginnings in 1987, whale-watching has taken off in a big way, and there are now many operators providing trips by air or sea to view sperm whales. More than 40 new businesses have been created in order to

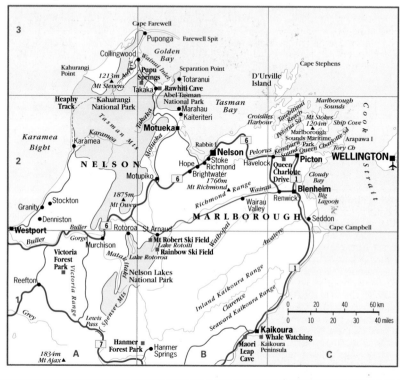

158

cater for the tourists. Ironically, the town has not enjoyed such prosperity since the days when it was a major whaling port.

NELSON At the head of Tasman Bay, with views over the Tasman Range to the west, Nelson is the northernmost city in the South Island, on the same latitude as Wellington. However, the climate in Nelson is more equable, and it has the second-highest amount of sunshine in the country (averaging 2,500 hours a year).

Nelson was one of the first European settlements in New Zealand, and its early days were dogged by problems. The land had been bought by Colonel William Wakefield on behalf of the New Zealand Company, but even after the first ships full of settlers had set sail from England there were disputes as to where they were going to create their new town: Governor Hobson wanted it near Auckland and the Company wanted it at Lyttelton, but eventually Wakefield had no option but to head for Tasman Bay.

After discovering Nelson Haven (a sheltered anchorage that still protects the present-day harbour), Wakefield landed in December 1841; the first migrant ships arrived the following February. By May 1842, some 2,000 migrants had landed; very few had any capital, however, and economic depression soon set in. With the collapse of the New Zealand Company in 1844, many families were reduced to near starvation.

But Nelson struggled through, and in 1858 Queen Victoria signed a charter granting it city status—the second in the country—even though the population was still only 2,700 people. Today it has a population of 47,000 and is a prosperous hub for horticulture (particularly fruit), forestry and fishing.

In the **Richmond Ranges** to the south of Nelson there are opportunities for tramping, fishing, hunting or just taking it easy in the extensive **Nelson Lakes National Park**, centred around two scenic glacial lakes.

Beyond Nelson to the west is **Abel Tasman National Park**. Embracing a glorious stretch of coastline in the sheltered northwestern corner of the South Island, Abel Tasman is the smallest national park in New Zealand (covering just over 200sq km/77sq miles), yet its scenic attractions and remarkably mild and sunny climate have turned it into one of the most popular in the country.

Next to Abel Tasman National Park to the south, and protected from the open ocean by Farewell Spit to the north, are the superb sandy beaches of **Golden Bay**, popular for family holidays. **Farewell Spit**, which curves around the top of Golden Bay and extends for about 26km (16 miles) out into the sea, is a bird sanctuary of international importance, with over 90 recorded species. Southwest of Farewell Spit is Kahurangi National Park (see page 186).

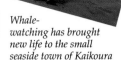

Whale-watching has brought new life to the small seaside town of Kaikoura

159

TASMAN'S LANDFALL
Abel Tasman anchored in what is now Golden Bay on 18 December 1642. That evening, two Maori canoes pulled out to inspect his ships, then departed. The next morning they returned, just as a small boat was crossing between the two Dutch vessels. Maori attacked the boat, killing four sailors. Tasman named the bay Murderers' Bay because of this 'detestable deed', and never set foot here or anywhere else in the country he named Staten Landt.

COASTAL WALK
The Abel Tasman Coastal Track, which takes walkers around the coastal bays and along the magnificent beaches, is one of the easiest in the country, with hardly any steep hills to climb. If you want to do just one walk in New Zealand, this is a good choice. Altogether, it is 51km (32 miles) long and takes between three and five days, though you can, of course, walk shorter sections (see pages 174–175).

Setting off from Marahau at the start of the Abel Tasman Coastal Track

Marlborough

▶▶▶ Abel Tasman National Park 158B2

It is not difficult to understand the popularity of this park, which has a succession of beautiful sandy beaches gently curving around wooded inlets and bays, with wildlife including seals, blue penguins and dolphins in the offshore waters, and shags, gannets and other sea birds nesting on the rocky headlands. Oystercatchers, herons and stilts feed in the park's many large estuaries.

There is great variety in its vegetation too; the coast is cloaked in fertile rain forest, rich with perching plants, vines and tree ferns, while farther inland beech forests are the predominant feature.

For many visitors, Abel Tasman National Park combines much of what is best about New Zealand—sun, sea, wildlife, beaches and bush—in one convenient, handy package. And it *is* both convenient and accessible (and can be crowded). You do not need to be a hardened hiker to reach the best parts, and there is the additional bonus of frequent water taxis and other boats hopping between the beaches. If you were feeling really lazy, you

could just stay on the boat and see it all without having to walk anywhere. In fact, experiencing the park from the sea is now an increasingly popular option, with plenty of opportunities for kayaking along the coast.

The main point of access to the park from the south is Marahau, to the north of Motueka (see page 169), while the northern half can be reached via either Wainui Bay or Totaranui, both accessible from Takaka in Golden Bay (see page 162).

▶ Blenheim 158C2

Famous for the wineries that surround it, Blenheim is the capital of the Marlborough region. Set on the Wairau Plains, it was originally the heart of a sheep-rearing district, but has now been given a new lease of life thanks to the Marlborough vineyards. The high annual sunshine rate (one of the best in the country), long summers and low autumn rainfall led to the planting of the first vines in the 1970s. Many fine wines are now produced here, and grapes are also exported to North Island wineries from this region.

Within a 14km (9-mile) radius of Blenheim there are over 20 wineries, ranging from the country's biggest producers to the small boutique vineyards, which can be visited for tastings. The information centre at the railway station (tel: 03 577 8080; www.destinationmarlborough.com. *Open* daily 8:30–5) has details of a Scenic Wine Tour, or alternatively you can pick up a copy of their *Wine Trail Guide* and set off on your own. The vineyards of Cloudy Bay, Hunter's, Vavasour and Montana are all well worth visiting.

PANORAMIC WALK
The Wither Hills Walkway, just outside Blenheim, has a network of trails with extensive panoramas over Blenheim and the Wairau Valley. This once-barren area has been replanted to create a nature reserve, and several short circular walks are now signposted; a complete circuit takes about two to three hours. The entrance is off Taylor Pass Road (7km/4.5 miles south of central Blenheim).

The countryside around Blenheim, which enjoys one of the best annual sunshine rates in the South Island

Blenheim also has a growing reputation for fine food, from cheeses to venison. Crayfish, green-lipped mussels and salmon come from the nearby sounds, and hazelnuts, olives, garlic, cherries and berry fruits from the plains. The twin pleasures of eating and drinking are highlighted by the popular **BMW Wine Marlborough Wine Festival** (tel: 03 577 9299; www.bmw-winemarlborough-festival.co.nz), held in early February at Brancott Estate.

Blenheim's modern, compact town has several pleasant gardens for relaxation: in the heart of the town is **Seymour Square** (*Open* daylight hours. *Admission: free*), with floral displays and lawns surrounding a clock tower and a multicoloured fountain. On the other side of the Taylor River (reached via a footbridge) is **Pollard Park** (*Open* daylight hours. *Admission: free*), with water gardens, rose gardens, rhododendrons and a native rock garden.

About 2km (1.25 miles) from the town at Brayshaw Park is the **Marlborough Provincial Museum** (tel: 03 578 1712; www.marlborough-museum.co.nz. *Open* daylight hours. *Admission: inexpensive*), with old farming equipment, a mock colonial village and a miniature railway.

FAREWELL SPIT TOURS
The oldest operator of tours to Farewell Spit is The Original Farewell Spit Safari, who has been carrying mail out to the lighthouse at the end of the spit since 1946; several tours are available, depending on the tides and other factors (booking essential, tel: 0800 808257; www.farewellspit.co.nz). Trips to the lighthouse are run by Farewell Spit Nature Tours (tel: 03 524 8188; www.farewell-spit.co.nz), and you can also join them in the Mail Bus for the daily mail run (departing at 9:30AM Mon–Fri) for a scenic five-hour trip around outlying farms and communities.

HEAPHY TRACK
The Heaphy Track links Golden Bay inland from Collingwood with the west coast north of Karamea, and has been described as one of the finest walks in the country. It is named after New Zealand Company draughtsman Charles Heaphy VC, and is 69km (43 miles) long with seven huts on the way: walkers normally take three to five days. Ferns, nikau palms and birdlife abound. You can get full details from DoC in Takaka (tel: 03 525 8026) or Nelson (tel: 03 546 9335).

▶▶ Golden Bay · · · · · · · · · · · · 158B3

In early Maori times, Golden Bay (then known as Mohua) was fairly heavily populated, owing to the presence of resources such as quartzite (quarried for knives), valuable red and black pigments, flints and the rare aromatic herb *kakara taramea* (karamea). The bay was also strategically placed on the supply routes to Westland, as a result of which there are signs of early habitation to be found on almost every promontory and headland. It was at the hands of the local Tumatakori tribe that Abel Tasman lost four of his sailors when he anchored in the bay in 1642. In the 19th century coal and timber were exploited here, and there was a mini gold rush in 1857. Dairy farming is now the main activity, and this tranquil area has also attracted a number of craftspeople and artists.

The principal township in Golden Bay is **Takaka▶**, with a number of good beaches within striking distance. Most of the town's facilities are on Commercial Street, where there is also a **Museum and Gallery** (tel: 03 525 9990. *Open daily, summer 10–4; winter Mon–Sat 10–4. Admission: inexpensive*) with objects and relics of the colonial era alongside paintings, arts and crafts in the converted post office next door. At the southern entrance to the town is the visitor centre (tel: 03 525 9136. *Open daily 9–5*) and the DoC office (tel: 03 525 8026. *Open Mon–Fri 8:30–noon, 1–4*); if you want to visit craft workshops in town or in the outlying areas, pick up a *Golden Bay Craft Trail* leaflet from the visitor centre for details.

Other attractions in the area include the massive **Rawhiti Cave▶**, the entrance to which, some 50m (164ft) wide, is adorned with hundreds of stalactites; a guided tour takes about three hours (*Open on demand.* tel: 03 525 9061. *Admission: expensive*; booking essential).

Another very popular place to visit is **Pupu Springs▶▶**, the largest freshwater spring in New Zealand. The name is an abbreviation of Waikoropupu ('bubbling waters') and the water flows up from underground at a rate of up to 21cu m (740cu ft) per second. Its chief source is the Takaka River, which sometimes disappears underground in the summer, flowing through caves and sinkholes before bursting through the eroded sandstone at this point. There are also vents offshore in the bay, so that sea water is sucked back into the system only to re-emerge at Pupu Springs, making the water slightly salty. Walkways through the Pupu Springs Reserve (5km/3 miles from Takaka, signposted off SH60) also encompass old gold workings in the bush.

Continuing from Takaka, after 27km (17 miles) you reach the tiny settlement of **Collingwood►** at the mouth of the Aorere River. In 1842 a surveyor came across three Europeans living here and building trading ships; later, it boomed briefly during the 1850s gold rush (with no fewer than seven hotels) and was named Gibbstown, after a pioneer settler, William Gibbs. In those heady days there was even a proposal to site the capital here, but once the miners had drifted away it reverted to being the quiet backwater that it remains today. It has an old church (St. Cuthbert's, built in 1873), a courthouse, a dairy/café and two adventure-tour operators.

Collingwood is the jumping-off point for the northern end of the Heaphy Track (see panel opposite), but the focus for most of the activities here is **Farewell Spit►►►**. Bird species seen here range from kea to gannets and spoonbills, but the most notable are the waders. Each year hundreds of thousands of migratory waders arrive here to feed in the inter-tidal zones, the best known of the many regular species being the bar-tailed godwit and the knot.

The spit was considerably overgrazed in earlier years, and much of it is now bare, unstable sand, with frequent high winds (80kph/50mph is not unusual) whipping the tops off the shifting dunes and sending curtains of stinging sand along the wide open beaches. Farewell Spit was declared a nature reserve in 1938, and access is limited to licensed operators (see panel).

BEACHED WHALES
Farewell Spit has always been a navigational hazard for ships (it has claimed around a dozen vessels) and also, it would seem, for whales, which often get stranded on the innermost curve of the spit, near Puponga Point. On at least four occasions (in 1937, 1948, 1977 and 1991) pods of more than 100 pilot whales have been stranded *en masse*, and others found beached up here have included sperm, minke and fin whales. Dolphins have also been stranded, and seals (which usually prefer rocky sites) often come ashore on the oceanside beach.

163

The crystal-clear waters of Pupu Springs, near Takaka

The tranquil township of Kaikoura nestling in the bay beneath the Kaikoura Ranges

PELORUS MAIL BOAT
The boat departs from Havelock on Tuesdays, Thursdays and Fridays at 9:30AM. Booking is essential; contact: Beachcomber Cruises, The Waterfront, Picton, tel: 03 573 6175; fax: 03 573 6176; www.beachcomber cruises.co.nz.

MAORI ENTERPRISE
The first whale-watching operation was set up in Kaikoura in 1987, eventually evolving into Whale Watch Kaikoura with the help of funding from the local Ngai Tahu tribe. Since then the company has expanded rapidly. Wholly Maori-owned, it has given a massive boost to the local economy, funded schemes to improve community education and health, and above all given the local Maori community a sense of self-esteem and pride.

▶ Havelock
158C2

It is hard to believe that this tiny port once had 23 hotels, but just over a century ago it was indeed a boom town, thanks to the nearby Cullen Creek and Wakamarina gold fields. When gold fever subsided, Havelock reverted to its former life as a sleepy fishing village, relying then (as it does now) on the famous green-lipped mussels that are grown in the Sounds. At the only point where the main road (SH6) joins the shoreline of Pelorus Sound, it is a charming little spot that invites you to linger.

You can explore the superb scenery of the Sounds from Havelock by joining the long-serving Pelorus Mail Boat, which visits isolated homesteads in the many quiet, secluded bays, dropping off supplies and mail (see panel).

▶▶▶ Kaikoura
158B1

One of New Zealand's best-known ecotourism destinations, Kaikoura has become famous for whale-watching, thanks to the deep trenches in the sea-bed that start less than 2km (1 mile) from the shore. Cold, north-moving currents are met here by warm, southward-moving currents, creating a constant upwelling of nutrients that supports a complex food web—an all-you-can-eat banquet for seals, dolphins, birds, shellfish, sharks and, of course, whales. In some places these canyons exceed 1,600m (5,250ft) in depth and contain many of the deepwater fish and squid that make up much of the sperm whale diet.

The sperm whales are present throughout the year, although at some seasons there are more of them, for example between April and August when they come inshore to feed on spawning grouper. Conditions in the open sea mean that it is not always possible to reach them, so if you are looking forward to a whale-watching trip, be prepared to allow an extra day or two. Do not plan to go whale-watching if you have a flight to catch.

Sperm whales are not the only cetaceans to take advantage of these rich feeding grounds. In the summer, orca (killer whales) pass through every three weeks or so, usually in pods of between 6 and 18 individuals, and their territory is thought to extend from Cook Strait down as far as Christchurch. Longfin pilot whales, sometimes in groups of up to 300 individuals, have also been spotted. Humpbacks pass through on their annual migration (during June and July) from Tonga to the Antarctic, although they are now few in number.

Dusky dolphins are another highlight of Kaikoura, and these charming, playful creatures appear in their hundreds between October and April. The endangered Hector's dolphin (of which there are only 2,000 to 3,000 left in the world) can be seen here, with two populations living near Kaikoura throughout the year. Fur seals are also plentiful.

Kaikoura was a major pre-European Maori stronghold, since the peninsula was easily defended and food was plentiful; there are numerous *pā* sites scattered across the peninsula. In the 19th century, sealers and whalers reaped the harvest from the offshore waters. The first whaling station was established here in 1842 by Robert Fyffe. He was later joined by his cousin George, and between them they pioneered sheep farming around Kaikoura.

The only surviving building from the whaling days is **Fyffe House**▶▶ (tel: 03 319 5835. *Open* Nov–May daily 10–6; Jun–Oct Mon–Fri 10–4. *Admission: inexpensive*) at Avoca Point, 2km (1.25 miles) southeast of the town. Originally a cooper's cottage built between 1842 and 1852, it was constructed on whalebone piles that can still be seen. George Fyffe and his wife Catherine moved in and extended it in the early 1860s, and it has changed little since then; the house was renovated (using traditional techniques) in 1993 by the Historic Places Trust, and the garden around it was re-created as a cottage garden of the time.

Whaling relics are a prominent feature in the small **Museum** (tel: 03 319 7440. *Open* Mon–Fri 12:30–4:30, Sat, Sun 2–4. *Admission: inexpensive*) on Ludstone Road, which also contains Maori objects and a replica of the largest moa eggshell ever found, discovered by George Fyffe near his house (see above).

The other main attraction in the vicinity is **Maori Leap Cave** behind the Caves Restaurant (tel: 03 319 5023), 3km (2 miles) south of Kaikoura. The origin of the name of this cave is obscure, but it has no basis in Maori mythology; the cave was only discovered during a lime-crushing operation in 1958. Thought to be around two million years old, the cave is 90m (295ft) long, with numerous delicate limestone formations (tours depart from the Caves Restaurant six times daily. *Admission: moderate*).

WHALE-WATCHING
Trips leave Kaikoura for the two-and-a-half-hour whale-watching excursion four times daily between 6:30AM and 2PM. The cost is NZ$95 (adults), NZ$60 (children). Booking (preferably three to four days in advance) is essential. Contact: Whale Watch Kaikoura, the Whaleway Station, Kaikoura, tel: 03 319 5045; freephone: 0800 655 121; fax: 03 319 6767; www.whalewatch.co.nz. You can fly over the whales by plane or helicopter (the DoC licences specify that they remain a certain distance away so their noise footprint does not disturb the whales). Contact Wings over Whales, tel: 03 319 6580; www.whales.co.nz; or Kaikoura Helicopters, tel: 03 319 6609; www. kaikourahelicopters.co.nz.

165

The sea has been the mainstay of Kaikoura since the earliest Maori settlement

There are about 76 species of whales and dolphins in the world, and of these 34 have been sighted in the waters around New Zealand: 15 different species have been identified off Kaikoura alone, and the regularity of their appearances has turned this small town into the main base for the country's whale-watching.

Hydrophones are used to locate the whales

First sightings Dawn spreads an orange glow over South Bay at Kaikoura as the first whale-watching trip of the day sets out. The rigid-hulled inflatable Naiad slips out of the harbour, past a seal colony at the end of the rocky peninsula, and in 20 minutes it has reached the edge of the continental shelf and the search for whales begins. The crew dip a hydrophone (underwater microphone) into the water, sweeping it around in search of the telltale clicks, amplified for all to hear, that betray the presence of sperm whales. Passengers soon discern the slow click of a whale about to surface, and the boat moves closer to the source of the sound. All eyes are on the look-out for the distinguishing jets of spray, and sure enough up comes a massive, 15m (50ft)-long sperm whale, to gasps of appreciation. It rests on the surface for about 10 minutes, then, having absorbed enough oxygen for its next dive, takes one last breath and lifts its mighty tail flukes in the air before sliding down into the depths again. If you are lucky you might experience several such sightings on a two-hour trip.

Sperm whales When it is resting on the surface, most of the sperm whale is invisible; its bulk really only becomes apparent when it performs spectacular leaps (known as 'breaches') out of the water. The sperm whale can dive down as far as 2,010m (6,600ft), using echolocation (sound beams emanating from its oil-filled jawbone) to pin-point squid and other prey. The average dive usually lasts about 40–45 minutes.

An adult male can weigh up to 35–50 tonnes, the smaller females up to 22 tonnes, and they are believed to have a lifespan of between 50 and 70 years. The females breed every four to six years and nurse their young

SEALS AND DOLPHINS
Usually aggressively territorial on land, fur seals are far more approachable in the water, and you can go snorkelling with these friendly, playful creatures; for guided snorkelling tours (including wetsuits and snorkelling equipment) contact Seal Swim Kaikoura, tel: 03 319 6182; www.sealsswim kaikoura.co.nz. Trips to swim with dolphins are also popular, with all equipment (snorkels etc) supplied. You can also just view the dolphins: contact Dolphin Encounter, tel: 03 319 6777; www.dolphin.co.nz or Dive Kaikoura, tel: 03 319 6622; www.scubadive.co.nz.

for two years; at between 4 and 15 years of age, the young whales form groups with others of the same age but remain in the same areas as the females. As they reach sexual maturity (at between 14 and 20 years of age), they leave the 'family' and set out on their own. The dilemma for the young males is that the acceptable breeding age is 25—so for the next five or ten years they simply hang out in groups with other bachelors, staying in the feeding areas all year round instead of migrating to the breeding grounds in winter. It is thought that most of the whales seen off Kaikoura are young males between 15 and 25 years old.

Sperm whales have a distinctive scalloped pattern on their tail flukes, and photo-identification has enabled researchers to identify at least 40 individuals (all of whom have been given names) within the range of the whale-watching operation, which covers around 15sq km (6sq miles). Another 20 or 30 whales move in and out of this area, and sometimes female sperm whales are spotted.

A sperm whale prepares to dive

168

Wonderful views of the Marlborough Sounds unfold along the length of Queen Charlotte Drive

▶▶ Marlborough Sounds   158C2

Crossing Cook Strait by ferry from the North Island, your first taste of the South Island will be of the convoluted waterways of the Marlborough Sounds (see panel page 172). Regrettably, many visitors get off the ferry at Picton and head straight down the highway to points farther south, missing out on this wonderful area.

The Sounds were formed by the sea drowning an intricate system of branching river valleys, and were first explored by Captain Cook, who visited them five times between 1770 and 1777. On each occasion he anchored at Ship Cove (where there is now a memorial to him) to replenish supplies and rest his crew. The French explorer Dumont d'Urville followed in 1827, discovering the passage now known as French Pass.

The two main inlets are **Pelorus Sound** and **Queen Charlotte Sound**, while **Havelock** (see page 164) and **Picton** (see page 173) are the main port and service centre for each one.

One of the most spectacular walks in the region is the 68km (42-mile) Queen Charlotte Track (www.qctrack. co.nz) along the north shore of the sound from Anakiwa to Ship Cove. It passes through lush coastal forests and skirts historic bays with superb views over both Queen Charlotte Sound and Kenepuru Sound (off Pelorus Sound). There are frequent boat services from Picton, so you can either walk it in day-trips or make a two- to five-day journey of it.

Equally enjoyable (and as strenuous) is the Queen Charlotte Drive along the south shore, a superb route that winds around the hills from Picton with magnificent views of the wooded sounds, beaches and bays ending up in Havelock. It is just over 100km (62 miles) as a round trip, or you can make it part of your onward journey and continue from Havelock to Nelson and points west and south.

▶ Motueka 158B2

Surrounded by a patchwork of orchards and fields producing crops as diverse as hops, kiwifruit and green tea, Motueka is a busy agricultural area set on the fertile plains behind Tasman Bay, 51km (32 miles) northwest of Nelson. As the nearest sizeable town to Abel Tasman National Park, it is also a service centre for trekkers and day-trippers; Kahurangi National Park (including the former North West Nelson Forest Park, see page 186) is also accessible from here.

Motueka's long main street has all the usual facilities, including a DoC centre (corner of King Edward and High streets, tel: 03 528 1810. *Open* daily 8–noon, 1–4:30) for track information and a visitor centre (20 Wallace Street, tel: 03 528 6543. *Open* Mon–Fri 8:30–7, Sat–Sun 9:30–7) where you can book local activities such as Abel Tasman trips, kayaking and so on. If you are interested in visiting local craft workshops, the visitor centre can provide a *Craft Trail* leaflet that describes a 70km (43-mile) tour around a dozen or more in the vicinity.

Although the superb beaches of Abel Tasman National Park are not far away, there are others nearer town, such as the popular **Kaiteriteri Beach▶**, a long strip of golden sand 14km (8.5 miles) to the north.

169

▶ Murchison 158A1

Surrounded by rugged mountains, Murchison lies on a small plain at the confluence of the Buller and Matakitaki rivers. Because of its strategic position between Nelson and Westland on the Buller Gorge Heritage Highway (SH6), it is often treated as no more than a refreshment stop by people passing in either direction. However, the town has developed an enormous range of adventure activities and is ideally placed for exploring the surrounding bush-clad ranges, fast-flowing rivers and unspoiled lakes.

The information centre (Waller Street, tel: 03 523 9350. *Open* daily 10–5) can provide details on gold-panning, mountain-biking, hunting, fishing, 4WD safaris, caving, horse-riding and much else besides.

Just off the main street is the **Murchison Museum▶** (tel: 03 523 9392. *Open* daily 10–4. *Admission: donation*) with a collection of antique telephones and a section devoted to the Murchison earthquake (see panel opposite).

The wharf at Motueka, the base town for both Abel Tasman and Kahurangi national parks

The shoreline at Nelson heading towards the city's main beach at Tahunanui

Nelson

▶▶ **Nelson**   *158B2*

Nelson is a popular holiday destination for many New Zealanders. The climate is the most equable of any New Zealand city, with the highest sunshine rate in the country. It has its own golden beach at Tahunanui, and Kahurangi, Nelson Lakes and Abel Tasman National parks are all within easy reach. One of the oldest settlements in the country, Nelson can also claim a number of firsts for New Zealand, including the first Rugby Club in the country, formed on 14 May 1870, with the first match being played the same day on the grounds of the Botanic Gardens. The first commercial brewery in New Zealand (Paolo and Pelham) opened here in 1842, and the first recognized racecourse in the country was built at Stoke in 1845. The first commercial thoroughbred horse-breeding stud was opened in 1852, and the country's oldest state secondary school, Nelson College, was opened in 1856.

Leading up from the seafront is the central axis of the city, **Trafalgar Street**, where you will find most of the shops and the helpful visitor centre (corner of Trafalgar and Halifax streets, tel: 03 548 2304. *Open* Mon–Fri 8:15–5:30, Sat 9–5, Sun 10–4). Near by is **Montgomery Square**, where there is a good weekend market with crafts, plants, bric-à-brac and fresh produce stalls.

Dominating Trafalgar Street at its southern end is **Christ Church Cathedral** (tel: 03 548 1008. *Open* 7AM–8PM), an unmissable monolith built on top of a small hill. Local

ARTS AND CRAFTS

The enormous range of arts and crafts produced in and around Nelson is detailed in the *Arts Trail and Gallery Guide* from the visitor centre. Near the heart of the city are South Street Gallery (10 Nile Street West, tel: 03 548 8117; www.nelsonpottery. co.nz) and the Bead Gallery (18 Parere Street, tel: 03 546 7807; www.beads.co.nz). Out of town, the long-established Craft Habitat (at Richmond, 10 minutes south on SH6) contains half a dozen or more workshops.

people tend to stress the 'beautiful gardens' that surround it, thereby sidestepping a description of the building. Started in Takaka marble but finished in concrete blocks, the cathedral took nearly 40 years to complete (it was begun in 1925, completed in 1967, but not consecrated until 1972), and it looks as though it was designed by a committee. The most polite thing you can say about it is that it has some nice stained glass—and lovely gardens.

Nelson is noted for its arts, music and crafts (particularly pottery), and there are plenty of outlets for browsing or buying around town. The city's best showcase is the **Suter Art Gallery**▶ (Queens Gardens, Bridge Street, tel: 03 548 4699; www.thesuter.org.nz. *Open* daily 10:30–4:30. *Admission: inexpensive*), which houses a permanent collection (with works by Wollaston, Lindauer, Van der Velden and others), and also touring and local exhibitions covering everything from sculpture to fibre crafts.

Nelson is home to a unique event, the Montana Wearable Art Awards. Started by sculptor Suzie Moncrieff in 1987 as a publicity stunt when she opened a gallery, this has since grown into an international event that is now staged in the **World of Wearable Art and Collectible Car Complex** (95 Quarantine Road, Annesbrook, tel: 03 548 9299. *Open* daily summer 10–6:30; winter 10–5. *Admission: moderate*) in September every year. It is an explosion of creativity and anarchic design, and the concept is still evolving, with categories including a Visual Arts section.

Nelson also has its fair share of historic buildings, albeit scattered quite widely across the city and its suburbs. One of the most interesting streets within the city is **South Street**▶ (off Nile Street West, just behind the cathedral), with 16 working-class cottages built between 1863 and 1867; most are private dwellings, but some house small galleries or craft shops. Many of the older buildings have been re-erected (or re-created) in **Founders Historic Park**▶ (87 Atawhai Drive, five minutes' walk from central Nelson, tel: 03 548 2649; www.founderspark.co.nz. *Open* daily 10–4:30. *Admission: moderate*), where there is also a three-dimensional maze, train rides and an audio-visual exhibition on Port Nelson.

One of Nelson's most beautiful historic homes is **Isel House**▶▶ (Marsden Road, Stoke, tel: 03 547 5222. *Open* summer, Sat–Sun 2–4. *Admission: inexpensive*), a two-floor homestead containing a collection of porcelain and furniture. Opposite Isel House, but moving to the middle of the city in 2005, is the **Nelson Provincial Museum**▶ (tel: 03 547 9740; www.mus eumnp.org.nz. *Open* Mon–Fri 10–4, Sat, Sun 12–4. *Admission: inexpensive*), which has some interesting Maori items as well as an extensive collection of photographs. Both buildings are within the grounds of the 6ha (15-acre) **Isel Park**▶▶, which has extensive plantations of exotic trees.

Near by is **Broadgreen House**▶▶ (Nayland Road, Stoke, tel: 03 547 0403. *Open* daily 10:30–4:30. *Admission: inexpensive*), a good example of a restored early 'cob' house, built in 1855.

ERNEST RUTHERFORD
Sir Ernest Rutherford, the father of nuclear physics, was born at Brightwater (19km/12 miles south of Nelson) in 1871, and educated at Nelson College before moving on to Canterbury University College in Christchurch and then to Cambridge University, England. His main achievement was in discovering how to split the atom, but he also made many other outstanding discoveries during over 40 years of experimentation with atomic physics. He took the title Baron Rutherford of Nelson on his elevation to the peerage in 1931, and on his death (1937) was buried in Westminster Abbey in London.

Marlborough and Nelson

ON THE SOUNDS

There are various ways to explore the Marlborough Sounds from Picton, including by kayak, which is highly recommended (Marlborough Sounds Adventure Co., tel: 03 573 6078; www.marlboroughsounds. co.nz; Sea Kayaking Adventure Tours, tel: 03 574 2765; www.nzseakayaking.com); on a three-hour cruise to Endeavour Inlet (Cougar Line, tel: 03 573 7925; www.cougarlinecruises.co. nz); or on a special dolphin-spotting cruise (Dolphin Watch Marlborough, tel: 03 573 8040; www.dolphinwatch-marlborough.co.nz).

172

The scow Echo *is a distinctive landmark in the background, on the eastern side of Picton Harbour: in the fore-ground the* Edwin Fox *can be glimpsed next to its interpretation centre*

▶▶ **Nelson Lakes National Park**   *158B1*

This lovely park is easily reached from Nelson, or can be visited by making a detour off SH6 on routes to Westland. In 1859, the explorer von Haast exclaimed 'I had no idea such a jewel in point of landscape existed so near to Nelson, and I am sure that the time is not far distant when this spot will become the favourite abode of those whose means and leisure will permit them to admire picturesque scenery.' And so it is, with fishing, trekking, mountain-biking, hunting and skiing all popular.

Covering 102,000ha (252,000 acres) of rugged terrain, the park has a diverse range of habitats, from tranquil lakeside beech forests to open tussock lands beneath craggy peaks. The most popular area is around beautiful **Lake Rotoiti▶▶**, where you can swim from the lakeside picnic areas with the forested hills as a backdrop. The main gateway to the park and the focus for activities is the alpine village of **St. Arnaud** (121km/75 miles from Nelson) on the shores of the lake, where hotel accommo-dation, camping and shops are all available at the lake-side. There is also a DoC visitor centre (tel: 03 521 1806. *Open* daily 8–5; closed Sat–Sun May–Aug).

The park has 270km (168 miles) of tracks and 21 huts, with the longest tramp being the 80km (50-mile) Travers-Sabine Circuit (four to seven days). For day visitors there are plenty of short walks around the shores of the lake, most of them well signposted and graded. You can also take a water taxi to the far shore and walk back from there.

Lake Rotoroa▶ is slightly harder to reach (down an 11km/7-mile gravel road) and has fewer facilities; it is more popular with those who want to go hunting or

trout-fishing. There are also short walks around Rotoroa, but be warned, as the lakeshore has a tendency to be plagued by sandflies.

▶ Picton 158C2

Primarily a transit point for ferry passengers crossing to or from the North Island, Picton sits near the head of Queen Charlotte Sound and is often bypassed in favour of more exciting destinations. In fact, it is a pleasant little port that makes a good base for visiting the Marlborough Sounds.

While catamarans, yachts and speedboats ply the harbour, one of the world's oldest ships is in its dock by the quayside. The **Edwin Fox▶▶▶** (tel: 03 573 6868; www.nzmaritime.co.nz/edwinfox.htm. *Open* daily 8:45–5. *Admission: inexpensive*) was built in 1853, and carried tea from the colonies, troops to the Indian Mutiny, convicts to Australia, immigrants to New Zealand and frozen meat back to Britain before ending up as a coal hulk in Picton harbour. There is a superb new interpretation centre alongside the ship.

On the other side of the harbour, the scow **Echo▶**, a 90-year-old coastal trader, is now a café/bar (tel: 03 573 7498. *Open* daily, summer 10–10; winter 10–5).

Overlooking the harbour is the **Picton Museum▶** (tel: 03 573 8283. *Open* daily 10–4. *Admission: inexpensive*), containing whaling relics and equipment and a small but unusual Maori collection.

WALKING TRACKS
Around Picton there are plenty of short to moderate walks that take you through scenic bush areas or up to vantage points over the Sounds. If you are short of time, one of the easiest is the 1km (0.5-mile) shoreline track to Bobs Bay, round the eastern side of the harbour. The visitor centre has a detailed leaflet on *Walkways and Mountain Bike Tracks*.

The only remaining East Indiaman, the Edwin Fox

Walk

Abel Tasman Coastal Track

This easy walk follows the popular coastal track around one of the most scenic sections of Abel Tasman National Park. Allow four hours for the walk back to Marahau from The Anchorage.

The Anchorage

After stepping ashore in The Anchorage, turn right past the DoC camping area and continue until you see a track heading inland. After a short climb you reach a ridge, where there are terrific views back across The Anchorage and Torrent Bay, with the headlands, beaches and coastal inlets of the park stretching northwards. In front of you, the view encompasses Astrolabe Roadstead and Adele Island, with the Richmond Mountains visible across Tasman Bay in the distance.

From here the track crosses one of the most arid sections of the park, a testament to the many fires (dating back to pre-European times) that have destroyed the original vegetation. In the poor soil even gorse and the hardy manuka struggle to survive.

Although the park is named after Abel Tasman, it was the French explorer Dumont d'Urville who was the true European discoverer of this coast, which he charted and explored in January 1827 while his corvette *Astrolabe* was anchored between Adele Island and the mainland. In contrast to Tasman, d'Urville established good relations with Maori.

Take the track down to **Watering Cove ▶ ▶**, another delightful beach seaward side. Just before Yellow Point, turn down towards **Akersten Bay▶▶**, another beautiful beach where you can cool off with a swim or a paddle in the warm waters of the Astrolabe Roadstead. An early surveyor, Frederick Carrington, understandably fell in love with this superb coastline in 1841: 'Certain it is that if I ever settle for life in New Zealand, Astrolabe Roads would be the place I give preference to.' It is easy to agree with him as you relax on the sand admiring this magnificent environment.

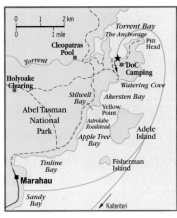

Coastal scenery in Abel Tasman National Park at Marahau

with a stream running down behind it. D'Urville replenished the ship's water supplies here, and an engraving of the time shows the *Astrolabe's* sailors relaxing and doing their washing in the 'charming stream of very clear water'.

There is evidence of fire everywhere in the park, with blackened tree trunks and scorched scrub, but after the junction branching off up to Holyoake Clearing (which leads to the inland section of the track) the vegetation becomes greener, with a variety of broad-leaved species, rimu and kamahi shading the track, and tree-ferns spreading their fronds over the moist gullies on the hillsides.

This is one of the prettiest sections of the track as it follows round the hillside, crossing tumbling brooks with glimpses of sandy coves on the

Past Yellow Point another track leads down alongside the stream bed of Lesson Creek to **Stilwell Bay▶▶**, also a gorgeous beach. Finally you come to **Apple Tree Bay▶▶**, which d'Urville described as 'the pleasantest spot on the whole coast...a narrow sandy belt, covered with nothing but herbaceous plants, runs along the edge of the sea...a magnificent stream crosses it from one end to the other, dashing its plenteous waters over a bed formed of enormous blocks of granite.' It is little changed today, apart from a strand of trees on the foreshore, and it is the last in this succession of splendid beaches.

Beyond here the track continues to **Tinline Bay**, surrounded by hillsides of bracken and gorse, until finally you emerge in the estuary of **Sandy Bay**, where a causeway leads across the tidal flats to the Park Café and bus stop at **Marahau.**

Cut off by the towering mass of the Southern Alps (above), the West Coast has numerous historic gold workings; in some you can try your hand at panning

South Island

The West Coast

177

THE WEST COAST A narrow strip of land hemmed in on one side by the Tasman Sea and on the other by the Southern Alps, the West Coast is characterized by wild, magnificent scenery and has several national parks. The coastal flats are scattered with the remnants of the gold-rush era of the 1860s, with walking tracks around many of the old workings. Visitors can still sometimes have a go at gold-panning here themselves.

The weather is often the topic of conversation on the West Coast, which has a reputation for almost continuous rain. The high rainfall is caused by westerly winds coming off the sea and rising up to the mountains, where they condense to dump their watery cargo on the narrow coastal belt—thus encouraging the region's lush vegetation. Nevertheless, most of the rain tends to fall at night with the clouds parting during the day to reveal the peaks of the Southern Alps sparkling in the clear light. But don't forget your water-proofs—just in case.

178

Kahurangi National Park was created in 1996. Covering some 5,000sq km (1,930sq miles) of diverse and largely untouched terrain in the northwest corner of the South Island, it stretches from Murchison all the way up to Farewell Spit in Nelson, and contains a greater variety of plant and animal life, geology and landforms than any other national park in the country. The coastline encompasses everything from palm-fringed beaches north of Karamea to the rugged cliffs beyond the Heaphy River, while inland lie countless caves, river canyons and jagged peaks reaching up to 1,875m (6,152ft).

The main point of access for the park, and a good base for a variety of activities, is **Karamea** (98km/61 miles north of Westport) at the end of the road in the far north of the West Coast region.

Paparoa National Park, 47km (29 miles) north of Greymouth, is one of the most popular areas on the West Coast. Extending from the coast to the crest of the Paparoa Range, the park is fairly compact (covering just 300sq km/116sq miles), but has a wide variety of features including delightful beaches, numerous lime-stone caves and cave systems, awesome gorges bordered by towering cliffs and forested valleys. Sheltered by the mountains and warmed by ocean currents from the Coral Sea, it has a mild, moist microclimate that is good for luxuriant subtropical vegetation, with masses of perching plants, tangled vines and nikan palms. In combination with the dramatic 300m (1,000ft)-high coastal cliffs, this gives the park tremendous appeal.

Other natural attractions on the West Coast include seal colonies at **Cape Foulwind** and **Gillespies Beach**, a black-petrel colony in Paparoa National Park and the white-heron colony near **Whataroa**.

To the southeast of Greymouth, **Arthur's Pass National Park** straddles the Southern Alps and is equally accessible from both the West Coast and Canterbury, either by car or on the famous TranzAlpine express.

About half-way down the coast, Fox and Franz Josef glaciers form part of **Westland National Park**, which has guided ice walks or thrilling helicopter sight-seeing trips.

The **Haast** area at the southern end of the West Coast is beautiful, but all too often neglected as people speed through on their way to Otago and Fiordland. Connected by a through route to the rest of the country only in 1965, this rugged, unspoiled wilderness has a spectacular coastline backed by the towering peaks of the Southern Alps, with foaming glacial rivers and a series of forest-fringed lakes inland.

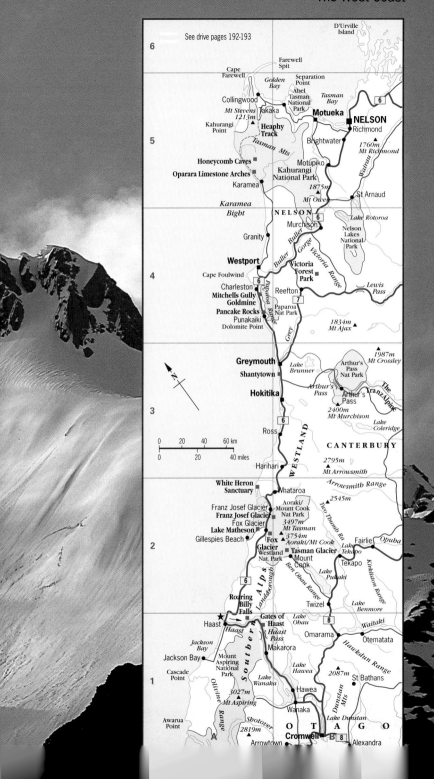

6

See drive pages 192–193

D'Urville
Island

Farewell
Spit

Cape
Farewell

Golden
Bay

Separation
Point

Abel
Tasman
National
Park

Tasman
Bay

Collingwood
Takaka

Motueka

NELSON

Mt Stevens
1213m

Richmond

Kahurangi
Point

**Heaphy
Track**

Brightwater

1760m
Mt Richmond

5

Honeycomb Caves

Motupiko

Oparara Limestone Arches

Kahurangi
National
Park

Karamea

1875m
Mt Owen

St Arnaud

Karamea
Bight

N E L S O N

6

Murchison

Lake Rotoroa

Granity

Buller
Gorge

Nelson
Lakes
National
Park

Westport

Buller

Victoria Range

Cape Foulwind

6

Charleston

**Victoria
Forest
Park**

Reefton

Lewis
Pass

**Mitchells Gully
Goldmine**

7

Pancake Rocks

Paparoa Nat Park

Punakaiki
Dolomite Point

Paparoa Range

Paparoa Nat Park

Grey

4

1834m
Mt Ajax

Greymouth

Lake
Brunner

Arthur's
Pass
Nat Park

1987m
Mt Crossley

Shantytown

Arthur's
Pass

Hokitika

Arthur's
Pass

The
TranzAlpine

6

2400m
Mt Murchison

Lake
Coleridge

3

Ross

C A N T E R B U R Y

0   20   40   60 km

0   20   40 miles

Harihari

2795m
Mt Arrowsmith

W E S T L A N D

**White Heron
Sanctuary**

Whataroa

Arrowsmith Range

Aoraki/
Mount Cook
Nat Park

2545m

Franz Josef Glacier
Franz Josef Glacier

3497m
Mt Tasman

Two Thumb Rd

Fox Glacier

3754m

Lake Matheson

Gillespies Beach

**Fox
Glacier**

Aoraki/Mt Cook

Fairlie

Opuha

Westland
Nat. Park

Tasman Glacier

Lake
Tekapo

2

Mount
Cook

Tekapo

Ben Ohau Range

Lake
Pukaki

Kirkliston Range

6

Lake Ohau Range

Twizel

Lake
Benmore

**Roaring
Billy
Falls**

Lake
Ohau

**Gates of
Haast**

8

Haast

Haast

Haast
Pass

Omarama

Waitaki

Otematata

Jackson
Bay

Makarora

Hawkdun Range

Jackson Bay

Mount
Aspiring
National
Park

Cascade
Point

Lake
Hawea

2087m

St Bathans

1

Olivine Range

Southern Alps

Lake
Wanaka

Hawea

Dunstan Mts

Awarua
Point

3027m
Mt Aspiring

Shotover

Wanaka

Lake Dunstan

2819m

O T A G O

Arrowtown

Cromwell

8

Alexandra

A

The West Coast

THE TRANZALPINE EXPRESS

One of the great railway adventures of the world, the TranzAlpine connects the east and west coasts via mountain passes, tunnels and impressive viaducts. The 233km (145-mile) narrow-gauge, single-track line climbs via six viaducts and 16 tunnels to the station at Arthur's Pass, then descends through the 8km (5-mile) Otira Tunnel to Greymouth. The TranzAlpine departs from Christchurch daily at 8:15AM, arriving at 12:45PM; from Greymouth it departs at 1:45PM, returning to Christchurch at 6:05PM. Bookings through Tranz Scenic agents or Central Reservations (tel: 0800 TRAINS, or www.tranzscenic.co.nz).

▶▶ Arthur's Pass National Park   *179B3*

Straddling the mountainous spine of the Southern Alps, Arthur's Pass National Park covers 990sq km (383sq miles) and is one of the most popular walking areas in the South Island. With many peaks rising above 2,000m (6,500ft) it is a dramatic and beautiful region, yet there are plenty of easy walks to waterfalls, scenic look-out points and mountain tarns. The beech forests provide a haven for birds such as the tui, bellbird and shining cuckoo, while the cheeky alpine parrot, the kea, can be seen at higher altitudes.

The small alpine community of **Arthur's Pass** has basic accommodation, a couple of café/restaurants and the National Park visitor centre (tel: 03 318 9211. *Open* daily 8–5). From June to September it becomes a skiing centre.

Arthur's Pass is 153km (95 miles) from Christchurch and 98km (61 miles) from the port of Greymouth, and you can reach the latter by travelling down the dramatic new viaduct to the north through the Otira Gorge, one of New Zealand's most exciting mountain routes.

▶ Cape Foulwind   *179A4*

Unjustly named by Cook, the Cape shelters Westport from westerly winds and was known to Maori as Tauranga, 'a sheltered anchorage'. **Tauranga Bay▶** (15km/9 miles from Westport) has a seal colony at its northern end, where pups are born in late November and early December. The clifftop path forms part of the **Cape Foulwind Walkway**, noted for its wildlife, views and rugged coastline.

▶▶▶ Fox and Franz Josef Glaciers 179A2

Among the highlights of the West Coast, the Fox and Franz Josef glaciers are unusual, since nowhere else in the world do glaciers descend this far down into rain forest, crunching their way down through the valleys from the peaks of the Southern Alps until they are a mere 12km (7.5 miles) from the sea. The reason for this is their unusual position: A huge tract of land at the head of both glaciers tapers down to two narrow valleys, so channelling the snow and ice down towards the sea. They are a spectacular sight, with huge blocks of ice breaking off at the terminal face and floating off downstream during floods.

Franz Josef Glacier was named in 1864 by the explorer Julius von Haast after the emperor of his native Hungary; it plunges 2,700m (8,860ft) from the alpine peaks to just 300m (985ft) above sea-level at the terminal face. The township of **Franz Josef Glacier** has a wide range of services and accommodation. The DoC visitor centre (tel: 03 751 0807. *Open* daily 8–5) has displays on the glaciers and details on local walks. From the town it is 6km (4 miles) to the parking area at the **glacier terminal▶▶**, along a road that passes through overhanging rain forests along the way.

The township of **Fox Glacier** has similar facilities for visitors, including a visitor centre (tel: 03 752 0796. *Open* daily, summer 8:30–7; winter 8:30–noon, 1–4:30). From Fox it is 6km (4 miles) to the **glacier terminal▶▶**.

GLACIAL TRIPS

Guided ice walks leave from both Fox and Franz Josef twice daily, with a range of options depending on your level of fitness: The shorter trips (suitable for most people) take about three hours, with 30 or so minutes on the glacier itself. More adventurous options include day-long glacier walks and heli-hikes to higher levels. Alpine Guides have bases in both townships (tel: 0800 111 600; www.foxguides. co.nz). Helicopter flights are also popular; contact Glacier Southern Lakes Helicopters, tel: 0800 800 732; www.heli-flights.co.nz; Fox and Franz Josef Heliservices, tel: 0800 800 793; www.scenic-flights.co.nz. Because of the weather, cancellations are frequent, and conditions are best around mid-year, in the southern winter.

181

Fox Glacier, named after politician Sir William Fox, who painted it in 1872, starts at a slightly higher altitude than Franz Josef

Whether global warming is a reality or not, both Fox and Franz Josef glaciers are bucking the worldwide trend and advancing at an unprecedented rate. In fact, they have followed a pattern of advance and retreat for centuries.

BEWARE ICEFALLS
The current hazardous state of the glacier terminals means that visitors should pay particular attention to the warning signs and barriers erected by park officials. Do not be tempted to step over the boundary ropes to pose for photographs: The terminus may look solid but in fact it is extremely fragile, and towering blocks of ice (seracs) have been crashing down with increasing frequency.

182

Crevasses on Fox Glacier

On the move Glaciers are very sensitive to the balance between the volume of snow and ice accumulating on the upper slopes and the amount of ice melting at the terminus: Only when both factors remain relatively constant over a number of years will the terminus remain stationary.

During the last great Ice Age, some 18,000 years ago, both Fox and Franz Josef glaciers reached down as far as the present-day coastline and beyond. About 1,000 years ago they were reduced to mere pockets of ice on their névés (upper slopes), but then a deterioration in the climate caused them to advance again. Since the beginning of the latest period of global warming they have been receding, with minor advances at roughly 20-year intervals.

During the last decade the terminal face of Franz Josef has advanced 1.6km (1 mile) down the valley, reaching a point it last occupied some 30 years ago, while Fox Glacier has advanced nearly 1km (over 0.5 mile) in the same period.

Measuring change The movement of the glaciers can be measured by following the progress of markers or debris on the glacial surface. In 1943, for instance, an aircraft crashed about 4km (2.5 miles) up from the terminus of Franz Josef Glacier; six years later parts of the wreckage appeared at the glacier front.

Because glaciers are so sensitive to climate change, they are used by scientists as indicators of climatic conditions. Both Fox and Franz Josef are particularly useful indicators because their large catchment areas feed into narrow valleys, so that small changes in the accumulation of snow and ice at the head can result in dramatic increases at the snout. But the response to climate change is not instantaneous: Fox Glacier takes about seven years to translate increased snowfalls into an advance at the terminus, while Franz Josef has a response time of around five years.

▶ Gillespies Beach 179A2

The area surrounding Gillespies Beach, a 19km (12-mile) drive to the coast from Fox Glacier, was mostly formed from the moraine dumped by the glacier some 18,000 years ago. The rimu forests that fringe the shore here are some of the best examples of their kind in the country, and the forest, lagoon and shoreline are rich in birdlife.

The Gillespies Beach **fur seal colony**▶ is a resting place for many different seal species during the non-breeding winter season, and can contain up to 1,500 seals. During the summer, it is home to around 30 immature bull seals. There is an excellent walk from the small settlement at Gillespies Beach to the seal colony: The round trip from the parking area in front of Gillespies Lagoon takes around three hours, with spectacular views of the coast, mountains, glaciers and rimu forests from Trig Point HU on Waikowhai Bluff. It is only possible two hours either side of low tide: Check tide tables at the Fox DoC office.

▶ Greymouth 179B3

As well as being the West Coast terminus for the TranzAlpine express, the port of Greymouth is the region's main hub for coal, timber and brewing. Tours of **Monteith's Brewery** are one of the few things to do in town (tel: 03 768 4149; www.monteiths.co.nz. *Tours:* Mon–Fri 10, 11:30, noon, Sat, Sun 11:30, 2. Brewery operates Mon–Fri only. *Admission: inexpensive*). **Jade Boulder Gallery** has a range of knitwear alongside its jade displays (corner of Tainui and Guinness streets, tel: 03 768 0700; www.jadeboulder.com. *Open* summer, Mon–Fri 8:30AM–9PM, Sat–Sun 9–9; winter, Mon–Fri 8:30–5, Sat–Sun 9–5).

The lagoons at Gillespies Beach are backed by rimu forests, home to a wealth of birds

BEWARE OF TRAINS
It may come as something of a shock to see a train coming towards you over road bridges on the West Coast highway, but there are combined road–rail bridges along this part of the coastline: across the Taramakau, 14km (8.5 miles) south of Greymouth, and across the Arahura, 8km (5 miles) north of Hokitika. The bridges used to have gates to stop road traffic while trains crossed, but these have been removed—so be careful.

The steam train at Shantytown takes visitors into the surrounding bush

Canoeing on the Moeraki River, running from Lake Moeraki to the coast 25km (16 miles) north of Haast

South of Greymouth (13km/8 miles) is **Shantytown**▶▶, a large open-air complex (tel: 03 762 6634; www.shanty-town.co.nz. *Open* daily 8.30–5. *Admission: moderate*) that includes steam-train rides, a stamper battery, a working sawmill, gold panning and horse-drawn vehicle rides. But the star attraction here is a reconstruction of a gold-rush town of the 1880s, complete with shops, livery stables, jail, post office, hotel and church (which originally came from the genuine gold rush settlement of Notown).

▶▶▶ Haast   *179A1*

The Haast area has the most extensive wetlands in New Zealand, with coastal lagoons and swamps dominated by giant kahikatea and rimu forests, where native grey and paradise duck, bittern and shag can be spotted. The silver and mountain beech lowland forests are home to the largest population of kaka (bush parrots) in the country, as well as to fantail, tui, bellbird, morepork (owls), falcon, warbler and kiwi. Trout and quinnat salmon abound in the Okuru, Turnbull, Arawata and Jackson rivers, with trout-fishing available all year round. The area is famous for its whitebait, fur seals and blue penguins, and Fiordland crested penguins inhabit the rocky sections of the coast.

At **Haast Junction**, where the coast road (SH6) crosses the Haast River and becomes the trans-alpine road to Otago, is the **South West New Zealand World Heritage Visitor Centre** (tel: 03 750 0809. *Open* daily 8–5:30. *Admission: inexpensive*), with imaginative displays and regular screenings of a film on the human and natural history of the area. The Centre can also provide a leaflet detailing a dozen or so short, easy walks in the vicinity and take bookings to view penguins, seals, dolphins and other marine wildlife along the coast.

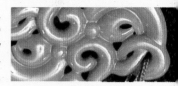

Intricately carved into elaborate ornaments, pendants and sculptures, greentone (or jade) is a beautiful material that is traditionally revered by Maori, who journeyed great distances to seek it out on the wild West Coast.

Jade nephrite True jade nephrite is a rare mineral, known to Maori as *pounamu*. Jade is found only in the South Island, which in Maori is called Te Wai Pounamu ('the waters in which pounamu dwelt'). The main source of greentone is in the remote headwaters of the Arahura River, about 40km (25 miles) inland from Hokitika. When Europeans arrived they used the terms 'green talc' and 'greenstone' for both jade and bowenite (a softer stone found mostly around Milford Sound).

A prized commodity Maori always prize greentone, partly because of its usefulness in a culture that possessed no hard metals. It could be carved into tools (such as adzes, fish-hooks, axe-heads and chisels) and weapons of war (such as the impressive *mere* or fighting clubs), as well as being used extensively for personal adornment, in the form either of ear ornaments or of pendants such as the celebrated *heitiki*.

Maori even endowed *pounamu* with life itself, tracing its origins back to the creation. They valued it more highly than gold, and the great importance attached to it is reflected in the number of names that they used for different types of jade, with 18 different expressions to cover the numerous subtle variations in its delicate shades.

Modern carvers follow the tradition of Maori greentone ornaments

Hard to find The difficulties of obtaining and transporting greentone from the remote Westland sites where it was found only added to its allure. Expeditions to recover it were fraught with danger: few tracks penetrated the forests, and the unpredictable Tasman Sea made arrival by canoe hazardous. A *tohunga* (ritual expert) was often taken along to help in the search for jade boulders (*papa pounamu*), for it takes a discerning eye to detect the heightened colour of a boulder containing jade among the many similar looking rocks and stones in the riverbed.

NO TRADE
Prized jade possessions were never traded. Captain Cook tried, unsuccessfuly, to barter for *pounamu*, reflecting ruefully: 'These green talc axes that are whole and good they set much value upon, and never would part with them for anything we could offer.'

The West Coast

A TRICKY HARBOUR

During the 1860s it was a major spectator sport in Hokitika to stand on the shoreline and watch sailing ships attempt to 'run the blockade' across the treacherous sand bar. The north/south orientation of the river estuary forced ships to enter almost broadside to the sea, and unless there was a good breeze they often had insufficient steerage to negotiate the sand bar. Between 1865 and 1867 a ship was beached on average once every ten days, and of these no fewer than 42 were wrecked completely. Craft that were beached undamaged were raised by screwjacks and dragged across to the river in an operation known as 'making the overland trip'.

KAHURANGI FLORA AND FAUNA

Kahurangi National Park is a rich storehouse of plant and animal life. Effectively isolated during the last Ice Age, the region became a major refuge in which new species and varieties of New Zealand's native plant species can be found here, with nearly 70 endemic species. Among the 100 native bird species are several that are threatened, including the great spotted kiwi, South Island kaka, kereru, blue duck and rock wren. New Zealand's only two native land mammals, the long-tailed and short-tailed bat, have both been recorded in the area. There are also three seal colonies along the coast.

▶▶ Hokitika   179B3

Built on the back of the 1860s gold rush, Hokitika was once one of the busiest ports in New Zealand. On one fine spring day in 1865 no fewer than 19 ships either entered or left the port. The quayside often bristled with the masts of up to 40 ships at any one time, but as well as being one of the busiest harbours, it was also one of the most notorious (see panel). One of the earliest ships wrecked here was the schooner *Tambo*, which has now been re-created as a **Shipwreck Memorial** at the northern tip of the Hokitika spit (five minutes' walk from town).

The quayside itself is also being refurbished, with the old **Custom House** standing at the heart of the Heritage Area. Hokitika's heritage is traced in the **West Coast Historical Museum▶▶** (Tancred Street, tel: 03 755 6898. *Open* daily 9:30–5. *Admission: inexpensive*). You can try gold panning here or at the **Phelps' Goldmine▶** 2km (1.25 miles) to the south of town (tel: 03 755 7766. *Open* daily 9–5. *Admission: inexpensive*). It's worth being in Hokitika in March for the Wild Foods Festival, to sample such dishes as huhu grubs and possum.

Try to stay until after dark in order to visit the magical **Glow-worm Dell▶** (beside the main road on the northern outskirts of the town), said to be the largest outdoor colony of glow-worms in the country.

▶▶ Kahurangi National Park   179B5

The second-largest park in the country after Fiordland, Kahurangi National Park is crisscrossed with 600km (375 miles) of walking tracks, the best known of which is the 78km (48-mile)-long Heaphy Track; others include the Wangapeka and Leslie tracks. But you do not have to be a hardened hiker to enjoy this wonderful park, since some of the most scenic parts can be reached easily from the West Coast village of Karamea.

▶▶ Karamea   179A5

Literally at the end of the road, this remote coastal settlement is 98km (61 miles) north of Westport on the northern continuation of SH67. Most of its visitors were walkers emerging from the wilderness at the southern end of the Heaphy Track, but the creation of Kahurangi National Park has set it firmly on the map.

Until now, Karamea has had a rough ride. The first settlers arrived here in 1874, but after three years of toil clearing the bush they discovered the land was useless. They moved farther up the river valley, only to have their first crops destroyed by floods.

Until the building of the road to Westport in 1915, the only link with the outside world was an erratic steamer service. In 1929 the Murchison earthquake destroyed the harbour and cut the community's road link for a couple of years (see page 168).

Flanked by bush-clad mountains, this tranquil backwater with its particularly mild climate now has an expanding range of activities, including canoeing, white-water rafting, fishing and some enjoyable day walks. The area's unusual geology also provides some interesting excursions to nearby limestone caves and arches. The most spectacular of these are the **Oparara Limestone Arches▶▶**, which are reached by driving to the very end of the road and then following a logging track (16km/10 miles from the North Beach turn-off in Karamea); it is then a 20-minute walk from the parking area.

Another essential sight is the **Honeycomb Caves▶▶**, which contain a remarkable assortment of subfossil remains, including moa, the giant New Zealand eagle, the giant flightless goose and the flightless rail. The caves are also home to cave-dwelling spiders and giant carnivorous snails. Access is restricted to guided tours (contact the Last Resort in Karamea, tel: 03 782 6617; www.lastresort.co.nz).

If time is limited, one of the best ways to experience the Kahurangi is to walk the first part of the Heaphy Track north of Karamea. From the town, drive 13km (8 miles) north to the Kohaihai River parking area. Cross the swing bridge to start a pleasant 40-minute circular walk through nikau palm groves; beyond the Nikau Grove Track the path continues up and over the hill through the forest, opening out on to a magnificent section of the coastline to reach Scott Beach (90 minutes round trip).

▶ Lake Matheson   179A2

One of the most photographed panoramas in the vicinity of Fox Glacier is the reflection of the peaks of the Southern Alps in the waters of Lake Matheson, a 'kettle' lake formed from the melting of glacial ice. Make a detour off the road to Gillespies Beach, 6km (4 miles) west of Fox, and follow the path to the jetty (one-hour round trip). You can also carry on until you reach the View of Views (two-hour round trip) on the far side of the lake. The reflections are at their best in the still of early morning.

JADE WORKSHOPS
Jade is a difficult material to work, but the results can be fabulous. You can watch jade carvers in several workshops in Hokitika, and prices for finished pieces are often far lower here than elsewhere in the country. The best jade shops are Mountain Jade Co (41 Weld Street, tel: 03 755 8007; www.mountainjade. co.nz) and Westland Greenstone (34 Tancred Street, tel: 03 755 8713).

187

Moa bones in the Honeycomb Caves (below); the Southern Alps reflected in Lake Matheson (bottom)

▶▶▶ Paparoa National Park   *179B4*

Paparoa National Park, embracing one of the most scenic sections of this coastline, is best known for the Pancake Rocks at Punakaiki, but there is much more here and it is well worth lingering a day or two to explore the area.

The focal point of the park is **Punakaiki** (47km/29 miles north of Greymouth), which has limited accommodation, tea rooms and a visitor centre (tel: 03 731 1895. *Open* daily 8:30–6, later in summer); the centre provides leaflets on local walks and activities and also screens a short audio-visual presentation (on demand) about the park.

Just across the road from the visitor centre, a track (suitable for wheelchairs) leads to the **Pancake Rocks and Blowholes**▶▶▶ at Dolomite Point. These spectacular formations of stratified limestone were formed on the sea-bed millions of years ago by a chemical process known as 'stylobedding'. Since being uplifted they have also been eroded by the waves, so that they are now undercut with arches and underwater caverns with blowholes. The blowholes are at their most spectacular when rough southwesterly storms combine with a high spring tide.

The bridge carrying the main Westport–Greymouth road over the Fox River in Paparoa National Park

It requires a little more effort to visit the **Fox River Caves**▶, which were first opened to the public in 1906 and became a tourist attraction long before the Pancake Rocks. It is a scenic walk of about an hour and a half to reach them, and you can explore about 100m (300ft) into the upper cave, which is decorated with intriguing calcite formations.

Other interesting walks include the **Truman Track** (signposted 3km/2 miles north of Punakaiki), which leads down through subtropical forest to a lovely beach with sea caves, an islet and limestone overhangs. You can also meander up a delightful forested gorge along the **Pororari River Track** (signposted 1km/0.5 mile north of Punakaiki); the Pororari River is also popular for canoeing.

Paparoa is home to a huge colony of Westland petrels, which spends most of the year soaring across the southern seas. They come here to breed between April and November and can be seen in the greatest numbers between April and June, when they congregate offshore every evening at dusk, ready to return to the colony. Watch them from beside the road at the Nikau Scenic Reserve 4km (2.5 miles) south of Punakaiki, or take a tour of the colony itself (contact Paparoa Nature Tours, tel: 03 731 1826).

In 1995 Paparoa was the scene of a terrible disaster, when a cliffside viewing platform collapsed, sending 14 people—students on a geology trip to Cave Creek and a ranger—to their deaths on the rocks 30m (100ft) below. All DoC structures have been checked, which is why you will often see signs limiting the number of people allowed on a structure at any one time.

SEA VIEWS
Home to a variety of wildlife, some sections of the Paparoa coastline are inaccessible from land and are best seen from a boat. Kiwa Sea Adventures operate two custom-built Naiad inflatables from Punakaiki, with two-hour trips to view a breeding colony of spotted shags at Perpendicular Point and a seal colony on Seal Island. If you are lucky you may also see rare Hector's dolphins riding the bow waves of the boat. Book at Punakaiki Visitor Centre (tel: 03 731 1895).

▶ Reefton
179B4

Reefton is one of the few inland towns in Westland (everywhere else the only flat land is the narrow coastal strip, so settlements inevitably grew up on the coast), set in forested hills beside the Inangahau River. The town boomed in 1870, when rich gold-bearing quartz reefs were discovered in the surrounding hills. By 1872 it had been dubbed Quartzopolis, and even had its own stock exchange (one of only a handful in the country); by 1888 it had the first electric street-lighting in New Zealand (only six years later than New York), powered by a small hydroelectric plant.

But New York went one way and Reefton another, and now it is little more than a whistle-stop on the routes from Greymouth and Westport over to Canterbury via the Lewis Pass. There are gold- and coal-mining relics in and around the town, and if you were tempted to stay longer there is tramping, hunting and fishing in the nearby Victoria Forest Park, as well as walks to old gold-mining sites.

The spectacular stratified limestone columns of the Pancake Rocks at Dolomite Point

The West Coast

Pointing the way in Ross

▶ **Ross**   *179B3*

This historic gold-mining town sits on some of the richest deposits of gold in New Zealand, and in 1907 it yielded the largest gold nugget ever found in the country (see panel). Unlike other gold-mining towns, such as Arrowtown, there is no tourist razzmatazz here, and the quiet main street has just one shop, one café and one pub. A fork off the main highway leads to the mining areas, where the old Bank of New South Wales building (1870) is now a visitor centre (tel: 03 755 4077; www.ross.org.nz. *Open* daily 9–4).

Close by is a **Miner's Cottage**▶ (*Open* daily 9–4), built in 1885 by a Belgian couple who had profited handsomely from the gold strikes: theirs was the most solid house in the old township, and the only one that survives today. Within the same area is the old town jail and **St. Patrick's Church**▶, a little cross-shaped chapel built in 1866 and ranked among the oldest buildings on the West Coast.

Two interesting short walks lead off from here through the goldfields. The **Jones Flat Walkway** and the **Water Race Walkway** each make a circuit of about an hour and a half, passing by dams, sluices, mining machinery and other relics from Ross's heady heyday.

Just behind the visitor centre you can hear the rumble of heavy machinery from a large open-cast gold mine; 800cu m (28,500cu ft) of gold-bearing gravel are processed here every day, and geologists report that there may still be some £30 million ($48 million) worth of gold below Ross township itself. If it is decided to dig the gold out, the town will have to be demolished. But locals are stoical about their fate—Ross has already moved once for the sake of gold, and it may yet have to do so again.

▶ **Westport**   *179A4*

The largest town at the northern end of Westland, Westport lies just beyond the junction at which SH6 heads inland through the Buller Gorge to Murchison. The surrounding region is the country's main source of bituminous coal, which is shipped out mostly through Lyttelton; the story of coal mining in the region is told through various displays and reconstructions at the **Coaltown Museum**▶ (Queen Street South, signposted from the town, tel: 03 789 8204. *Open* daily 8:30–4:30. *Admission: inexpensive*). The Buller Coalfield Heritage Trail starts on the wharfside at Westport and leads through the bush and past a number of coal settlements north to Seddonville.

One of the most popular walks in the vicinity is the **Denniston Walkway**, a bush walk (five hours round trip) along an old bridle track leading to the historic Denniston Incline, an ingenious rail system used to bring coal down from the mines to the bottom of the plateau. Surrounded by dense bush and forest, the track crosses several tumbling watercourses, with views out to the coast on a clear day. A leaflet is available from the visitor centre in Westport (Brougham Street, tel: 03 789 6658; www.westport.org.nz. *Open* daily 9–5).

To the west of Westport are the **Cape Foulwind Walkway** and seal colony (see page 180), while inland there is white-water rafting and jet-boating on the Buller River (contact Buller Adventure Tours, tel: 03 789 7286; www.adventuretours.co.nz), pony-trekking, fishing and caving trips in the surrounding hills.

▶▶ Whataroa   179B2

Whataroa (114km/71 miles south of Hokitika, 32km/20 miles north of Franz Josef Glacier) is the base for trips to the nearby **White Heron Sanctuary**▶▶ beside the Waitangitaona River. This is the only breeding site in New Zealand for these elegant birds (known to Maori as *kōtuku*), which nest here from November to February. On average around 50 chicks are fledged in the colony each year, with 70 or more in a good season. In late February the herons fan out to their winter feeding grounds in estuaries elsewhere in Westland and all over New Zealand. The sanctuary is also a nesting ground for royal spoonbills and little shags. Access to the colony is via a jet-boat ride followed by a short walk through native bush along a boardwalk to the colony itself. The round trip from Whataroa takes about two hours (contact White Heron Sanctuary Tours, PO Box 19, Whataroa, tel: 0800 523 456; www.whiteherontours.co.nz).

Anybody could strike lucky

191

Open-cast gold mining behind the township of Ross

Drive

See map on page 179.

The Haast Pass Highway (SH6)

This transalpine route is the only crossing between Otago and Westland, a superb drive past numerous spectacular waterfalls, with lake views and panoramas of the surrounding peaks. From the World Heritage Centre at the Haast River bridge it is about 150km (93 miles) to Wanaka.

Heading inland from Haast, the road traverses dense rain forest before snaking alongside the wide silt and gravel bed of the **Haast River**. At **Depot Creek**, a set of waterfalls tumbles down the steep sides of the valley within a minute's walk of the road. About 5km (3 miles) farther on, a track (30 minutes round trip) leads through silver beech and podocarp forest to the **Roaring Billy Falls▶**. The Roaring Billy River tumbles over a jumble of boulders before dissipating itself in the gravel beds of the Haast River.

After several twists and turns the road now reaches **Pleasant Flat** (48km/30 miles from the bridge), where there is a picnic and camping area with good views of Mount Hooker. From here a short bush walk makes a loop beside a bubbling mountain stream. Another 4km (2.5 miles) farther on are the impressive **Thunder Creek Falls▶▶**, which drop 28m (92ft) from the bluff down to the Haast River bed; a track leads to the falls (100m/110 yards from the road) through stands of kamahi and silver beech. At the **Gates of Haast▶** (55km/34 miles from the bridge) the river drops dramatically into a gorge. Another 6.5km (4 miles) farther on are the **Fantail Falls▶▶**, which spread out in a fan shape at the foot of Fantail Creek; the Haast River itself is already much reduced in volume here.

The main divide between the western and eastern sides of the Alps comes at **Haast Pass▶▶** (562m/1,844ft), where a plaque commemorates the

first explorers to cross the pass. In 1836, a northern chief, Te Puoho, used it to conduct a raid on the southern Kai Tahu and Kati Mamoe tribes, and a gold prospector named Charles Cameron is credited with being the first European to traverse the pass in 1863. Just a few weeks later Julius von Haast led a party of four all the way across to the coast, and by 1876 a narrow pack track linked the two sides. Work on upgrading the track to a road began in the 1880s, but was not completed until 1965.

Beyond Davis Flat is **Cameron Flat**, with a short walk leading up through silver beech forest to a platform overlooking the surrounding peaks and the Makarora valley to the east. Just beyond this, at the outlet of the Blue River, is a parking area, where an easy track (30 minutes round trip) leads through more silver beech to a viewing platform over the **Blue**

Pools▶▶ at the mouth of the river. You can see large rainbow and brown trout feeding in these pools.

The landscape changes dramatically from green rain forest to tawny tussock, and opens out into the flat expanses of the **Makarora valley**▶, where the small hamlet of Makarora boasts a grocery shop, café and petrol station. Maori would camp here on their hazardous journey across the pass to the West Coast, and its Maori name, Kaika Paekai, means 'the place of abundant food'. The forests that once carpeted the valley floor were extensively logged from the 1860s onwards, but a few remnants survive in the **Makarora Bush**▶, where an easy track leads from the parking area in Makarora through podocarp and silver beech forest; a pitsaw display on the track shows how the forest giants were dealt with before being floated down Lake Wanaka to the sawmills.

Glorious mountain and lake scenery on the road between the Haast Pass and Wanaka

The Makarora River flows out into **Lake Wanaka**▶▶▶ at the end of the valley. This is one of the most scenic sections of the road, traversing the bluffs high above the lake waters, with the peaks of Mount Aspiring National Park rising up on the far shore. Turning southeast from Lake Wanaka, the road cuts across **The Neck**, a narrow valley that leads through to **Lake Hawea**▶▶▶, another expanse of shimmering water stretching across to the steep glaciated slopes. Most of the remainder of the route from The Neck to Wanaka (43km/27 miles) follows the picturesque lake shores. Past the settlement of Lake Hawea, the road crosses farmland before descending again to the shores of Lake Wanaka.

The foothills and valleys of the Southern Alps near Hanmer Springs in North Canterbury

Canterbury affords a host of adventure activities among its mountains and rivers—jet-boating was invented here

CANTERBURY Stretching from the heights of the Southern Alps across the wide-open expanses of the Canterbury Plains to the Pacific Ocean, the Canterbury region is a vast rectangular block encompassing both the flattest and the steepest landforms in the country. At its heart are the extensive farmlands of the Canterbury Plains, a rolling patchwork of fertile fields where sheep and racehorses are raised alongside extensive grain crops.

Threading through the plains are a number of wide, braided rivers, with numerous shallow channels and shingle banks that support trout- and salmon-fishing: These meandering rivers were virtually unnavigable until the jet-boat, invented by a Canterbury engineer (see pages 210–211), opened them up to adventure activities.

Beyond the plains, the alpine foothills have a number of well-known ski fields (such as **Mount Hutt**), while horse-trekking, hiking, rafting and mountain-biking are popular around areas such as **Hanmer Springs**, a thermal resort in North Canterbury.

Canterbury

CHRISTCHURCH The first farmers settled this area in the 1840s, and the city of Christchurch began to take shape in the 1850s as one of the last major planned settlements in the country. The driving force behind the new colony was a devout Anglican, the appropriately named John Robert Godley, who formed the Canterbury Association in London with the aim of attracting migrants who were to include 'all the elements, including the very highest, of a good and right state of society'. The first four ships docked at Lyttelton harbour in 1850, and by 1853 over 3,500 carefully vetted migrants had arrived. By 1855 the Canterbury Association had foundered, having failed to meet its religious objectives, but Christchurch itself was prospering.

BANKS PENINSULA, a distinctive knobby peninsula jutting out to sea to the southeast of Christchurch, is the South Island's main volcanic area, and the two massive craters that form the peninsula now shelter two main harbour areas—Lyttelton (the port for Christchurch) and Akaroa, almost a former French colony. The peninsula itself has a rugged, dramatic coastline indented with small bays, with wonderful views from the crater rims. It makes an interesting day-trip from Christchurch or, even better, a weekend excursion (there are plenty of places to stay in Akaroa) with a bit of walking or sea-kayaking thrown in.

AORAKI/MOUNT COOK NATIONAL PARK This vast alpine wilderness covers some 70,000ha (172,970 acres) on the east side of the Southern Alps, and has some of the most

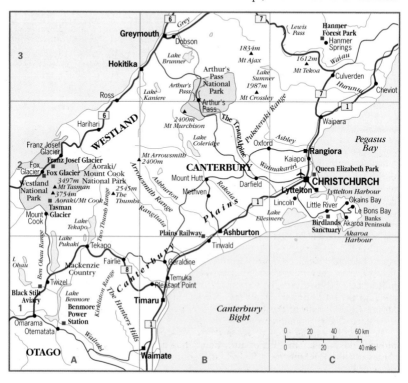

dramatic mountain scenery in the country. All except one of New Zealand's peaks over 3,000m (9,850ft) are found here, including mighty Aoraki/Mount Cook itself, at 3,754m (12,317ft) the highest in New Zealand. More than a third of the park is permanently covered in snow and ice, while Tasman Glacier, stretching some 29km (18 miles) down the south face of Mount Cook, is one of the largest glaciers outside of the Himalayas.

The first mention of Mount Cook by a European was made by the explorer Charles Heaphy, who sketched it in 1846. In 1851, the survey ship HMS *Acheron* named the peak after Cook, and its neighbour Mount Tasman (3,497m/11,474ft) was named after the Dutch explorer in 1862 by Julius von Haast—although paradoxically neither Cook nor Tasman had seen these mighty mountains from the sea. Mount Cook is one of the unmissable sights and it is essential to book accommodation well in advance.

The beautiful glacial lakes of **South Canterbury**, below Mount Cook, are another major attraction, while on the shores of **Lake Ruataniwha** at Twizel you can see one of the world's rarest wading birds, the black stilt.

Hikers set off up the Hooker Valley track in Aoraki/Mount Cook National Park

THE FIRST FOUR SHIPS
The Canterbury Association was founded to create an Anglican settlement that was typically English. The association provided assisted passages for suitably sober and industrious men and their families, and initial settlers came out in what are still known as the first four ships: the *Charlotte Jane*, the *Randolph*, the *Sir George Seymour* and the *Cressy*, all arriving in December 1850.

198

Christchurch was one of the first cities in New Zealand to have a horse tramway system, and electric trams began operating here in 1905. The system was shut down in 1954, but elegant trams have now been painstakingly restored and new track has been laid in a 2.5km (1.5-mile) loop around the heart of the city. The tramway provides a convenient 'hop on, hop off' service for visitors (tel: 03 366 7830; www.tram.co.nz. *Open* daily, Nov–Mar 9–9; Apr–Oct 9–6).

The modern heritage tram system (right) harks back to the time of Queen Victoria, who presides over Victoria Square in the heart of the city

Christchurch

New Zealand's third-largest city (after Auckland and Wellington), Christchurch is the capital of Canterbury and the main international gateway to the South Island. Whether or not it is your first port of call, it is well worth setting aside a few days to explore this lovely city packed with things to see and do.

The Canterbury Association brought over 3,500 carefully chosen immigrants to Christchurch in its early years. But all did not go according to plan: Land intended for crops did not sell and drought in Australia brought many sheep farmers to the area. They were not popular (the Association was accused of giving the land over to 'squatting and barbarism') but the injection of capital saved the settlement from economic ruin.

New Zealand's English heritage is perhaps more evident in Christchurch than it is almost anywhere else in the country. The first pilgrims had not forgotten to pack their cricket bats, and ever since the establishment of the Christchurch Cricket Club the city has been the country's headquarters for the game. A rowing club had been set up by 1864, and an archery club established by 1873. The first lawn tennis courts were built in Cranmer Square in 1881. The solid, Gothic-style stone buildings, the uniformed schoolboys at the famous Christ's College school, and above all the punts gliding down the sinuous River Avon in the heart of the city, between overhanging willows and sycamores—all evoke images of traditional English university towns.

Christchurch is also renowned as a garden city, with over a third of its central area devoted to beautiful parks and gardens. Combined with the compactness of the city, this makes it a pleasurable place to explore on foot (see pages 202–203), or you can hop on and off the tramway between sightseeing. For a more leisurely tour, take to the Avon in a punt.

The city has a lively arts and cultural scene, with several theatres, frequent concerts and musical festivals, and probably the greatest concentration of arts and crafts talent in the country. Christchurch also has excellent shopping, numerous restaurants, cafés and wine bars and plenty of good-quality accommodation.

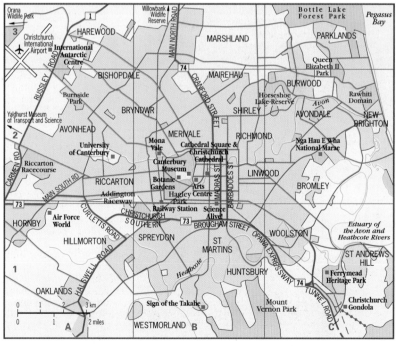

199A1

ARTS CENTRE EVENTS

The Arts Centre is home to the Court Theatre (New Zealand's most successful professional theatre group), the Christchurch School of Music and the Southern Ballet. In the summer months, jazz, classical music, exhibitions and theatre performances spill out through the cloisters and courtyards during the Summertime Festival. Friday lunchtime concerts take place throughout the year in the Great Hall, the grandest building in the Arts Centre. Details of events are available from the information centre (tel: 03 366 0989; www.artscentre.org.nz. *Open* daily 9:30–5).

▶ Air Force World   *199A1*

Wigram Aerodrome, tel: 03 343 9532; www.airforceworld.co.nz
Open: daily 10–5. Admission: moderate
Air Force World, 15 minutes' drive west of the city, is worth a stop if you are heading south on SH1. The museum covers the history of military aviation in New Zealand from the earliest days.

▶▶▶ Arts Centre   *199B2*

Worcester Boulevard
Open: daily 8:30–5. Admission: free
One of the main focal points of Christchurch, the Arts Centre is housed in the old University of Canterbury buildings, which were completed in 1929; the university had outgrown the premises by the 1950s, and this rambling, neo-Gothic complex has become the biggest and busiest cultural centre in New Zealand (see panel).

Nobel Prize-winning physicist Sir Ernest Rutherford (1871–1937) studied here in the 1890s, and his 'den' in the North Quadrangle has been preserved, complete with its laboratory equipment, as a tribute to the man who split the atom in 1919.

Now some of the country's leading painters and sculptors work in the galleries and studios, alongside musicians, actors, dancers and craftspeople. Here you will find specialists in stained glass, Maori carvings, ceramics, embroidery, leatherwork, handmade clothing of all kinds, wooden toys,

caneware and jade, bone and silver jewellery and much more besides.

The complex also hosts a weekend market and food fair (*Open* Sat, Sun 10–4) with more than 100 outdoor stalls selling everything from antiques to Asian foods.

▶▶▶ Botanic Gardens
199B2

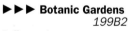

Rolleston Avenue
Open: daily 7AM–one hour before dusk. Admission: free
These magnificent gardens covering 30ha (74 acres), mostly within a loop of the River Avon on the west side of the central city, contain many fine old trees, including the Albert Edward Oak—the first tree planted here, to commemorate the marriage of Prince Albert Edward to Princess Alexandra of Denmark in July 1863.

Claiming the finest collection of indigenous and exotic plants found anywhere in the country, the gardens are divided into a number of different planting areas, with sections devoted to roses, herbs, rock plants and New Zealand native plants. The lovely conservatories (*Open* daily 10:15–4. *Admission: free*) are also well worth a visit, with numerous varieties of ferns, palms, flowering plants, cacti and alpines. There is also an information centre (opposite the Rolleston Avenue car park, tel: 03 941 7590. *Open* daily 10:15–4).

CANTERBURY TALES

Te Puna Ora storytelling and water ceremony tours recount the history and mythology of Canterbury during a leisurely stroll through the Botanic Gardens (*Open* Aug–Apr, fine weather only. *Admission: moderate*; book at the information centre or tel: 03 377 2025).

▶ ▶ ▶ Canterbury Museum
199B2

Rolleston Avenue, tel: 03 366 5000
Open: daily, winter 9–5; summer 9–6;
free guided tours four times daily.
Admission: free
Backing on to the Botanic Gardens, this museum is the most comprehensive in the South Island. The excellent Hall of the Moa and Moa Hunters has several graphic dioramas depicting the lifestyles of early Maori, and the Hall of Asian Decorative Arts has Chinese and Japanese objects from different periods. There is a new Whalespace exhibition, and the eternally fascinating and highly acclaimed Hall of Antarctic Discovery has also been refurbished.

▶ ▶ ▶ Cathedral Square
199B2

At the heart of the city, Cathedral Square is an attractive open space that can always be relied on for entertainment, from buskers (street musicians) to breakdancers, or from open-air preachers to eccentrics, and anyone else who cares to mount a soapbox (see panel).

Among the fine old buildings, apart from the cathedral itself, is **Four Ships Court** (next to the old Post Office) with the names of all the pilgrims who arrived on the 'first four ships' engraved on marble slabs on its walls.

It's all happening in Cathedral Square; leafy Hagley Park (left) is a more tranquil spot

▶ ▶ Christchurch Cathedral
199B2

Cathedral Square
Open: daily 8:30–4. Admission: inexpensive
The copper-sheathed spire of the cathedral dominates Cathedral Square, and from the viewing platform 30m (98ft) (and 133 narrow steps) up you get a good view of the city. The cathedral itself was planned shortly after the arrival of the 'first four ships' and construction began in 1864; work was then halted owing to lack of funds, and the building was not finally consecrated until 1904. There are daily guided tours at 11 and 2.

▶ ▶ Christchurch Gondola
199C1

Base station, 10 Bridle Path Road, tel: 03 384 0700;
www.gondola.co.nz
Open: 10AM–late. Admission: expensive
Rising to the top of the Port Hills, 500m (1,640ft) above sea-level, the gondola terminates at the Mount Cavendish complex, from where there are unrivalled views across Lyttelton harbour and Banks Peninsula to the south, with the sweep of Pegasus Bay and the Pacific Ocean leading to the distant Kaikoura Peninsula in the north—and Christchurch, of course, in the foreground.

Continued on page 204

THE INIMITABLE WIZARD
He is a Christchurch institution, a flamboyant figure in black velvet robes and pointed wizard's hat who mounts his stepladder to poke fun and deflate pomposity amid the rhetoric of the Cathedral Square preachers. The wizard (alias Ian Brackenbury Channell; www.wizard.gen.nz) has been a thorn in the flesh of the authorities since his arrival in Christchurch in 1974; it was ten years before he was allowed to harangue the crowds in Cathedral Square, a freedom he now exploits with considerable glee on most days at about 1PM—a performance not to be missed.

Walk

An imposing figure sits among the flowerbeds of the Botanic Gardens

Christchurch

Christchurch is an enjoyable city for strolling, and there is plenty to see on this circular walk from Cathedral Square. Allow two to three hours, not counting visits to the Canterbury Museum, the Botanic Gardens or the Arts Centre. To save energy, the tramway covers a large part of the route.

Starting from Cathedral Square, head west down Worcester Boulevard. After one block you will find the old **Municipal Chambers**, an elegant red-brick building of Queen Anne design that now houses the visitor centre. Opposite is a statue of **Captain Scott**, the Antarctic explorer, sculpted by his widow. Cross the River Avon over Worcester Street bridge, with wrought-iron balustrades, and turn left to follow the Avon upstream.

Immediately on your right is the **Canterbury Club**; built in 1872, this long-established gentlemen's club still has a gas lamp standard and a hitching post outside. The next bridge along but one is the **Bridge of Remembrance**, a memorial to Kiwi troops who died in World War I.

On the opposite bank of a bend in the river you can now see the superb church of **St. Michael and All Angels▶▶**, built in 1872 with a detached belfry (1860) alongside, housing a bell from one of the 'first four ships'. Continuing beneath the sycamores and willows that line the riverbank you reach the **Antigua Boatsheds▶**, built in 1882 and the sole survivor of half a dozen or more similar boatsheds that once stood on the riverbank.

Carry on down Rolleston Avenue, with the entrance to the **Botanic Gardens** and the **Canterbury Museum** on your left, and the **Arts Centre** on the right. Just past the museum is **Christ's College▶** (www.christscollege.com),

Exercising freedom of speech

the city's oldest school, with several attractive buildings grouped around a grassy quadrangle.

At the junction with Armagh Street another attractive old bridge leads over the Avon into **North Hagley Park►**, a huge area of sports grounds and playing fields. Follow the tramline down Armagh Street, then cross leafy **Cranmer Square**, with the Gothic edifice of the old **Christchurch Girls' High School**, onto Chester Street West. Near the end of the street stands the city's oldest stone church, the **Durham Street Methodist Church**, with the new court buildings opposite.

Turning right down Durham Street you reach the **Provincial Council Buildings►►►**, a fine ensemble of Gothic architecture in stone and wood around a courtyard, and dominated by

a redstone tower (*Open* Mon–Fri 9–4. *Admission: free*). Follow the riverbank around to the impressive modern **Town Hall►** (www.nccnz.co.nz. *Open* Mon–Fri 9–5, Sat–Sun 10–5. *Admission: free*), which has a fountain like a globe on the river's edge.

Cross another lovely old bridge to reach **Victoria Square►►**, a charming open space on the riverbank that was once the commercial heart of the city. Within the square are statues of **Queen Victoria** and **Captain Cook**, and by the riverbank itself you can also see an old stone ramp leading down to the Avon, formerly used for watering horses.

Follow the river along a gently winding stretch of Oxford Terrace; on the opposite bank you can see the fine Italianate **Edmonds Band Rotunda**, built in 1929 and now a restaurant. Past the Manchester Street bridge the Avon flows between a double row of stately poplars, with the **Centennial Pool** on your right-hand side. The **Oxford Terrace Baptist Church►**, on the corner of Chester Street East and Madras Street, has an imposing façade, and behind it on Chester Street East itself there is an interesting row of two-storey wooden houses.

Continue down Madras Street to **Latimer Square►**, where you will find the stone-built **St. John's Church** and the venerable **Occidental Hotel►** (www.occidental.co.nz). Follow Hereford Street to return to Cathedral Square.

203

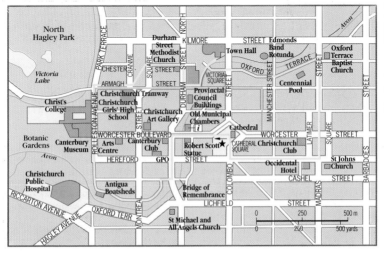

On a clear day the views from Mount Cavendish are unsurpassable

Continued from page 201

There are nature walks through the alpine tussock of the Mount Cavendish Scenic Reserve around the complex, while inside, a multimedia **Time Tunnel**▶▶ (*Open* noon–late. *Admission: inexpensive*) has displays on the early history of the area and on volcanoes, and a first-rate replica of the interior of an early immigrant ship. To get there, take the shuttle from the visitor centre, Explorer Bus or No. 28 bus.

▶ Ferrymead Heritage Park 199C1

269 Bridle Path Road, tel: 03 384 1970; www.ferrymead.org.nz Open: daily 10–4:30. Admission: moderate
This re-created 19th-century township has a long main street with a livery stables, a blacksmith's forge and a jail, among other premises, with small museums on transport, sound, printing, rural history and phonographs. Admission includes a steam train or tram ride.

▶▶▶ International Antarctic Centre 199A3

Orchard Road, Christchurch Airport, tel: 03 353 7798; www.iceberg.co.nz Open: daily summer 9–8; winter 9–5:30. Admission: expensive
The visitor centre here contains one of the two most outstanding displays on Antarctica in New Zealand (the other being Kelly Tarlton's Antarctic Encounter in Auckland, see page 52), and gains added prestige from its position within the International Antarctic Centre, which serves as the supply and administration base for the New Zealand, American and Italian research projects. Highlights include an Antarctic Experience audiovisual presentation on the changing seasons of the frozen continent, a walk-through ice cave, a replica of the current Scott

HOMAGE TO DAME NGAIO
Dame Ngaio Marsh (1899–1982), one of New Zealand's most prolific and successful authors, is best known throughout the world for her crime thrillers. But on her home patch of Christchurch it was as a director of Shakespeare that she was celebrated. Many of her productions were staged at the Christchurch Arts Centre, which was the focus for celebrations in 1995 to commemorate her birth in 1899. The house in Christchurch's Cashmere Hills, where she penned most of her detective novels, has been converted into a museum (*Open* daily except Mon by appointment only, tel: 03 337 9248; www.ngaio-marsh.org.nz).

Base, an Antarctic aquarium and a stunning finale in the form of a 12-minute film entitled *The Great White South*.

▶▶ Mona Vale 199B2

63 Fendalton Road, tel: 03 941 7590
Open: Gardens daylight hours. Admission: free
Mona Vale is an attractive, late-Victorian house in 6ha (13 acres) of beautiful gardens. For a memorable experience, take one of their picnic lunches (with wine) on a leisurely punt on the River Avon. Reservations are advisable (tel: 03 348 9660).

▶ Ngā Hau E Whā National Marae 199C2

250 Pages Road, Aranui 5km (3 miles) from the city,
tel: 03 388 7685; www.nationalmarae.co.nz
Ngā Hau E Whā (Four Winds) National Marae is said to be the largest *marae* in New Zealand, and has many fine carved buildings, such as the Wharenui (meeting house) and Whare Wānanga (house of learning). It also has a splendid carved gateway that tells the story of Maori and of European colonization.

▶▶ Orana Wildlife Park 199A3

McLeans Island Road, 18km (11 miles) northwest,
tel: 03 359 7109; www.oranawildlifepark.co.nz
Open: daily 10–4:30. Admission: expensive
New Zealand's largest safari park, Orana Wildlife Park is known for the breeding of endangered and rare species, including exotic animals and native fauna. The New Zealand section has a nocturnal kiwi house, a native reptile house (with tuatara, skinks and geckos) and native bird aviaries. Elsewhere in the 80ha (200-acre) reserve are kangaroos, emus, pelicans and cockatoos from Australia; tigers and Himalayan thar from Asia; spider monkeys, llamas and wolves from the Americas; and lions, zebras, monkeys and rhinos from Africa.

An unusual experience is hand-feeding giraffes from a tall platform, and there are regular 'cheetah chases', when cheetahs are exercised by racing after a baited lure.

▶▶▶ River Avon 199C2

The lovely River Avon, which meanders at a leisurely pace through the middle of Christchurch, is perfect for exploring by canoe, punt or paddle-boat. You can either rent your own from the Antigua Boatsheds (2 Cambridge Terrace, tel: 03 366 0337. *Open* summer 9:30–5:30; winter 9:30–4 *Admission: moderate*) or relax in an upholstered punt and glide along with a boatman in charge. You can choose from several departure points, the main one being behind the information centre on Oxford Terrace (trips operate daily 9–dusk in summer, 10–4 in

ANOTHER ADRENALIN RUSH
'The South Island's only dignified adrenalin rush' is how they like to describe the Christchurch Casino. The casino houses two restaurants, three bars, 30 gaming tables and 350 gaming machines (30 Victoria Street, tel: 03 365 9999; www.chchcasino.co.nz. *Open* daily 24 hours).

205

A leisurely punt along the River Avon is a good introduction to Christchurch

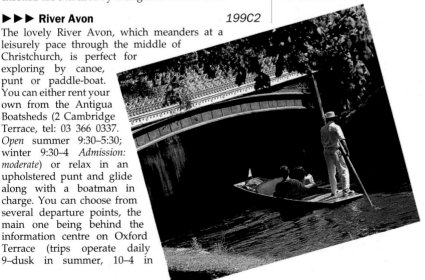

OUT-OF-TOWN TRIPS
Although most central sights are within walking distance, those on the outskirts require a bit more planning. If you have your own transport, you can drive northwest (towards the airport), devoting a day to the International Antarctic Centre, Orana Wildlife Park and Willowbank Wildlife Reserve. To the west, transport enthusiasts can combine the Yaldhurst Transport Museum with Air Force World. To the southeast, the Ferrymead Heritage Park and Christchurch Gondola are conveniently close together.

Akaroa's distinctive Dalys Wharf, with Saddle Hill (841m/ 2,759ft) on the other side of the harbour

winter. *Admission: moderate*). The Canterbury information centre is in the old Post Office building, Cathedral Square (tel: 03 379 9629. *Open* Mon–Fri 8:30–5, Sat–Sun 9–4).

▶ Science Alive! 199B1
392 Moorhouse Avenue, tel: 03 365 5199;
www.sciencealive.co.nz
Open: daily 9–5. Admission: moderate
A great one for the kids, containing over 50 hands-on, fun exhibits including a 3D Discovery Area. As well as its permanent displays, the centre also has visiting exhibitions on the same 'learn through fun' theme.

▶▶ Te Puna O Wariwhetu/ Christchurch Art Gallery 199B2
Worcester Boulevard, tel: 03 941 7300;
www.christchurchartgallery.org.nz
Open: daily 10–4:30. Admission: free
This gallery, focusing mainly on art with a connection to Canterbury, has over 5,500 items in its collection, including works by Rita Angus, Charles Goldie, Frances Hodgkins, L. S. Lowry, Dick Frizzell, Ralph Hotere and Colin McCahon.

▶▶ Willowbank Wildlife Reserve 199B3
60 Hussey Road, Harewood, tel: 03 359 6226;
www.willowbank.co.nz
Open: 10–10. Admission: moderate
This compact wildlife park includes a zoo with exotic species, a farmyard with some interesting and rare breeds of colonial domestic animals (such as kunae pigs and Hokonui sheep) and a New Zealand Experience section

with endangered species. It is also open in the evening for a 'Wildlife by Night' guided tour, where you can see kiwi and other nocturnal beasts. Willowbank is about 20 minutes from the city.

▶ Yaldhurst Museum of Transport and Science
199, off A2

School Road, Yaldhurst,
tel: 03 342 7914;
www.yaldhurstmuseum.co.nz
Open: daily 10–5. Admission: moderate
From being the proud possessor of just one 1910 two-cylinder Renault in the 1960s, this museum has grown to include hundreds of displays, from fire engines to motor bikes, carts, racing cars and more. It is 11km (7 miles) from the city, off SH73 near the airport.

The French failed in their claim to New Zealand, but their legacy lingers on in Akaroa

Canterbury

▶ Ashburton
196B2

Ashburton, mid-Canterbury's main town, is surrounded by the Canterbury Plains, with the snow-capped Southern Alps as a backdrop. At Tinwald, just to the south, the **Plains Railway▶** (tel: 03 308 9621; www.plainsrailway.co.nz) and **Vintage Car Club Museums** (tel: 03 308 4595. *Open* Sun 2–4. *Admission: inexpensive*) share a site. The former is notable for the restoration of the 120-year-old Rogers K-class 2-4-2 locomotive *Washington*, which spent 50 years dumped in the Oreti River in Southland as flood protection.

▶▶▶ Banks Peninsula
196C2

When he circumnavigated New Zealand, Captain Cook mapped Banks Peninsula as an island, an understandable mistake as the spit connecting the peninsula to the mainland is very low-lying. This land-bridge is bordered on its south side by **Lake Ellesmere**, a broad expanse of water rich in eels and flounders which, though one of New Zealand's largest lakes by area, is no more than 2m (6ft) deep.

The waters around Banks Peninsula abound in marine life such as seals and penguins, with thousands of spotted shags nesting on the steep sea cliffs. The country's first marine mammal sanctuary (covering over 1,100sq km/425sq miles around the shoreline) was established here in 1988 to protect one of the world's rarest marine mammals, the Hector's dolphin.

The first Maori to live here were assured of a plentiful food supply and easily defended villages, but a major feud in the 1820s virtually wiped out the local Ngai Tahu population. The numerous bays and inlets made perfect shelters for the early

HARBOUR TOURS
Cruises around Akaroa harbour on the *Canterbury Cat* are highly popular: the trip includes volcanic sea caves, a salmon farm, bird-nesting sites and the chance of seeing Hector's dolphins riding the bow wave (usually from November to April). Tours depart daily at 1:30, plus 11:30AM in Nov –Mar (bookings at the main wharf or tel: 03 304 7641; www.canterburycat.co.nz). You can also take a day-long sea-kayak tour of the harbour with Banks Experience Canterbury (tel: 0800 89 69 89).

Colonial-style architecture graces the quiet streets of Akaroa

THE FRENCH CONNECTION
In 1838 Jean Langlois bought a tract of land from the Ngai Tahu before returning home to France and assembling a shipload of immigrants to colonize the peninsula. The French government supported his venture, and even sent along a warship, *L'Aube*, to accompany him. But while Langlois was on the high seas the Treaty of Waitangi was signed, and he arrived to find British sovereignty a *fait accompli*. So concerned were the British at the impending arrival of the French that they immediately dispatched a ship to Akaroa, setting up a magistrate's court and hoisting the flag just five days before Langlois and his followers landed.

whalers, one of whom, Captain Jean Langlois, tried to establish French sovereignty by colonizing the peninsula.

The French legacy lingers on in the charming port of **Akaroa►►►**, with its French street names and the 'French' bakeries and restaurants. One of the early French settlers' cottages, the Langlois-Eteveneaux House, now forms part of the excellent **Akaroa Museum►►►** (tel: 03 304 7414. *Open* summer, Mon–Sat 10–5, Sun 10:30–4:30; winter, daily 10:30–4. *Admission: inexpensive*) near the seafront. The old courthouse and the nearby Custom House are also part of the complex.

Akaroa is a lovely spot to wander around, with a handful of good cafés and restaurants, interesting craft shops (Rue Lavaud, in particular, has at least nine galleries) and many picturesque old houses and cottages lining its quiet streets. A *Historic Village Walk* leaflet gives details of more than 40 historic buildings (available from the information centre, 80 Rue Lavaud and Rue Balguerie, tel: 03 304 8600; www.akaroa.com. *Open* daily 9–5).

Elsewhere on the peninsula, **Le Bons Bay►** is a good swimming spot (21km/13 miles from Akaroa), as is **Okains Bay►** (25km/15 miles from Akaroa), home to the intriguing **Maori and Colonial Museum►►** (tel: 03 304 8611. *Open* daily 10–5. *Admission: inexpensive*). The Maori collection includes many *heitiki*, war clubs, flax cloaks, musical instruments and fishing implements, kumara gods (placed in the fields to ensure a good crop) and a rare 'god stick' that is thought to be over 500 years old. There is also a war canoe dating back to 1867, a carved meeting house (one of the few in the South Island), a 'slab cottage' built from totara wood, and other old colonial buildings. It is a demanding drive over the twisting summit road from Akaroa to Okains Bay, but well worth it if you have the time.

Banks Peninsula was one of the first regions in the country to export cheese, and at the turn of the 20th century there were at least eight cheese factories here. Traditional cheesemaking continues today at **Barrys Bay Cheese** (tel: 03 304 5809) 11km (7 miles) outside Akaroa, where they produce and sell a wide range of tasty cheeses. From August to May you can watch the cheesemakers at work (*Open* Mon–Fri 8–5, Sat–Sun 9:30–5).

For those with two to four days to spare, the Banks Peninsula Track (tel: 03 304 7612; www.bankstrack.co.nz) takes you to volcanic cliffs, penguin breeding grounds, native bush, waterfalls—and a dunny (Kiwi for toilet) with a view. Don't forget the sunblock and sunhat.

▶ Geraldine 196B1

Between Mount Cook and Christchurch the SH79 passes through Geraldine, a small town where you can stretch your legs and find refreshments.

The **Vintage Car & Machinery Museum▶** (178 Talbot Street, tel: 03 693 8756. *Open* Nov–Apr, daily 10–4. *Admission: inexpensive*) has several curiosities, including a Harley Davidson with a coffin-carrying sidecar that was once used by the Geraldine undertaker, one of the oldest working tractors in the country, an early Mount Cook Line charabanc and a 1928 biplane which is the sole survivor of its kind in the world.

▶▶ Hanmer Springs 196C3

This thermal resort is set in a beautiful wooded area on the edge of the Hanmer Plain about 120km (75 miles) north of Christchurch, with the mountains rising up behind. The regal Hanmer Lodge Hotel, built in 1897, was used as a convalescent home for soldiers returning from World War I; the Queen Mary Hospital (1916) served the same purpose.

Nowadays the focal point is the redeveloped **Thermal Reserve▶▶** (tel: 03 315 7511; www.hotfun.co.nz. *Open* daily 10–9. *Admission: inexpensive*), with several attractively landscaped hot pools, an outdoor café, a health and fitness centre and aqua-therapy rooms. Across the road the comfortable old Lodge is nearly fully restored.

Continued on page 212

The geothermal waters of Hanmer Springs are used to treat a variety of conditions—or simply for a relaxing soak

No one should visit New Zealand without taking a ride in a jet-boat—a fast, shallow-draught craft that was perfected by New Zealanders to navigate the country's extensive river system.

A thrilling ride Almost anywhere in the country where there is a navigable river you will find jet-boat operations. The beauty of the design is that jet-boats can go into much shallower waters than any other type of craft—they can navigate with ease the shallow, braided rivers of Canterbury, for instance, where conventional boats would not dare to venture. When planing, a jet-boat draws as little as 10cm (4in) of water.

Propelled at top speeds of up to 97kph (60mph), they slide around boulders, bounce their way down shallow rapids, skim across gravel banks and bank sharply to avoid floating logs and other hazards. The noise, the wind and the spray can seem overwhelming, but then suddenly you are on a tranquil stretch of the river and all is quiet—and you are aware of the fact that you are far into the wilderness, with no one else around. It is this ability to go almost anywhere that makes jet-boats so special.

Not really a jet? Although they have always been known as jet-boats, in fact these craft are propelled by a jet of water, not a jet of air. Many are simply powered by old car engines that drive the jet unit: an internal propeller (impeller) that is little more than a sophisticated pump. Water is drawn in through an intake in the bottom of the hull and then driven out at high pressure through a nozzle at the back of the boat. Steering is accomplished simply by turning the nozzle laterally, with braking and reversing achieved by a deflector that drops down behind the nozzle. The boat is propelled along by the force of water, and has no rudder or propeller.

Early beginnings Jet-boats are usually thought of as a New Zealand invention, but in fact the idea had been around for more than 200 years. In 1769, two British inventors designed a steam-driven pump that drew in water at the bow of a vessel and ejected it at the stern, and in Queen Victoria's time the Admiralty designed a gunboat fitted with a similar means of propulsion.

Dressed for a jet-boat safari into the wilds of the Dart River Valley

In 1888, Britain's Royal National Lifeboat Institution commissioned the world's first jet-lifeboat, which was built with a back-up jet system in case the main prop became fouled. By 1900, however, marine architects had decided the system was inefficient, and jet-boats fell out of favour.

It was left to a Canterbury sheep farmer, Bill Hamilton, to perfect the system. A prolific inventor, he had played on the local rivers from an early age, but decided that he wanted to go upstream instead of just downriver. His first attempt at a boat to navigate shallow rivers (which had a retractable screw) was not successful, and it was not until the 1950s that he realized that the jet propulsion unit had to have the nozzle above the water-line to work efficiently. Following this breakthrough jet-boats capable of 80kph (50mph) or more were soon developed using an axial flow design in the pump. The first boats had plywood hulls, but as these were easily damaged on shingle banks, fibreglass hulls soon became standard.

Masters of the river In just over 30 years since the jet-boat was invented, New Zealanders have become the most skilled drivers in the world, conquering the most difficult rivers and winning international river marathons hands down. As you watch the skipper on your jet-boat trip it may look deceptively easy, but a jet-boat race over unfamiliar waters with hidden hazards is a different matter altogether. You can learn how to drive a jet-boat in five minutes, but 'reading a river' requires considerable skill and judgement: you have to anticipate at speed, looking for ripples that might indicate a sandbank, white-water crests that betray a hidden rock, and much else besides. It is a subtle, exacting sport.

THE NOISE FACTOR
Some people consider it incongruous that these noisy machines should be used to explore the country's wildest natural areas, but Sir Edmund Hillary, for one, gives them his whole-hearted endorsement: 'Somehow the roar of the engine has never worried me. The jet-boat seems to fit into its environment. The constant change of direction, the struggle against steep rapids, the long, deep, fast stretches, the sharp corners—all seem to tune into the engine from a gentle hum to the scream of power in a difficult section. Rivers are exciting, noisy things anyway.' (Foreword to *The Jet Boat—the Making of a New Zealand Legend* by Les Bloxham and Anne Stark, Reed Books 1994.)

211

Agility and speed are the key elements of jet-boating

FLYING AND CLIMBING
One of the most popular activities around Aoraki/ Mount Cook is to take a flight-seeing trip; several available options include a glacier landing on the Tasman, a Grand Circle flight (crossing the divide over to the Fox and Franz Josef glaciers) or a short Tasman Glacier flight. Contact Mount Cook Ski Planes (tel: 0800 800 702; www.skiplanes.co.nz). Potential mountaineers can obtain information on routes, huts and weather conditions from the visitor centre, or contact Alpine Guides (tel: 03 435 1834; www.alpineguides.co.nz), who rent equipment, supply guides and run courses.

Aoraki/Mount Cook National Park offers great scope for climbers

Continued from page 209

Otherwise, this peaceful village has a scattering of discreet motels and a few bars and restaurants: there are plenty of activities available, including horse-trekking, mountain-biking, canoeing, jet-boating, rafting, kayaking, hunting and fishing. Less demanding activities include safari tours of the nearby **Molesworth Station**, New Zealand's largest high-country farm station (covering 182,000ha/450,000 acres), or walks in the beech and pine forests of the **Hanmer Forest Park►►**. Details on walks and activities are available from the information centre next to the Thermal Reserve (tel: 03 315 7128).

►►► Aoraki/Mount Cook National Park
196A2

The first recorded attempt to scale Aoraki/Mount Cook was made in 1882 by the Rev. William Green, a young Irish clergyman. A storm prevented him from reaching the summit, but from that day the race to conquer the peak was on. In 1894 an English climber, Edward Fitzgerald, announced plans to make another attempt, but on hearing of his plans three New Zealanders (Fyfe, Graham and Clarke) decided to beat him to the top. At 1:30PM on Christmas Day they finally made it, leaving Fitzgerald—who was fishing at the time—fuming. Since then, many famous climbers (including Sir Edmund Hillary) have trained on these awesome slopes.

Inevitably, Aoraki/Mount Cook National Park has become one of the great tourist attractions of the South Island, exceeded in annual visitors only by Fiordland National Park. Most of the 20,000

visitors drawn each year to this great amphitheatre of snow, rock and ice pass through **Mount Cook Village** (tel: 03 435 1809; www.mount-cook.com), a rather haphazard scattering of buildings including the Hermitage Hotel, the Alpine Guides shop, a hostel, a motel and the DoC visitor centre (tel: 03 435 1819. *Open* daily 8–5).

This is primarily climbers' country, with few hiking tracks; there are nevertheless some lovely walks on the valley floor, particularly the famous **Hooker Valley Walk**, an easy three- or four-hour round trip up to the terminal lake of the Hooker Glacier, with stunning views of Aoraki/Mount Cook and the surrounding ranges. Several other short walks are described in the *Walks in Mount Cook National Park* leaflet available from the visitor centre. Other activities include four-wheel-drive safaris, horse-trekking, mountain-biking and hunting. The hunting of introduced animals such as deer, chamois and tahr (mountain goats)—considered pests—is encouraged.

The most notable of the park's flora is the Mount Cook lily (*Ranunculus lyallii*), actually the world's largest buttercup, while smaller buttercups, snow gentians and mountain ribbonwood flower on the alpine slopes. Native birds include the kea, kereru, tomtit, rifleman and grey warbler.

At 29km (18 miles), **Tasman Glacier▶ ▶** is the longest in the southern hemisphere. Its average width is 2km (1 mile), and the terminal is in much the same place as it was when Julius von Haast first explored the area, although the ablation zone (where the ice starts to melt) is much thinner and consists mostly of a jumble of rocks and debris at the terminal. The Tasman is notable for the numerous large sinkholes in the ablation zone, probably above glacial streams. Three-hour sightseeing trips (bus, short walk and boat) are organized by Glacier Explorers (tel: 03 435 1077; www.glacierexplorers.co.nz).

Beautiful Lake Pukaki, fed by the melt waters of Tasman Glacier, lies beneath Aoraki/ Mount Cook

The Mount Cook lily

In the early days of tourism to Mount Cook, a simple 'cob' building called the Hermitage sufficed to welcome visitors. Destroyed by floods in 1913, it was rebuilt as an elegant Edwardian building, which in turn was destroyed by fire in 1957 and replaced by the present hotel of the same name. In the face of the huge numbers now visiting the park, its facilities and infrastructure are no longer able to cope. But should any new facilities be in the Mount Cook village or farther back down the valley in order to spread the impact? The debate treads a familiar fine line between development and conservation. A review is currently under way to try to find solutions to these problems and their effect on one of the country's most spectacular parks.

▶ Mount Hutt   196B2

One of the most popular ski areas in the South Island, Mount Hutt overlooks the Canterbury Plains 25km (16 miles) north of Methven. It not only has an excellent range of runs suitable for all levels of ability, but also has one of the longest seasons of any New Zealand ski field. There are restaurants, a café and equipment rental. Telephone 03 302 8811 or www.nzski.com/mthutt for more details.

▶ Tekapo   196A2

To the east of Aoraki/Mount Cook National Park lies Mackenzie Country, a vast basin of tawny tussock grass with the glacier-fed **Lake Tekapo**▶▶ at its northern end. Finely ground rock in the outflows of the Macauley and Godley rivers, which feed the lake, give it a luminescent turquoise hue, creating a stunning view from the lakehead village of Tekapo up towards the mountains.

214

The remote Church of the Good Shepherd, built in the 1930s to commemorate the pioneer farmers of Mackenzie County

The name Tekapo derives from the Maori Taka-po (*taka* = sleeping mat, *po* = night), recalling an incident when a group of sleeping Maori awoke with a fright in the night, rolled up their mats and fled. They were probably on a hunting expedition for moa, birds and eels, which were taken to the coast to be traded. The first Europeans settled here in the 1850s, and a guest-house was built in the 1880s: it was demolished in 1954 when the lake waters were raised for power generation.

The control gates for the dam lie beneath the road bridge connecting the two halves of the village: The outflow travels from here down a series of canals to eight power stations, also fed by other lakes. One of these, **Benmore Power Station**, is open for guided tours (tel: 03 438 9212; daily 11, 1, 3. *Admission: inexpensive*, booking essential).

On the eastern side of the lake outlet is the picturesque **Church of the Good Shepherd**▶▶, built in the 1930s to commemorate the pioneer farmers of Mackenzie Country. The view of the lake and the mountains through the east window of this simple chapel is sublime. Near by is a bronze statue of a sheepdog, sculpted in 1968 by a Mackenzie farmer's wife (see panel).

The lake waters are too cold for swimming, but you can fish for rainbow or brown trout; there are windsurfers, kayaks and mountain-bikes for rent, and in the winter months ski facilities are available for the nearby Round Hill and Mount Dobson ski fields.

▶ Temuka
196B1

The pottery hub of the south, Temuka has a long association with ceramics. Early settlers noted the many earthenware ovens adjacent to the *pā* sites of Nga Tahu, and Temuka is a contraction of *te umu kaha*, meaning 'fierce strong ovens'. The biggest local manufacturer, New Zealand Insulators, produces tableware and industrial components. Just off the main road is the **Temuka Domain**▶, an attractive park with stately trees, statues, fountains and roses.

BOUNDARY DOGS
The bronze statue next to the Church of the Good Shepherd in Tekapo is a memorial to the faithful sheepdogs of Mackenzie Country, 'without the help of which the grazing of the mountainous country would have been impossible'. Many of them were 'boundary dogs', tethered at crucial points on the outskirts of unfenced farmland to keep the flocks from straying. Sometimes provided with a small kennel for shelter, they were often left for days on end to do their work. You can still sometimes see boundary dogs posted at strategic points either side of the road next to a bridge, for instance, to stop the sheep from wandering into danger.

215

The bronze statue of a 'boundary dog'

THE UNSUNG AVIATOR

A South Canterbury farmer and inventor, Richard Pearse, may well have been the first person in the world to achieve powered flight. He is thought to have flown his home-built aircraft several months before Orville Wright made his historic flight in the USA in 1903: Eyewitnesses recall Pearse making a hopping flight above Waitohi at Easter 1903. After serving in World War I, he returned to live in Christchurch, and focused his ambitions on developing an aircraft capable of hovering. He built a prototype but it never flew. Having spent two years in a mental home, Pearse died in 1953, his place in history sadly unrecognized.

▶ Timaru   196B1

South Canterbury's largest town and port, Timaru is a busy industrial place that has little in the way of visitor attractions; however, since it is about half-way between Christchurch and Dunedin on the main coast road, you might want to stop on the way through.

Originally named Te Maru ('place of shelter'), the harbour was used by Maori travelling by canoe along this otherwise shelterless coastline. A whaling station was established in the 1830s, but the difficulties of berthing—dozens of ships were wrecked here in subsequent years, and on one fateful day, 14 May 1882, no fewer than four sailing ships came to grief on the shore—led to the building of an artificial harbour in the 1870s. The sand that built up behind the harbour breakwaters eventually became the beach of **Caroline Bay▶** one of the few protected and safe swimming beaches on the east coast.

Behind the beach are a park, a maze and a small aviary (tel: 03 686 2136; www.carolinebay.org.nz.

Open daily 10–5. *Admission: free*).

If you have half an hour to spare, it is worth visiting **South Canterbury Museum▶** (tel: 03 684 2212. *Open* Tue–Fri 10–4:30, Sun and holidays 1:30–4:30. *Admission: free*), which has displays relating the story of South Canterbury from early Maori times onwards; it

Midway between Christchurch and Dunedin, Timaru is South Canterbury's largest town and has a busy port

also has a replica of possibly the first aeroplane in the world ever to fly, built by Richard Pearse (see panel).

Several town walks are described in leaflets available free from the visitor centre. You can also take a free tour of the huge **D. B. Mainland Brewery** (tel: 03 688 2059, Sheffield Street, Washdyke. *Open* Mon–Thu by appointment).

▶ Twizel   196A1

Originally built to house workers constructing the Upper Waitaki hydroelectric scheme in the 1960s, Twizel is a rather featureless place that has developed as a holiday base for the nearby lakes (Ruataniwha, Ohau and

Benmore), with facilities for camping, boating, fishing and other outdoor activities. It is also a convenient base for visits to Aoraki/Mount Cook National Park, which is just 40 minutes' drive around the shores of Lake Pukaki.

The chief attraction in the area is the **Black Stilt Visitor Hide►►** (see panel), on the shores of Lake Ruataniwha. Once common throughout New Zealand, the black stilt (or kaki) is now the world's rarest wading bird. A captive breeding programme was established in 1979 at Mount Bruce National Wildlife Centre in order to try to halt the decline in numbers, and the Twizel aviaries were built in 1987 to continue this project in an environment nearer to the birds' natural home. Viewing hides have been built and the guided tours also include viewing of breeding pairs with binoculars, and a close look at captive (nonbreeding) stilts. (Tours daily, Twizel visitor centre, tel: 03 435 3124 for times. *Admission: moderate*.)

► Waimate   196B1

This small town 45km (28 miles) south of Timaru is the hub of a flourishing soft fruit and flower-growing district, and has a huge white horse (a tribute to the Clydesdale horses that once ploughed these lands) outlined on the slopes of Mount John behind it. Waimate has an old wooden church and an unusual mud-floored cottage, known as **The Cuddy►**, constructed using slabs from a single totara tree. Built in 1854, it was the first European dwelling in the area. (*Open* by arrangement, tel: 03 689 7199; www.waimate.org.nz/tewaimate).

Hydroelectric development has destroyed much of the black stilt's breeding grounds

BLACK STILTS
Found only in New Zealand, black stilts were once widespread, but their numbers have been decimated by predation of eggs and chicks and the loss of breeding habitats. Their last remaining natural home is among the braided rivers of South Canterbury's Mackenzie Country. There are currently only about 80 of these birds left in the wild, with a dozen pairs nesting each spring on the side channels of the rivers. Artificial incubation, as part of the black stilt recovery programme, has raised the survival rate of the fledglings from 1 per cent to 35 per cent, and numbers are now steadily increasing.

New Zealand was the third country (after Australia and the USA) to experience a gold rush in the late 19th century, an event that significantly affected the economic fortunes of the South Island.

THE POWER OF THE PRESS

Australian miner Gabriel Read claimed the reward for discovering gold offered by the Otago Provincial Council, and the news was published in July 1861 in the *Otago Witness*, precipitating a rush to Tuapeka. By the end of the month over 11,000 people were camping in the district, and gold fever had gripped the Otago capital, Dunedin.

218

First strike Maori had long been aware that there was gold in New Zealand, but they valued jade more highly. The first gold rush was in the Coromandel in 1852, a time when settlers were being lured to the recently discovered goldfields of California and Australia. When rumours of gold near Thames first emerged, an Auckland committee was quick to offer a reward of £500 to anyone who could find a 'payable' goldfield in New Zealand. Within two days Charles Ring, a Coromandel sawmiller, raced to Auckland with some gold-bearing quartz to claim the reward. Land around Thames was immediately leased from Maori by hopeful prospectors; unfortunately for them, expensive machinery proved necessary to extract the gold, and within a few months the excitement had fizzled out—so Charles Ring was denied his reward since the goldfields were not considered payable.

Gold rush The Coromandel finds were followed by others in the South Island, notably in Golden Bay in 1856, when there were major strikes in the Aorere River. More than 2,000 miners and hangers-on flooded into the area, but by 1859 most of the gold had been worked out.

Prompted by these finds, the Otago Provincial Council also offered a reward to anyone who could find a payable field. An Australian miner, Gabriel Read, set off for the Tuapeka area (now Lawrence), where he had heard that a miner called Black Peter had found gold at Woolshed Creek. On 23 May 1861 he finally struck lucky, panning 200g (7oz) of gold from a creek in what became known as Gabriels Gully.

The following year two prospectors, one Irish and one American, arrived in Dunedin with 40kg (87lb) of gold. A reward tempted them to reveal their source, the Clutha River near Dunstan (now Clyde), and the next great rush was on.

Fox-hunting Meanwhile, suspicions were aroused in Dunstan by the behaviour of a tight-lipped miner named William Fox, who would appear periodically to sell quantities of gold and then

vanish into the bush again. When a group of miners followed him, he managed to give them the slip, and it was some time before he was discovered with some 40 companions working the rich deposits of the Arrow River. Then came the first finds in the Shotover River (later described as 'the richest river in the world'), and the rush was on again—this time the largest the country had seen. Queenstown, Arrowtown and several other settlements sprang up in the wake of the prospectors, and Dunedin became the richest and biggest settlement in the country.

Last strikes By 1863 it was almost over in Otago, and in 1865 reports of new finds in Westland led to swarms of miners crossing the Southern Alps via Arthur's Pass to try their luck there. Prospecting on the West Coast was hard work, hampered by thick bush, heavy rain and the ubiquitous sandflies, but Greymouth and Hokitika boomed nevertheless, with the latter's port becoming the busiest in the country as thousands more miners arrived from Australia.

The last major gold rush was in the Coromandel in 1867–68, but this time the quartz reefs were worked mostly by companies who could afford to invest in stamper batteries to beat out the gold.

In just under a decade the gold rush was over, with only isolated graves, battered shacks and heaps of tailings to show where thousands of hopeful prospectors had toiled. But short-lived though it was, it had a profound effect on the New Zealand economy, bringing instant wealth to many areas; in 1863 gold had accounted for 70 per cent of all overseas exports.

POPULATION GROWTH
The European population of the country was given an enormous boost by the influx of miners, many of whom stayed on, particularly in Otago, where they founded fruit farms and other businesses.

219

Miners camped close to rivers to pan for gold, but flash floods were always a danger

THE DEEP SOUTH The southernmost region of the South Island embraces a great diversity of landscapes, from semi-arid, high-country basins to fertile plains and forested mountains. The range of fascinating things to see and do in the Deep South is no less varied, from the stunning scenery of Fiordland to historic gold-mining sites in Central Otago and wildlife-viewing on the Otago Peninsula. Adventure tourism is probably better represented here than almost anywhere else in New Zealand, with action-packed thrills available all year round.

FIORDLAND The glacial landscapes of Fiordland National Park are icons of New Zealand's wilderness areas. Covering 1.2 million hectares (3 million acres), this is one of the largest national parks in the world: parts of it are so mountainous they have yet to be fully explored. The famous **Milford Sound** is just one of 14 fiords along the coastline, while inland are numerous freshwater lakes (the biggest of which are **Manapouri** and **Te Anau**), tumbling waterfalls and virgin forests beneath the mountain peaks.

One way of exploring this wilderness is by walking (either independently or with a guide) along well-known walking tracks such as the Milford, Kepler, Routeburn, Greenstone or Hollyford; climbing, hunting and fishing are other possibilities, while flightseeing (sightseeing by air) and cruising on the fiords and lakes are more relaxing ways to enjoy this splendid natural environment. The main gateway to Fiordland National Park is the township of Te Anau, on the shores of Lake Te Anau.

OTAGO Central Otago was the scene of one of New Zealand's greatest gold rushes (see pages 218–219), and there are still remnants of those heady days scattered around the towns and countryside. Today fruit-growing is almost as lucrative, with peaches, apricots and other stonefruit thriving on the well-irrigated plains.

Queenstown, the busiest resort in the South Island, lies at the foot of the Remarkables Range, on the shores of glittering Lake Wakatipu. In winter skiing is the main attraction, but in the summer months there are almost endless opportunities for outdoor adventure and sports—name almost any thrill you can imagine, from bungee-jumping to surfing down rapids, and they do it here. The second main resort area is **Wanaka**, on the shores of Lake Wanaka, which has almost as many adventure options as Queenstown, but has a much more laid-back atmosphere.

While Central Otago typically has hot summers and frosty winters, Coastal Otago has a somewhat milder climate. The coastal areas were settled by Scottish migrants in the 19th century, a heritage that is evident in the well-preserved architecture of the regional capital, **Dunedin**. On the city's doorstep is the **Otago Peninsula**, where royal albatross and rare penguins can be seen at remarkably close range.

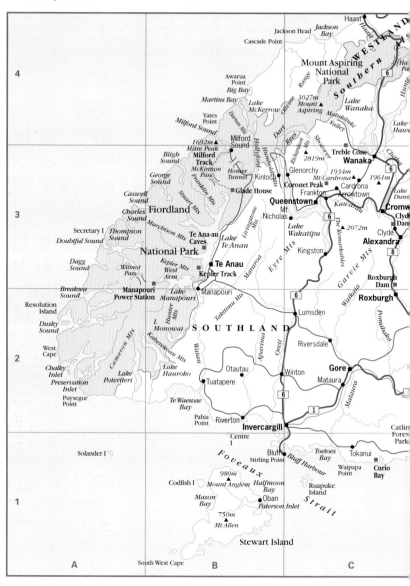

SOUTHLAND AND STEWART ISLAND Adjoining Fiordland is the rest of the province of Southland, a triangular wedge of sheep farms and trout streams. Like Dunedin, the region has strong Scottish connections: Inhabitants still display traces of a Scots burr, and many place-names are Gaelic in origin. At the bottom of this triangle, Invercargill is New Zealand's southernmost city and the jumping-off point for underrated Stewart Island where, in Rakiura National Park, rare birds outnumber people and trampers will find deserted coastline and bush to explore. This is one of the few places in New Zealand where you can be almost sure of seeing kiwi in the wild, with regular excursions to view a beach colony of these elusive birds.

Page 220: Milford Sound
Page 221: Canoeing the rapids

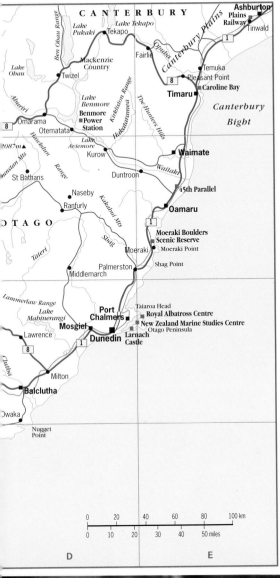

Paua *(abalone) shells*

Take a night safari to spot kiwi on remote Stewart Island

Coastal Otago and Southland

▶ Bluff

222B1

The southernmost town in the South Island, Bluff is a major port and fishing hub, with the massive Tiwai aluminium smelter dominating the far side of the harbour. From the top of **Bluff Hill▶** (265m/870ft) there is a breathtaking panorama of the harbour, with Foveaux Strait and Stewart Island to the south, while nearby **Stirling Point** has a compulsory photo-stop at an 'international signpost' showing the distances from Bluff to major cities all over the world.

Bluff is well known for its excellent seafood, principally Bluff oysters (see panel), but grouper, blue cod and crayfish are also fished locally. The late Fred and Myrtle Flutey put mollusc shells to good use in their amazing **Paua Shell House▶** (corner of Marine Parade and Henderson Street, tel: 03 212 8262. *Open* daily 9–5. *Admission: donation*), which contains an entire room lined with beautiful *paua* (abalone) shells and an enormous collection of shells from around the world.

BLUFF OYSTERS
These deepwater shellfish have a sweet, succulent taste and are much sought after; although supplies may be erratic elsewhere in the country, you can usually find oysters here during the season (1 March to 31 August). You can also visit dockside oyster sheds during this time, and oyster-opening and other competitions are part of the Bluff Oyster Festival, held in mid-April (tel: 0800 SEAFUN; www.bluffoysterfest.co.nz).

Stirling Point Lookout, the end of the road in the South Island

▶▶▶ Dunedin   *223D2*

There is no mistaking the ancestry of Dunedin's founding fathers: certainly not with a statue of Robert Burns at its heart and the only kilt shop in the country, not to mention an architectural heritage whose Scottish roots are plain to see. You may even hear the strained notes of a bagpipe during a haggis ceremony here; it comes as no surprise that Dunedin is the old Gaelic name for Edinburgh.

The early settlement, founded in 1848, struggled along with just a few hundred people attempting to carve a living from this difficult terrain. Thirteen years later the town was galvanized by the Central Otago gold finds. Although the goldfields were some 121km (75 miles) inland, Dunedin was the nearest port and its prosperity was soon assured (see pages 218–219). Between 1861 and 1865 the population leapt from some 2,000 to over 10,000, and it developed into New Zealand's wealthiest city. Great public buildings were erected, the country's first university (the University of Otago) was founded and Dunedin became the proud possessor of the first cable tramway outside the USA (this ran for over 70 years until it was closed down in 1957).

Although the Scottish heritage predominates, Dunedin is now demographically much more cosmopolitan, with a population including descendants of Irish and Dutch settlers, a large Chinese community (many of them descendants of gold-diggers), third- and fourth-generation Lebanese and newly settled Cambodians and Vietnamese. Similarly, although the city may be most famous for its architecture, it also has a lively artistic and cultural life and fine museums. The city's large student population (around 14,000 attend one of four higher-education institutions) has helped to foster a vibrant entertainment and music scene, and Dunedin has produced a number of successful rock bands. The Dunedin Sound gained international recognition in the 1980s, and numerous bands are now based here.

Recently, Dunedin has also capitalized on the accessibility of the nearby Otago Peninsula (see pages 232–233) to become a major place for ecotourism based on the region's unique wildlife.

An obvious place to start exploring Dunedin is the eight-sided **Octagon** at the heart of the city, where Robbie Burns gazes 'with his back to the kirk and his face to the pub'. The kirk in question is **St. Paul's Cathedral** (tel: 03 477 4931), which has an impressive vaulted nave and a rather less impressive 1970s chancel. On the north side of the Octagon, the Municipal Chambers contain the helpful and efficient Dunedin **visitor centre** (tel: 03 474 3300). *Open* winter,

Robbie Burns' statue, Dunedin

225

Dunedin's railway station, with its magnificent booking hall (top), gave the nickname 'Gingerbread George' to its architect Sir George Troup

Mon–Fri 8:30–5, Sat–Sun 9–5; longer hours in summer).

Opposite the visitor centre an old department store has been converted into the brilliant **Dunedin Public Art Gallery**▶▶▶ (tel: 03 477 4000; www.dunedin.art.museum. *Open* daily 10–5). The gallery has a wonderful glass façade providing a window onto the interior displays from the street. It has one of the two best collections in the country (the other is at the Auckland Art Gallery), a legacy that began with the early acquisition of Van der Vedlen's *Waterfall in the Otira Gorge*, considered to be the country's greatest 19th-century landscape painting. The gallery also has over 40 works by Frances Hodgkins (whose father was one of the gallery's founders), as well as paintings by Constable, Gainsborough, Reynolds, Monet, Lorrain and Landini. The decorative arts and modern works are also well represented in its collections.

Heading down Stuart Street from the Octagon you pass the magisterial **Law Courts**▶ to reach the splendid **railway station**▶▶, reputedly 'one of the most photographed railway buildings in the world'. Completed in 1907 and faced with Oamaru stone, the station is dominated by a massive tower and embellished with rampant lions and stained-glass windows depicting steam locomotives, while the foyer has an impressive Royal Doulton mosaic floor.

A short distance southwest of the station is the **Otago Settlers Museum**▶▶ (tel: 03 477 5052; www.otago.settlers.museum. *Open* daily 10–5. *Admission: moderate*), which has undergone a major and successful revamp. At the entrance, the main Hall of Otago History encompasses the story of early Maori settlers, European migrants and Chinese gold-diggers. Beyond, a fabulous Edwardian

Hall houses temporary exhibits, while the atmospheric Portrait Gallery, lined with hundreds of nostalgic photographs of early settlers in Dunedin and Otago, also has some fine Edwardian furniture and other antiques.

The museum's expansion is due largely to the acquisition of the former railways' bus station next door, where the fine art-deco booking hall is now the highlight of a permanent exhibition on transport in Otago.

If you visit only one museum in Dunedin it should be the main **Otago Museum▶▶▶**, a few minutes' walk on Great King Street (tel: 03 474 7474; www.otagomuseum. govt.nz. *Open* daily 10–5. *Admission: free*). Founded in 1868, this has outstanding collections on Maori and Pacific island culture, displays on New Zealand's natural history and exhibits of archaeological treasures from around the world—a legacy that reflects the wealth of the local community at the turn of the 20th century.

The museum includes a 'Discovery World' hands-on science exhibit on the ground floor, with galleries devoted to cultural objects from all over Oceania, and a comprehensive southern Maori collection.

On the top floor is the natural history collection, with a 'Survival and Extinction' section containing stuffed specimens of some of the 44 species and 32 genera of birds that have become extinct since humans first set foot in Aotearoa; ironically, many of these species vanished because they were over-zealously hunted by collectors for export to museums overseas. Also on this floor are

GORGE TRIP BY RAIL
To the west of Dunedin, the Taieri River wends its way through a picturesque gorge, which is for the most part accessible only aboard the Taieri Gorge Railway. Railway enthusiasts will also appreciate the many fine examples of Victorian stone bridges and iron latticework viaducts along the route. The four-hour round trip departs from Dunedin Railway Station daily in summer (tel: 03 477 4449 or see www.taieri.co.nz for times and bookings).

227

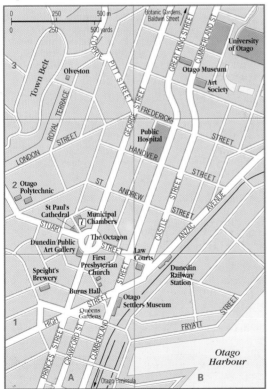

The Otago Settlers Museum's main entrance is on Queens Gardens

pottery, textiles and decorative arts, as well as a Maritime
Hall with ship models and a whale skeleton.

The distinctive natural history of Otago is recalled in the
Hall of Natural History, while at the top is the unusual
'Animal Attic'. Its ornate, arched, wooden structure re-
creates a Victorian natural history museum, with an
extensive collection of specimens from around the world.

One of the most popular historic buildings in Dunedin is
Olveston▶▶, a Jacobean-style mansion built in 1906 by
local businessman David Theomin. Bequeathed to the city
by his daughter in 1966, it had been left virtually
untouched since her father's death in 1933, and shows the
lifestyle of a prosperous Edwardian family. Complete with
billiard room, library and an impressive oak gallery and
stairway, this spacious family home is furnished with
items collected by the Theomins in Asia, ranging from
Chinese jade and ceramics to Persian carpets and
weaponry and helmets from Japan. There are also French
antiques, English silverware and early New Zealand paintings (42 Royal Terrace, tel: 03 477 3320; www.
olveston.co.nz. Guided tours daily 9:30, 10:45, noon, 1:30,
2:45 and 4. *Admission: moderate*).

Dunedin merits a place in *Guinness World Records* for
having the world's steepest street. A few minutes' drive
north from the city, **Baldwin Street** climbs dramatically
from the main road at a gradient of 1 in 2.7, only to come
to a dead end half-way up the hillside. The street remains
a secret, however, because its residents are fed up with the
sound of splintering fences
and crumpling metal as cars
career out of control down
the hill. So leave the driving
to the locals, and walk up
the 270 steps to the top.

228

*Furnishings from the
turn of the 20th century
in the historic family
home of Olveston*

▶ Invercargill

222C2

New Zealand's southernmost city, Invercargill, sprawls across wide open plains almost at the tip of the South Island—only the port of Bluff lies closer to Foveaux Strait and nearby Stewart Island. The capital of Southland (or Murihiku, 'the tail end of the land', as it was known to Maori), the city is as flat as a pancake, having been mostly reclaimed from swampland, and is laid out on a spacious grid pattern. The main transport centre for Southland, it is the departure point for flying to Stewart Island (see pages 234–235).

Invercargill's main attraction is the excellent **Southland Museum and Art Gallery▶▶** on the edge of Queens Park (tel: 03 218 9753; www.southlandmuseum.com. *Open Mon–Fri 9–5, Sat–Sun 1–5. Admission: donation*). Founded over a century ago, the museum was redeveloped in 1990, when it was roofed over with a gigantic pyramid. The complex includes displays on natural history, early colonial settlers and Maori heritage, including stone toolmaking and jade carving. The evocative 'Roaring Forties Experience' vividly brings to life the wild subantarctic territories administered by New Zealand. The unusual wildlife, giant alpine flowers, spectacular topography and appalling weather of these islands are convincingly conveyed in a 25-minute audiovisual show (Shows on the hour. *Admission: inexpensive*) and a new display gallery.

The museum is also home to a successful captive breeding programme for tuatara, an ancient reptile that has survived only in New Zealand.

229

'Henry', one of 40 tuatara in Southland Museum's Tuatara House

BOULDER FORMATION

There are about 50 boulders at Moeraki, the largest of which weighs about 7 tonnes and measures over 2m (6ft) in diameter. Although their position on the beach and their shape would seem to suggest that the boulders were formed by surf action, in fact they emerged from the mudstone cliffs behind the beach, having been created by chemicals crystallizing around a nucleus (like a pearl) when they were formed in the sediment some 65 million years ago. An informative leaflet on this process, published by the Institute of Geological and Nuclear Sciences, is available from the café shop.

The Moeraki boulders are strewn across a beach close to the coast road

▶ Moeraki Boulders   223E3

www.moeraki-nz.com/boulders.html

These unusual spherical boulders strewn along the beach in Moeraki Boulders Scenic Reserve are the finest examples of their kind to be found anywhere in the world (see panel). According to Maori legend they are the remains of food baskets washed overboard from a great canoe shipwrecked here on its way from Hawaiki. Geologists know them, more prosaically, as septarian concretions, and these are the last remaining ones on this coast; they were once plentiful on nearby Katiki Beach and around Shag Point, but all the smaller examples have long since been claimed as souvenirs. Perhaps the main reason for people's curiosity is their almost perfect roundness, combined with the veined surfaces that give them the appearance of a turtle's back.

There is a good café/restaurant just above the boulders at the parking area, and the nearby fishing village of Moeraki (77km/48 miles from Dunedin, 39km/24 miles from Oamaru) is also worth a visit for its walks and heritage trail.

▶▶ Nugget Point   223D1

Nugget Point rises some 130m (427ft) above the beach with a series of sea stacks—one with a lighthouse—extending out into the ocean beyond the South Otago coastline. A popular spot for viewing wildlife, this remote promontory is the only place on the mainland where fur seals, elephant seals and Hooker's sea lions are known to co-exist. Yellow-eyed penguins and little blue penguins both breed here, and other penguins (Fiordland crested, Snares crested and rockhopper penguins among them) are also sometimes seen. Birdlife includes spotted shags, gulls and Australian gannets; the largest known mainland colony of sooty shearwaters is also here.

There is a viewing hide for the yellow-eyed penguins (which come ashore in the evenings) in Roaring Bay, and a viewing platform at the lighthouse (binoculars recommended). Nugget Point is 29km (18 miles) southwest of Balclutha.

▶▶ Oamaru 223E3

Oamaru would probably be just another declining coastal port were it not for the timely discovery—soon after the town was founded—of large deposits of pure limestone in the surrounding area, which encouraged architects and stonemasons to design a magnificent series of buildings along its main street. Most of these still stand, earning Oamaru the title 'whitestone city', and a walk along Thames Street will reveal a bewildering variety of styles on historic buildings such as the National Bank and the courthouse.

Oamaru's port was dogged by early misadventures, but it nevertheless brought enough prosperity to lead to the development of the harbour area and, when it closed down in the 1970s, to bequeath a legacy of well-designed wool and grain stores, warehouses and other buildings. These now form the heart of the **Harbour-Tyne Street Historic Precinct▶▶** (tel: 03 434 1406; www.historicoamaru.co.nz), which is being gradually

Creamy limestone adds allure to Oamaru architecture

and sympathetically redeveloped as a Victorian town. The visitor centre (*Open* daily 9–5) is in the old Colonial Bank Building in this area, and architectural tours of the district can be arranged (tel: 03 434 1656).

The mild, sheltered climate has benefited the lovely **public gardens** (Severn Street. *Open* daylight hours. *Admission: free*), founded in 1876, with an oriental garden, Japanese bridge, rhododendron dell and wallaby park.

The **Oamaru Blue Penguin Colony** (tel: 03 433 1195; www.penguins.co.nz. Visitor centre and viewing platforms *Open* 7PM–10PM. *Admission: inexpensive*) on the harbour edge is probably the only one in the world in such close proximity to a main town—sometimes, indeed, the penguins get confused on their way home at night and wander downtown. A penguin refuge has been created in an old quarry at the end of Waterfront Road, with two viewing platforms for watching them as they waddle inland to their nests after a day's fishing out at sea, usually about half an hour after dark.

SOUTHERN SCENIC ROUTE
Part of the Southern Scenic Route traverses an almost-forgotten corner of the coastline between Invercargill and Balclutha, crossing ridges and valleys close to the coast and passing through tracts of native forest in the Catlins, with superb views of sandy bays, estuaries and rocky headlands. The numerous places of interest along the way include Nugget Point (see page 230) and Curio Bay, where the fossilized remains of an ancient forest can be seen embedded in the rocks along the foreshore. From Invercargill to Balcutha is 170km (106 miles), with 55km (34 miles) of this along unpaved roads.

Royal albatross breed on Taiaroa Head near Dunedin

THE ROYAL ALBATROSS
One of the largest of all sea birds, the royal albatross glides across the oceans on its enormous wings, sometimes staying aloft for days on end. Adults arrive at Taiaroa in late September, building their nests ready for egg-laying in November. The parents share incubation duties over 11 weeks—one of the longest incubation periods of any bird. The chicks hatch during January and early February, but are not ready to fly until eight months later.

DISAPPEARING GUN
Guided tours at Taiaroa Head include a visit to an underground military complex inside Fort Taiaroa, which was built to counter the (imagined) Tsarist threat in the 1880s. Inside is the world's only working example of an Armstrong Disappearing Gun.

'Seals for breakfast, albatross for lunch, penguins for dinner' as they say in Dunedin—not to be found on local menus, of course, but rather to be observed at close quarters on the adjoining Otago Peninsula. The concentration of wildlife here is even more remarkable because of its proximity to the city (it is, in fact, within the city limits), and it is with ample justification that Dunedin proclaims itself the wildlife capital of New Zealand.

The volcanic hills of the peninsula terminate in steep headlands on the ocean side, and with the edge of the continental shelf close to shore, wildlife such as seals and sea birds have a plentiful source of food as well as sheltered breeding and resting sites on the cliffs. Fur seals breed in several locations, as do Hooker's sea lions, which are twice the size of seals and among the world's rarest sea lions.

The most spectacular resident is the royal albatross, which breeds on the grassy slopes at Taiaroa Head at the tip of the peninsula, the only place in the world where these magnificent birds nest on a mainland site. The nesting colony can be viewed from an observation post, which is part of the **Royal Albatross Centre**▶▶▶ (tel: 03 478 0499; www.albatross.org.nz. *Open* daily summer 9–dusk; winter 10–dusk; tours on the hour and half-hour in summer, restricted hours during winter; colony closed mid-Sep to late Nov. *Admission: expensive*; booking recommended). Allow at least a couple of hours to visit the reserve and the centre, which also houses displays on the wildlife and history of the area (*Open* same hours. *Admission: free*).

The other main wildlife attraction on the peninsula is penguins: blue penguins breed at Taiaroa Head and elsewhere around the coast, and rare yellow-eyed penguins breed on just about every beach on the peninsula. There are two main viewing areas for the latter: the first is at the **Southlight Wildlife Reserve**▶, the entrance to which is just past Taiaroa Head. The penguins nest on a sandy bank some distance below the viewing area, but you can spend as much time as you want here (there are fixed binoculars, but bringing your own would be better). There are also fur seals and a spotted shag colony just down the beach (collect the key from Southlight Wildlife, Harington Point before arriving at Taiaroa Head, tel: 03 478 0287. *Open* daily dawn–dusk. *Admission: inexpensive*).

For a really close-up view of the penguins, take one of the tours at the excellent **Penguin Place**▶▶▶ (tel: 03 478 0286; www.penguin-place.co.nz. *Open* daily 9–dusk. *Admission: moderate*; booking essential). After an introductory talk, a short ride brings you to the reserve on the opposite coast of the peninsula, where a viewing platform allows you to watch the penguins as they waddle ashore. A series of covered sunken paths and viewing hides then leads to the nesting areas, giving an intimate insight into nesting activity.

Farther back down the north coast, the **New Zealand Marine Studies Centre**▶, at Portobello (tel: 03 479 5826; www.otago.ac.nz/marinestudies. *Open* daily noon–4:30. *Admission: inexpensive*) has a series of tanks containing plants, invertebrates and fish from the waters around this region, as well as a touch tank.

Near by, **Glenfalloch Woodland Gardens**▶ (tel: 03 476 1006. *Open* daily 9–dusk. *Admission: donation*) have a collection of fuchsias, roses, azaleas and rhododendrons, including species not found elsewhere in the country.

The Otago Peninsula's primary historical attraction is the impressive **Larnach Castle**▶▶ just over 10km (6 miles) east of Dunedin, built in 1871 in the Scottish baronial style, which displays some fine craftsmanship and has antique furniture inside (tel: 03 476 1616; www.larnarchcarstle. co.nz. *Open* daily 9–5. *Admission: moderate*). In the former ballroom is a café, and from the attractive grounds there are extensive views over the peninsula and out to sea.

VIEWING FROM THE SEA
Seals, albatross, penguins and birdlife on the peninsula can also be viewed on cruises such as those run by Monarch Wildlife Cruises (tel: 03 477 4276; www.wildlife.co.nz); naturalists Colleen and Fiona Black operate these highly recommended tours aboard the MV *Monarch*, with several options around the harbour and peninsula.

233

William Larnach, the builder of Larnach Castle, originally called it 'The Camp'; the name is still visible in the tiled entrance hall floor

The Deep South: Coastal Otago and Southland

GETTING THERE
Stewart Island can be reached in an hour aboard the *Foveaux Express* from Bluff (tel: 03 212 7660; www.foveauxexpress.co.nz), or in 20 minutes on board the frequent flights from Invercargill operated by Southern Air (tel: 03 218 9129; www.southernair.co.nz); accommodation, water taxis and excursions can be booked through Stewart Island visitor centre (tel: 03 219 1218).

A yellow-eyed penguin (below); Halfmoon Bay, Stewart Island (bottom)

234

►►► Stewart Island   222B1

Some 30km (18 miles) across Foveaux Strait from Bluff, Stewart Island is largely uninhabited by humans. Just 65km (40 miles) long and 40km (25 miles) at its widest point, it covers 172,000ha (425,000 acres) and has a local population of only 400, most of whom live in and around the one township, Oban, usually called Halfmoon Bay.

Captain Cook made a rare major mistake in mapping the coastline in 1770 when he drew the island as a peninsula. Whalers and sealers later sought the shelter of Paterson Inlet, and timber mills were established, with most settlements developing on the north side of the island.

Today there are only about 20km (12 miles) of roads on the entire island, so if you want to explore beyond the immediate vicinity of Halfmoon Bay, hiking (or a boat) is the only way to go. Most of the island has a dense cover of native bush and rain forest, with bush walks and tramping tracks spreading out from Halfmoon Bay around the coastline and into the interior. Trekking huts are strategically placed on the main hiking routes, which include the arduous North-West Circuit (a ten-day trip) and the Rakiura Track (three days). Launches can also be chartered to reach the more remote areas for hunting, track drop-offs, fishing or simply fossicking in isolated bays.

Nearly all the island is within **Rakiura National Park**, with the native birdlife including kaka, tui, bellbird, robin, fantail, longtail and shining cuckoo. Numerous sea birds breed around the shoreline and on surrounding islands, and yellow-eyed, little blue and Fiordland crested penguins are also found here. Most of the islanders make their living from fishing, with crayfish, abalone, blue cod and salmon exported overseas.

The pace of life on Stewart Island is relaxed, and the islanders are friendly. Halfmoon Bay has plenty of accommodation (from motels to homestays), a general store and

the venerable South Sea Hotel. Within the township there is also a small **museum** on Ayr Street (tel: 03 219 1049. *Open* Mon–Sat 10–noon, Sun noon–2. *Admission: inexpensive*), with displays on whaling, Maori history, fishing, timber-milling and so on. The natural history of the island is explored at the nearby Department of Conservation Centre (Main Road, tel: 03 219 0009. *Open* daily 9–5), which can also provide leaflets on tramping tracks and short walks around Halfmoon Bay.

Other activities include kayaking in Paterson Inlet (which has over 90sq km/35sq miles of sheltered waterways and 20 islands), and one-hour trips by minibus around (most) of the island's 20km (12 miles) or so of roads.

One of the highlights of a stay here is walking on **Ulva Island►►**, an almost paradise-like bird sanctuary; another is the rare chance to see kiwi in their natural environment. The southern tokoeka, the species found on Stewart Island, is unusual in that it forages both by day and by night: trampers may well spot them nosing out sand hoppers under washed-up kelp on the beaches (particularly in Mason Bay). Boat trips operate from Golden Bay cross Paterson Inlet to Ocean Beach, where a handful of kiwi can usually be seen—an opportunity not to be missed. Departures are every other day and numbers are limited, so booking is essential (with Bravo Adventure Cruises, tel: 03 219 1144).

► Waitaki Valley   223E3

Forming the boundary between South Canterbury and North Otago, the Waitaki River drains down from the Southern Alps and flows out to sea just north of Oamaru. A major source of hydroelectric power, it has three lakes created by dams along its length (Benmore, Aviemore and Waitaki), which are now stocked with trout and salmon.

At the head of the valley is **Omarama**, popular with anglers and famous as a gliding centre. Near by (10km/6 miles northwest, off SH8) are the **Clay Cliffs►►**, a spectacular natural example of badland erosion, with a series of elegant pinnacles, columns, ravines and ridges.

Farther downstream, **Benmore Power Station** (see page 215) is the first of three hydroelectric plants; the community of **Otematata** provides service facilities for all three. At the junction of the Waitaki and Hakataramea rivers, **Kurow** has some interesting old limestone buildings from the 1890s. Finally comes **Duntroon**, a farming area with good fishing near by. Just outside the township are some Maori **rock drawings►** (see panel page 214) on the walls of a limestone shelter (signposted 2.5km/1.5 miles west of town on SH83).

MUTTONBIRDS
If you fly into Stewart Island you will notice a small cluster of islands to the east of the flight path on approaching the coast. These are the northern Muttonbird Islands, so named after the fledglings of the sooty shearwaters that migrate here from the North Pacific during the summer months. Maori know them as titi and prize them as a gastronomic delicacy; most *pakeha* find them too rich and oily, which is perhaps why they were also called muttonbirds. Thousands nest here in burrows, and the fledglings are collected from April onwards only by Maori, who have inherited the ancestral right to do so.

235

Stewart Island is just one of the places to watch sea lions

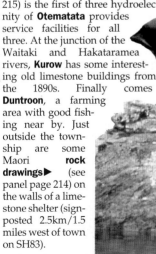

The kiwi, New Zealand's national symbol, is a one-off evolutionary design, a bird that holds all sorts of biological records. But now the unthinkable might be about to happen, and its very survival is threatened.

WHERE TO SEE KIWI
Places to see New Zealand's national bird include Auckland Zoo; Rainbow and Fairy Springs, Rotorua; Kiwi House and Native Bird Park, Otorohanga; National Aquarium, Napier; Wellington Zoo; Orana Wildlife Park, Christchurch; Willowbank Wildlife Reserve, Christchurch; Moana Zoo, near Greymouth; and Kiwi and Birdlife Park, Queenstown.

A great spotted kiwi foraging for food

A truly curious bird The flightless, nocturnal kiwi evolved some 70 million years ago, at about the time when the New Zealand landmass drifted away from Gondwanaland. A relation of Australia's emus and cassowaries, the kiwi thrived at ground level where there were then no mammals to hunt it. Its only predators at the time were New Zealand goshawks and the gigantic Haast's eagle (both now extinct), and it may have been this threat that turned it into a creature of the night.

The kiwi is one of the few birds with a highly developed sense of smell, and it is the only known bird with external nostrils at the end of its bill, with which it literally sniffs out its food below the surface of the ground. Its diet consists mostly of earthworms, spiders, seeds, fallen fruit and insect larvae. It lays simply enormous eggs, with a mature example averaging 20 per cent of the female body weight. Once laid, they take up to 80 days to hatch, and in some varieties the male does most of the incubating. Kiwi form monogamous pairs and bond until death; the females are bigger than the males and tend to dominate them. As they forage for food during the night they

call to each other, performing a duet that may last for hours on end, with the female giving a lower, hoarser call than the male. Kiwi are highly territorial and protect their patch (which can be as big as 40ha/100 acres) by calling or, if that fails, attacking the intruder. Generally considered gentle creatures, they are in fact often bad-tempered, and are capable of inflicting nasty wounds with their razor-sharp claws.

Types of kiwi There are six identified varieties of kiwi, the rarest of which is the **little spotted kiwi**, of which just 1,000 remain. The **great spotted kiwi** lives mainly in mountainous regions in northwest Nelson, central Westland and east Canterbury. One of the most bad-tempered is the **North Island brown kiwi**, which is found only in the upper two-thirds of the North Island. The **Okarito brown kiwi** is one of the most recent to be identified (in 1993), and lives in lowland forest just north of Franz Josef. Squat and round, **southern tokoeka** are found in Fiordland and Stewart Island. Finally, the **Haast tokoeka** was also identified (thanks to DNA testing) as a new species in 1993.

237

Under threat Forests all over the country, which once rang at night to the sound of kiwi calls, are now ominously silent. The little spotted kiwi is now extinct on mainland New Zealand and survives only on Kapiti Island. Other species are also at risk, partly because of the loss of their forest habitat, and extinction looms if effective action is not taken quickly.

The kiwi's main predators today are possums, stoats, ferrets and feral cats, which steal kiwi eggs and kill the young. Larger predators include pigs and dogs. In a single incident in 1987 a dog went on the rampage for six weeks in Waitangi State Forest; by the time the dog was found (and shot) it had killed as many as 500 to 1,000 kiwi.

The Kiwi Recovery Plan Started in 1991, the Kiwi Recovery Plan (www.kiwirecovery.org.nz) is a joint initiative by the Department of Conservation and the Royal Forest and Bird Protection Society, funded by the Bank of New Zealand. In an attempt to halt the kiwi's slide towards extinction, the project carries out research (surprisingly little is known about these birds, owing largely to their nocturnal habits), funds captive breeding programmes and transfers of endangered populations to predator-free offshore islands, and provides educational material to every school in New Zealand as well as to farmers, foresters—and dog owners. With luck, the unthinkable can be prevented and the kiwi saved.

KIWI FEATHER CLOAKS
According to Maori legend the kiwi is the oldest of Tanemahuta's bird family; as it was Tane who created most of the natural world, kiwi are in effect our elder siblings, and patrol the forest nightly to protect us. The *kahukiwi* (kiwi feather cloak) is donned as a symbol of high birth and chieftainship at important ceremonies relating to death, marriage and so on. The cloaks, which are nearly always named, are great *tohunga* (treasures), which carry the *wairua* (spirit) of the birds themselves. Nowadays *kahukiwi* are made only from feathers of kiwi that have died naturally or accidentally.

Central Otago and Fiordland

▶ Alexandra 222C3

Like so many other Otago towns, Alexandra was founded in the gold rush days; more recently it has prospered on the surrounding fruit orchards which were originally planted to feed the miners. This comfortable, conservative and little-visited town is attempting to put itself on the map with a series of events such as the annual Blossom Festival and the increasingly popular Easter Bunny Shoot. You can also visit wineries and the country's first freshwater crayfish farm; canoeing and other outdoor adventures are centred on the nearby Roxburgh Gorge.

▶▶▶ Arrowtown 222C3

Sheltered beneath the towering Crown Range, the historic settlement of Arrowtown is just 19km (12 miles) from Queenstown.

A Chinese miner's hut at the Chinese Settlement, reconstructed after excavation

The displays of the spacious and well-laid-out **Lakes District Museum**▶▶ (tel: 03 442 1824; www.museumqueenstown.com. *Open* daily 9–5. *Admission: inexpensive*) give a good impression of life during the pioneering and gold-rush days when Arrowtown was founded. The town has numerous historic buildings; among them are many picturesque gold-miners' cottages. A pamphlet on *Historic Arrowtown* (available from the information centre at the museum) details some 50 or so listed buildings, which must be a record for a township as small as this.

The **Chinese Settlement**▶▶ near Bush Creek is an evocative collection of rudimentary huts (reconstructed following an excavation in 1983) that speaks volumes about the hardships endured by the Chinese gold-seekers. In front of Ah Lum's store stands Ah Wak's lavatory—almost certainly the only one in New Zealand to sport a Historic Places plaque!

▶ Cromwell 222C3

A major fruit-growing area, Cromwell was redeveloped in the 1980s to house the workers on the nearby Clyde Dam, which was completed in 1989. The town lost some of its older streets to the flood waters but gained Lake Dunstan. The story of the dam, and of Cromwell's early days as a gold-mining town, is told in the well-presented displays at the **information centre and museum**▶▶ (tel: 03 445 0212; www.cromwell.org.nz. *Open* daily 10–4. *Admission: donation*) which is in the middle of the town, and closed to traffic.

Before the lake waters rose, many of Cromwell's historic buildings were salvaged, and a dozen or more have been reconstructed on the shores of Lake Dunstan as **Old Cromwell Town**▶▶ (*Admission: free*), where several craft-workers have taken up residence around the old buildings.

CHINESE MINERS
Arrowtown's boom years were relatively brief, lasting only from 1861 to 1865, when many gold-diggers left for richer fields in Westland. To bolster the goldfields' economy, Chinese miners were invited over from Australia, and within two years there were 1,200 Chinese in Otago. The Chinese made their living by sifting through the tailings, extracting the finer gold that others had left behind. The fascinating story of the Arrowtown community is told in *The Arrowtown Chinese Settlement*, available from the museum.

▶▶▶ Fiordland National Park 222B3

New Zealand's largest national park covers 12,000sq km (4,632sq miles) in the remote southwestern corner of the South Island. Fiordland is a rugged wilderness where dramatic coastal fiords allow the Tasman Sea to penetrate deep into the bush-clad hills and mountains. The majestic glacial lakes of **Te Anau▶▶▶** and **Manapouri▶▶** are the largest of scores of inland lakes.

The most accessible of the 14 fiords in the park is **Milford Sound▶▶▶**, which is surrounded by steep, forest-clad cliffs riven with waterfalls dropping vertically into the sound. Milford Sound has the highest average rainfall in the country, and it is after heavy rains that these falls are at their most spectacular. Rising sheer from the sea on the south side of the sound, dominating the inlet, is the 1,683m (5,522ft) pinnacle of Mitre Peak.

Milford Sound can be reached on foot, by road or by plane. The four-day **Milford Track▶▶▶** from Lake Te Anau is one of the most popular in the country and must be booked months in advance at peak times. The road route (119km/74 miles from Te Anau) is a spectacular drive. Flights operate from Te Anau and Queenstown, landing at tiny Milford Sound airstrip. From Milford launch cruises depart regularly for tours with commentary.

The next most frequently visited fiord is **Doubtful Sound▶▶▶** (see page 247). **Dusky Sound** and **Preservation Inlet** both require a five- to seven-day cruise.

(see page 247).

TOUR TIMES
Doubtful Sound tours depart from Manapouri wharf daily at 9:30AM for the 'Long Trip', which lasts eight hours. Connecting buses leave Te Anau at 8:45AM and Queenstown at 6:45AM (from Queenstown the tour makes a very long day, returning at around 7:30PM). You can also take a 'Short Trip', which cuts short the cruise down Doubtful Sound and just visits Hall Arm within the fiord. Contact Real Journeys, Lakefront, Te Anau (tel: 03 249 7416; www.realjourneys.co.nz); or Steamer Wharf, Queenstown (tel: 03 442 7500).

239

The magnificent glaciated landscape of Doubtful Sound in Fiordland National Park

Steamer Wharf Village on the edge of Lake Wakatipu

LAKE CRUISES
TSS *Earnslaw* departs
for up to six cruises
daily (every two hours
between 10AM and 8PM),
bookings through agen-
cies or Real Journeys,
tel: 03 442 7500;
www.realjourneys.co.nz.
For a bird's-eye view
76m (250ft) above the
surface, you can parafly
behind a boat, taking off
from a floating flight
deck so that you don't
get wet (Paraflights NZ,
tel: 03 409 0712;
www.parasail.co.nz).

▶▶▶ Queenstown   222C3

Queenstown is the South Island's liveliest adventure
resort, open all year round, with skiing in the nearby
Coronet Peak and Remarkables ranges in winter, and a
whole host of summer activities focusing on the mountains, lakes and rivers of Central Otago.

The first Maori settled here over 1,000 years ago, but
once the moa they hunted were gone, so too were the
Maori, who moved back to coastal encampments. Later
Maori passed through in search of greenstone in Westland, following the ancient 'greenstone route' from the
head of Lake Wakatipu across the Hollyford Valley to the
sea. When the explorer Nathaniel Chambers sighted the
lake from the heights of the Remarkables in 1853,
the area was deserted. In 1859, William Gilbert Rees
explored the lake and laid his claim to a run on its eastern
shores, thus deciding the future site of Queenstown.

During the 1860s, gold strikes in nearby Arrowtown
meant a huge influx of prospectors. Queenstown quickly
became a major supply depot for the miners, with sailing
boats and paddle-steamers plying the lake to bring in
supplies and to ship the gold out via Kingston, at the south
end of Lake Wakatipu. It was the biggest gold rush the
country had ever seen (one pair of prospectors, trying to
rescue their dog from the river, found 11kg (24 lb) of gold in
rock crevices in a single day), and the Shotover River
became known as the 'richest river in the world'.

By the turn of the 20th century the gold had started to
peter out, and a new influx of visitors started. The
paddle-steamers were put to good use ferrying sightseers around the lake, and buggy rides to Skippers
Canyon to see the miners at work were a popular attraction. A Scotsman, Donald Sutherland, built the first hotel
in Milford Sound, and people journeyed by boat and

overland to see the remarkable Sutherland Falls and the awe-inspiring fiord itself. Queenstown is still a big attraction, receiving just under half a million visitors annually.

At the heart of the town are traffic-free Mall and Church Street, running down to the lake's edge and parallel to Shotover Street, where you will find the visitor centre (tel: 03 442 4100; www.queenstown-vacation.com), DoC visitor centre (tel: 03 422 7934) and booking offices for many of the activity operators. At the end of Shotover Street is the modern Steamer Wharf Village, with chic boutiques, wine bars and restaurants.

Steamer Wharf is the departure point for lake trips aboard historic TSS *Earnslaw*, a vintage steamship that was built in Dunedin and then completely dismantled before being taken to Kingston by rail and reassembled. Launched in 1912, it is the last of the many steamships that once plied the lake, and still chugs across the waters at a rate of 13 knots, burning a tonne of coal every hour. Its destination is **Walter Peak Station**, founded in the 1860s, and one of the oldest sheep and cattle stations in the country, where sheep-shearing and other agricultural demonstrations are given before morning or afternoon tea in the old homestead.

For a view of what happens beneath the lake's waters, the **Underwater World Aquarium** on the main jetty (*Open daily 9–5:30. Admission: inexpensive*) has large viewing windows 5m (16ft) down, where rainbow and brown trout and long-finned eels come close to the glass to be fed, with the country's only diving duck, the scaup duck, popping down among them.

The **Skyline Gondola**▶▶▶ (tel: 03 441 0101; www.skyline.co.nz. *Open daily 10–10. Admission: moderate*) rides up 450m (1,475ft) from the base station at the end of Brecon Street to a viewing complex at the top, with a restaurant, café, viewing platform and the Skyline Showcase Theatre (tel: 03 442 7862), screening Kiwi Magic (www. kiwimagic.co.nz) on the hour 10–8. *Admission: moderate*. From here there are magnificent views of the town and the lake, set against a splendid backdrop of the Remarkables. The more energetic can walk up the track from Lomond Crescent, 1km (0.5 mile) west of the town.

TSS Earnslaw *(top) steams across to Walter Peak Station for sheep-shearing demonstrations (above)*

Also on Brecon Street is the **Motor Museum**▶ (*Open* daily 9–5:30. *Admission: moderate*), packed with marvellous machines and motoring memorabilia. Behind it, the **Kiwi and Birdlife Park**▶▶ has several aviaries with endangered species, waterfowl, a native bush area and a nocturnal kiwi house (tel: 03 442 8059; www.kiwibird.co. nz. *Open* daily, summer 9–late; winter 9–5. *Admission: moderate*).

One of the most peaceful areas on the lakeside is the **Queenstown Gardens**, founded in 1867 on a small promontory jutting out into the lake. At the entrance to the gardens, is **Williams Cottage** (tel: 03 442 2941; www.nzcountry. co.nz/williams), one of the town's last remaining early buildings, built between 1866 and 1867.

Eichardt's Tavern (Marine Parade, tel: 03 441 0450; www.eichardtshotel.co.nz), which has a long and vibrant history, is now a boutique hotel. The **Old Stone Library** on Ballarat Street dates back to the 1870s and has two giant sequoia trees outside.

Horse-riding amid the glorious scenery of Lake Wakatipu can be organized through the Queenstown Visitor Information Centre

Queenstown environs

There are a phenomenal number of adventure activities on offer in Queenstown, with fierce competition to provide yet more thrills and spills on the surrounding lakes, rivers and mountains. Many of these activities are suitable for everyone—whatever age, however unfit.

One of the most popular activities is **jet-boating**, with around ten operators offering a choice of different trips. The narrow chasms and shallow rapids on the lower reaches of the **Shotover River** provide an exciting ride, as does the **Kawarau River**—both within a short minibus ride of Queenstown.

But to experience the true potential of a jet-boat (see pages 210–211), consider a half-day safari across the top of Lake Wakatipu and up the broad expanses of the

The Shotover Jet powers up and down the river canyon north of Queenstown

BLACK SINGLET LITERATURE

As well as producing outstanding contemporary fiction by writers such as Keri Hulme, Patricia Grace, Alan Duff and Witi Ihimaera, New Zealand also has a tradition of honest, down-to-earth fiction about bush life, known as 'black singlet' literature. Its champion exponent was Barry Crump, whose entertaining tales started in 1960 with *A Good Keen Man*. Other black singlet writings are perhaps of more esoteric interest: *New Zealand Farm* and *Station Verse*, for instance, include poems with such alluring titles as 'Shorn Sheep', 'Wet Sheep' and 'Frozen Lamb'.

Take a tour down dramatic Skippers Canyon—and take turns to drive

Dart River▶▶—a longer trip but well worth it for the wilderness scenery of the Dart River Valley.

The Kawarau and Shotover rivers are equally popular for rafting. All trips involve a pre-departure briefing, full safety gear and the services of qualified guides; calm periods drifting down river are interspersed with the thrills of plunging over seething rapids. Other ways to get wet include kayaking, white-water sledging and river surfing.

Queenstown is the home of commercial bungee-jumping, and nearly all the bungee sites have observation platforms that give good vantage points for spectators. The original bungee jump is the 43m (141ft) drop from the **Kawarau Suspension Bridge** (tel: 03 442 1177; www.ajhackett.co.nz), 23km (14 miles) east of Queenstown along SH6. The most recent area to open up is Skippers Canyon (see below), where there is a spectacular 72m (236ft) drop from the Skippers Canyon Bridge above a narrow gorge, and an even more heart-stopping 102m (335ft) drop from the Pipeline Bungy (tel: 03 442 4007; www.ajhackett.co.nz) further downstream.

Alternative ways that you can take to the air above Queenstown include tandem hang-gliding, glider flying, helicopter sightseeing, paragliding, tandem parachuting and biplane rides.

The historic and fascinating **Skippers Canyon▶▶▶**, upstream on the Shotover River, was one of the main gold-rush areas in the 19th century. A levy on gold found here was used to build the tortuous road up through the canyon (it took eight years to complete). Bumpy and pot-holed, with sheer drops of 120m (394ft) to the river below in some places, this road is definitely not recommended as a self-drive route (indeed, signs at the entrance advise that rental-car insurance is invalid here).

Besides the dramatic scenery of the canyon there are many relics of gold-mining days and, at the head of the canyon, the remains of the old Skippers township, with a restored schoolhouse, homestead and other dwellings. Options on these safaris include jet-boat or helicopter rides or even mountain-biking down the canyon to base.

In winter, skiing is the activity, with **Coronet Peak** (tel: 03 442 4620; www.nzski.com/coronet) considered one of the country's premier ski areas. Regular shuttle buses make the 18km (11-mile) journey from the middle of town, and a series of chair-lifts and T-bars rise from the base station to the top of the runs at 1,585m and 1,620m (5,200 and 5,315ft). There is good skiing here for all levels, with snow-making equipment ensuring a long season (from mid-June to October).

It is a bizarre concept, jumping from a great height with nothing but a huge elastic band tied to your ankles. Welcome to the world of bungee-jumping (spelled bungy in New Zealand), a typically Kiwi phenomenon.

Polynesian origins Bungee-jumping is not a new sport: for many centuries leaping from a tall tower has formed part of the initiation ceremonies to manhood in Vanuatu. Young men traditionally plunge headlong from rickety bamboo structures, only to be pulled up short—just above the ground—by the stout vines attached firmly to their feet.

Inspired by this example, New Zealander A. J. Hackett set out to devise a safe, controlled method of jumping using the same principles. Experimenting with latex rubber and a parachute harness, he and his companions started leaping off New Zealand's bridges, including the Auckland Harbour Bridge. In 1987 Hackett captured the world's attention by jumping off the Eiffel Tower, and went on to set up a bungee empire with outposts in many parts of the globe. In 1998 he set a new world record by jumping off Auckland's Sky Tower.

The home of bungee Hackett opened the world's first professional bungee-jump operation in 1988 on the Kawarau Bridge, 43m (141ft) above the Kawarau River just east of Queenstown. And since then bungee-jumping has become an export to many countries.

Who can do it? All it takes is willpower. The oldest bungee-jumper so far was a 90-year-old in Normandy. Anyone from the age of 10 upwards is eligible (though children aged between 10 and 16 require parental supervision), and anyone over 60 years old pays a reduced price. At one stage, Hackett offered free jumps to anyone who went nude: demand was so great that the offer had to be discontinued.

Way to go—but don't forget to empty your pockets

You may need a Kiwi-style Swanndri bush shirt to keep warm on the lake!

Tour

Doubtful Sound

This boat and bus tour (see panel page 239) encompasses not only Doubtful Sound but also the island-studded waters of Lake Manapouri, the impressive Manapouri Power Station and the rain forests of Wilmot Pass. The all-day trip departs from Queenstown, Te Anau or Manapouri.

From Manapouri wharf the first boat ride takes you out of the Pearl Harbour Inlet and past Stoney Point Light onto the broad expanses of **Lake Manapouri►►**. Passing the lake islands, you get a fine view of the Hunter Mountains rising up to 1,768m (5,800ft) on the south bank, with the impressive peaks of the Kepler Range on the north shore. Half-way across, the boat skirts Pomona Island, the largest on the lake; the waters beneath the hull are at their deepest here (444m/1,456ft).

Disembarking at the wharf at the end of West Arm, you transfer to a bus for the tour of the **Manapouri Power Station►►**. Even for people who are not technically minded, this visit can be of great interest: above ground, only the transmission lines and a control centre are visible, but once you have descended the 2km (1.25-mile) spiral access tunnel the full extent of this engineering achievement becomes apparent. The machine hall and its seven humming turbine generators are a testament both to the dedication of the builders and to the power of the water, which flows through at a constant rate to generate around ten per cent of the country's electricity requirements.

Emerging into daylight once more, you continue over the **Wilmot Pass Road▶**. Constructed to provide access for heavy equipment to the power station, this 23km (14-mile)-long road took two and a half years to build and was at the time the most expensive road ever to be built in New Zealand. Today it serves as the only land access to Doubtful Sound, traversing a range of forest types with several spectacular waterfalls en route; there is a brief stop to admire the **Moss Gardens**, where some of the 500 varieties of moss and lichen found in Fiordland can be appreciated at close range.

The tour continues down one of the country's steepest roads (with a gradient of 1 in 5) to arrive at Deep Cove, where the tailrace, a 10km (6-mile) tunnel through the heart of the mountains, emerges from the power station. Here, you embark on a catamaran for the trip down the magnificent **Doubtful Sound▶▶**.

Captain James Cook sighted the entrance to Doubtful Sound in 1770, but refused to enter it as he believed that he would only get out again with a (rare) east wind. It was left to a Spanish scientific expedition, led by Alessandro Malaspina, to explore the inlet fully in 1793. During the early 19th century the area was a popular haunt of sealers and whalers, but once these animals had been depleted (which happened within the space of 20 years), Doubtful Sound was left in peace for a hundred years or more.

As you cruise down this superb fiord, various features become apparent: hanging valleys—the remnants of tributary glaciers—are one of the most obvious, and numerous waterfalls tumble down the sheer rock faces, with rainbows often adding to the enchantment of the magical scenery. The boat noses in close enough for passengers to capture a cup of pure drinking water from the mountain-fed falls, and to appreciate the extraordinarily tenacious hold of the moss, plants and trees that intertwine their roots on the sheer rock surfaces.

At Malaspina Reach, in the first section of the Sound, a resident pod of bottlenose dolphins often plays on the bow wave; beyond, where the turbulent Tasman Sea rolls in towards the coast, fur seals—returning after a long absence—bask on the rocks. At Shelter Island, near the mouth of the Sound, the rare Fiordland crested penguin can be seen at close quarters in the summer months.

247

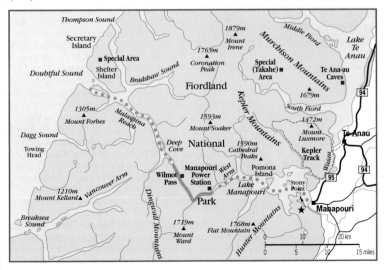

▶▶ Te Anau

Spreading across the eastern shoreline of Lake Te Anau, the township of Te Anau is the main departure point for tours into the wilds of Fiordland: The dense rain forests that mark the boundary of New Zealand's largest national park cloak the western shores of the lake, rising up into the dramatic mountains beyond.

Although for most people Te Anau is just a transit stop, there are a number of activities locally, should you have a day or half-day to spare. Top of the list of priorities should be a tour of the remarkable **Te Ana-au Glowworm Caves**▶▶▶ at the base of the Murchison Mountains, reached by boat across the lake (tours take two and a half hours and depart up to five times daily, depending on the season; tel: 03 249 7416. *Admission: moderate*).

A floatplane on the shores of Lake Te Anau

The caves are relatively young on the geological timescale, dating back a mere 15,000 years, and for this reason they lack the delicate limestone stalactites and stalagmites found in other cave systems. Instead they are a fine example of a 'living cave', where the stream that originally formed them (in this case the Tunnel Burn) is still actively eroding the rock, cascading through and chiselling away at a rate of around 1cu m (35cu ft) every 100 years.

The caves appeared in Maori legends as Te-Ana-hina-tore ('the cave of phosphorescence') and, later, as Te Ana-au ('the cave of rushing waters'), but they remained unknown to Europeans until rediscovered by local explorer Lawson Burrows in 1948.

Tranquil Lake Wanaka, backed by the peaks of Mount Aspiring National Park

Once inside the caves, walkways and two short boat journeys along the Tunnel Burn take you past whirlpools and underground waterfalls to the inner depths, where there is an enchanting glow-worm grotto, with the glow-worms' sticky threads twinkling in the silent darkness of the ledges and ceilings above.

There are several ways of exploring **Lake Te Anau** (the country's second largest, after Lake Taupo): by kayak, on a beautiful old handcrafted gaff ketch (the little ship *Manuska*) or by floatplane from the wharf. There are also lakeside walks (ranging from 15 minutes to eight hours).

The DoC visitor centre (tel: 03 249 7921. *Open* daily 8–6) on the southern edge of Te Anau has information on local walks and long-distance tracks (including the Milford and the Kepler); it also screens an audiovisual show (on the hour and half-hour. *Admission: inexpensive*) describing the formation of Fiordland and the flora and fauna of the area. On the first floor is a small museum (*Admission: free*) with displays on early mining and whaling along the coast, including a cannon from New Zealand's first-ever shipwreck, the *Endeavour*, which ran aground in 1795.

Continue past the DoC centre and you will come to the **Te Anau Wildlife Centre▶** (tel: 03 249 7921. *Open* daily 24 hours. *Admission: free*), one of the very few places in New Zealand where you can see the rare takahe (see panel page 250). Other enclosures house red deer, parrots, parakeets, morepork and lizards.

▶▶▶ Wanaka   222C3

A peaceful township surrounded by mountains, Wanaka is tucked into the southern end of Lake Wanaka. It could be an embryonic Queenstown, but locals are keen to emphasize the differences: it is unspoiled, uncommercialized and not overcrowded, and there is no pressure to do anything more strenuous here than put your feet up and enjoy a good book for a few days. This relaxed, pleasant resort remains very Kiwi in character: The majority of visitors are summer campers who come to swim, fish and boat on the lake or walk in nearby **Mount Aspiring**

WINGS OVER WANAKA
Wanaka Airport has developed into something of a focal point for aviation buffs, with the Fighter Pilots Museum now organizing the biennial 'Warbirds Over Wanaka' show with dozens of vintage, veteran and classic aircraft taking to the skies. At any time you can go flying in a number of unusual or old aircraft, such as a de Havilland Dominie biplane, an open-cockpit Tiger Moth biplane or a Pitts Special stunt plane (loop the loop, barrel rolls and inverted flight obligatory). Contact Bi-plane Adventures (tel: 03 443 1000).

AN UNUSUAL ISLAND
Lake Wanaka has the unusual attribute of an island—Mou Waho—with a lake in the middle of it—or, as they put it here, a lake in the middle of an island in the middle of a lake in the middle of an island. The largest of the Wanaka islands, Mou Waho is 16km (10 miles) from the town. The spectacular Arethusa Pool lies in a rock cradle within walking distance of the landing point.

THE TAKAHE
Once thought to be extinct, the takahe (*Notornis mantelli*) was rediscovered in the Murchison Mountains in 1948 by a local doctor, Geoffrey Orbell; it had not been sighted since the previous century, and even then only rarely. Following this discovery, a huge tract covering 530sq km (207 sq miles) of the mountains was declared a 'Special Area' to protect this flightless bird, about the size of a chicken, which lives for most of the year on alpine tussock grasslands. Currently there are only 120 takahe still in the wild, and ways are now being sought to prevent them from becoming extinct—including removing their eggs for artificial rearing.

The brilliantly hued takahe (right); helicopter charter is an exciting transport option (opposite)

National Park, whose headquarters is here. In the winter, skiers head for the renowned **Cardrona** (tel: 03 443 7411; www.cardrona.com) and **Treble Cone** (tel: 03 443 7443; www.treblecone.co.nz) ski fields.

The lake is fringed by a broad, grassy park lined with poplars and willows, with barbecue areas beside the beach. Good walks in the area include the popular **Diamond Lake–Rocky Mountain walking track**, which takes about two and a half hours and is considered one of the South Island's most stunning half-day walks.

Lake Wanaka is the country's fourth-largest lake, and the numerous ways of exploring it include trips on the country's only commercial hovercraft, or by kayak, jet-boat, catamaran or powerboat.

On the edge of Wanaka, **Puzzling World**▶ ▶ (tel: 03 443 7489; www.puzzlingworld.co.nz. *Open* daily, summer 8:30–6; winter 8:30–5. *Admission: inexpensive*) was the originator of the 'maze craze', which saw many imitators all over New Zealand. As well as the 1.5km (1-mile)-long, three-dimensional maze, it also has a hologram gallery and a 'Tilted House' that is truly disorientating.

The **NZ Fighter Pilots Museum** (tel: 03 443 7010; www.nzfpm.co.nz. *Open* daily 9:30–4. *Admission: moderate*) at Wanaka airfield has famous planes from both world wars, as well as a re-created briefing room (complete with authentic film footage) and displays on the country's fighter aces.

Travel Facts

Arriving and departing

By air

The majority of overseas visitors to New Zealand arrive at **Auckland International Airport** (www.auckland-airport.co.nz), which handles more than 20 international airlines. The national airline, Air New Zealand, has an enviable reputation worldwide and flies direct from Los Angeles, Honolulu, Japan, Hong Kong, Singapore, Taipei, Australia, Pacific Island, Taiwan and South Korea.

Christchurch (www.christchurch-airport.co.nz) has direct flights from Singapore, Tokyo, Brisbane, Sydney, Melbourne and Hobart. Because of restricted runway length, the only direct flights to **Wellington** (www.wellington-airport.co.nz) are from Australia, Fiji and some Pacific islands.

If you are flying from the USA or Europe, the flight times are long: 23 hours from London, 19 hours from New York and 12 hours from Los Angeles, the main US gateways. From Europe, it makes sense to break your journey along the way, either in Southeast Asia or in the Pacific. Airlines sometimes have enticing stopovers, including at Fiji, the Cook Islands, Tonga, Samoa and Hawaii.

Auckland Airport (AKL) has separate terminals for international, Qantas domestic and Air New Zealand domestic flights, with a shuttle bus operating between the three. Banking and exchange facilities are available for all international arrivals and departures. There are direct-line (free) telephones in the welcoming halls at all terminals for making hotel or motel reservations, and information offices in each terminal can help with reservations for accommodation, onward travel arrangements and other services. Luggage storage facilities are available. All terminals have elevators or escalators, and toilet facilities for visitors with disabilities.

The airport is 23km (14 miles) from downtown Auckland, with a taxi fare of around NZ$40 one way. The Airbus (www.airbus.co.nz) does a circuit of the middle of the city every 20–30 minutes. Door-to-door shared-ride shuttle services cost NZ$15–20 to downtown.

Both Wellington and Christchurch airports have similar facilities, including currency exchange and information desks. Wellington airport is 8km (5 miles) from downtown, with a taxi fare of around NZ$15–25, a shuttle bus fare of NZ$10–12 or a regular bus costing NZ$4.50. Christchurch airport is 10km (6 miles) from the city, with a taxi fare of around NZ$25–30 and a shuttle bus fare of NZ$12–18 or a regular bus costing NZ$4.

Customs Arriving passengers are entitled to bring in 200 cigarettes, 200g of tobacco or 50 cigars, or a mixture of all three weighing not more than 250g. Alcohol allowances are 4.5 litres of wine (equivalent to six 750ml bottles), and one 1,125ml bottle of spirits or liqueur. Apart from personal effects, goods up to a total of NZ$700 in value may be imported free of tax.

Note that New Zealand airports all have duty-free arrivals shops, so you can buy your duty-free goods on arrival or at your departure point.

There are restrictions on the import

of animal and plant materials (including foodstuffs), designed to protect the country from animal and plant diseases. You will be asked to fill out a declaration form on arrival stating whether your baggage contains any plant or animal materials.

You will be asked to declare on arrival if you have visited a farm recently and footwear is inspected for mud.

The import of wildlife souvenirs sourced from rare or endangered species may be either illegal or require a special permit. Before purchase you should check your home country's customs regulations.

There are no exchange controls or restrictions on the import or export of currency. Hunting rifles may be imported, although you will need to obtain a firearms permit on arrival. The import of narcotics is prohibited.

Vaccinations No certificates are required.

Visas Many nationals can enter New Zealand for up to six months without requiring a visa. You will need to be in possession of a passport valid for at least three months beyond the date when you intend to leave the country, a fully paid onward or return ticket and sufficient funds to support yourself during your stay.

Visas are required if you intend to work, study or seek medical treatment, or if you are being sponsored by a friend, relative or business organization during your stay.

Visa requirements are subject to change, so you should check with your home embassy before visiting.

Insurance Comprehensive travel insurance is recommended. If you are planning to take part in any adventure sports make sure that you are covered in case of accidents.

Departing There is an airport departure charge of NZ$20–25 payable on all international flights.

253

The waterfront buildings and skyline of Aukland viewed from the slopes of Devonport's Mount Victoria

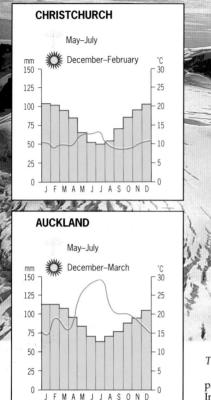

CHRISTCHURCH

May–July

December–February

mm		°C
150		30
125		25
100		20
75		15
50		10
25		5
0	J F M A M J J A S O N D	0

AUCKLAND

May–July

December–March

mm		°C
150		30
125		25
100		20
75		15
50		10
25		5
0	J F M A M J J A S O N D	0

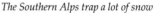

The Southern Alps trap a lot of snow

Essential facts

Climate and when to go

The seasons in New Zealand are the reverse of those in the northern hemisphere, with spring from September to November, summer from December to February/March, autumn from March to May, and winter from June to August.

Being nearer to the equator, the North Island has the warmer climate, often described as 'Mediterranean', with short, mild winters and long, warm summers. Northland ('the winterless north') and the Bay of Islands experience some of the highest summer temperatures in the North Island, with Auckland not far behind. The climate in the South Island is more variable, with the coldest winters and hottest summers usually being found in Central Otago.

New Zealand lies across the 'Roaring Forties' latitudes, and prevailing winds are from the west. In general, the western areas get higher rainfall and, conversely, many eastern areas can have drought conditions in the summer months; the most extensive vineyards and sheep stations are on the eastern sides of the islands.

In the South Island, the Southern Alps act as a natural barrier to the westerly winds, causing high rainfall on the west coast. The variation in rainfall either side of this north–south mountainous spine is extreme, with annual averages of 600cm (236in) on the west coast, compared to just over 28cm (11in) in Central Otago.

In the North Island, east–west variations are less marked, with the annual average rainfall of 130cm (51in) being fairly evenly spread across the island. Snow falls on the peaks of Egmont and Tongariro National parks in the winter months, but it is not nearly as reliable as the snowfalls in the Southern Alps, so if you are planning to ski in winter, head for the South Island.

closed on public holidays, but an increasing numbers of shops are open. Museums and visitor attractions are open on nearly all holidays except Christmas Day and Boxing Day (26 December).

- New Year Holiday
  1 and 2 January
- Waitangi Day
  6 February
- Easter
  March/April
- Anzac Day
  25 April
- Queen's Birthday
  First Monday in June
- Labour Day
  Fourth Monday in October
- Christmas
  25 and 26 December

255

Time differences
With the International Date Line just 300km (186 miles) east of the Chatham Islands, New Zealand is one of the first countries to witness the start of the new day. Local time is 12 hours ahead of Greenwich Mean Time (GMT), 2–4 hours ahead of Australia, 17–22 hours ahead of the USA, 15–20 hours ahead of Canada and 4 hours ahead of Hong Kong. New Zealand Daylight Saving Time (summer time) runs from 2AM on the first Sunday in October to 2AM on the third Sunday in March: clocks are set an hour forward.

Money matters
The New Zealand dollar (NZ$) is divided into 100 cents, with notes in denominations of $5, $10, $20, $50 and $100, and coins of 5c, 10c, 20c, 50c, $1 and $2.

There are no restrictions on the import or export of foreign currency in any form. Travellers' cheques can be changed at bureaux de change, banks and hotels and in major stores in resorts and large cities. All international credit cards (American Express, Diners' Club, JCB, Visa and MasterCard) are generally accepted. Cash points (ATMs) are widely available and can be used to obtain cash. EFTPOS (Electronic Funds Transfer at Point of Sale) is also common.

The annual sunshine hours are higher in central North Island (2,100) than in upper or lower North Island (1,900), and in upper South Island (2,400), averaging 1,700 elsewhere. Because of New Zealand's unpolluted atmosphere, ultraviolet radiation is high, and care must be taken to avoid sunburn (see page 263).

Holidays
New Zealanders are great travellers (both at home and abroad), and many families visit resorts or explore the countryside during school holidays. Pre-booking of accommodation during these periods is almost essential in the more popular resort areas, unless you are prepared to take pot luck or continue to somewhere less crowded. The worst period is during the summer holidays from mid-December to the end of January, which coincides with the peak tourist season. Other school holidays are in May, July and August. Accommodation can be quite difficult to find in resort areas on national holidays.

Most businesses (apart from those related to tourism) and all banks are

Getting around

Driving
New Zealand is ideally suited to exploring by car, with a good but winding road network giving safe, easy, but not very fast, driving. Driving is on the left and the wearing of seat-belts is compulsory. Speed limits are generally 100kph (62mph) on the open road and motorways (expressways), 50kph (31mph) in urban areas, but other limits may be indicated.

Most rural roads are well maintained, although sometimes narrow—often narrowing further on the approach to river bridges, many of which are one-lane (with signs indicating priorities). Many back-country roads are unsealed (metalled gravel), and a section of SH12 through Waipoua Kauri Forest was finally sealed over only in 1995, with considerable ingenuity being employed to avoid damaging the roots of the mighty kauri trees.

Unsealed roads have their own particular hazards (including large grading machines that seem to lurk around corners), and require care. Restrictions may apply to some unsealed roads if you are renting a car.

Driving documents
Drivers must have a current UK, USA, international or other approved over-seas licence, which must be carried at all times when driving. No further documentation is necessary.

Car rental
There are numerous car-rental companies operating in major cities and resorts, with competition ensuring rental rates are reasonable, particularly for long-term rent (one month or more). You must be over 21

256

Driving in New Zealand is easy, even in a campervan—but the roads can be winding

years of age to rent a car or campervan, and some companies insist on a minimum age of 25 unless the rental fee is pre-paid from overseas. Insurance is not compulsory, and is usually quoted separately on top of the rental cost.

Campervans are popular in New Zealand and represent an economical and flexible means of exploring the country. With a campervan you are by no means limited to campsites, although there are many excellent campsites for overnight stops.

All the major agencies are represented in New Zealand, and cars can also be booked through their offices overseas. Maui Tours are the biggest agency for campervans.

Many companies do not allow rental cars to travel between the North and South Islands, so turn your car in before crossing on the ferry, and pick up another car at the depot on the other side. The rental companies will organize this, but you will have to carry all your luggage across with you. Most companies can also arrange one-way rentals if, for instance, you wanted to drive from Auckland southwards and then return by plane from Christchurch.

Car rental from the major firms costs from around NZ$90 per day. Some of the best deals are available through smaller independents such as Ace Tourist Rentals, Trusty Rental and Pegasus Rentals: a small four-door vehicle can be rented for as little as NZ$35 per day, with some firms offering even lower prices for rental periods of over one month. These prices are inclusive of Goods and Services Tax (GST), insurance and unlimited mileage and represent a real bargain.

Standard campervans cost from NZ$144 per day for a two-person van, rising to around NZ$230 per day for a four- to six-person van in high season. Again, there are bargains to be had with the smaller companies; it is possible to rent a two-berth van from NZ$70 per day (low season) to NZ$99 (high season), inclusive of unlimited mileage, GST and insurance.

Ace Tourist Rentals, 39–43 The Strand, Parnell, Auckland freephone: 0800 502 277; www.acerentals.co.nz
Avis, 666 Great South Road, Penrose, Auckland tel: 0800 655 111; fax: 09 525 0309; www.avis.com
Budget, 83 Beach Road, Auckland freephone: 0800 652 227; www.budget.co.nz
Hertz, 154 Victoria Street West, Auckland tel: 0800 654 321; www.hertz.com
Maui, Richard Pearse Drive, Mangere, Auckland tel: 09 275 3013; freephone: 0800 651 080; fax: 09 275 9690; www.maui-rentals.com
Pegasus Rentals, 38 Customs Street East, Auckland tel: 09 358 5757; fax: 09 373 5727; www.rentalcars.co.nz
Trusty Car Rentals, 205 Lichfield Street, Christchurch tel: 03 366 6329; www.rentalvehicles.co.nz

257

Car breakdowns
Most rental companies include a free breakdown service as part of the package. Automobile Association members in the UK receive free reciprocal membership of the New Zealand AA, including breakdown assistance, the provision of maps, touring advice and accommodation guides. Further details from the New Zealand Automobile Association, PO Box 5, Auckland, tel: 0800 500 222; fax: 09 309 4563; www.nzaa.co.nz.

On two wheels
A good way of exploring New Zealand is by bicycle. Operators include Natural High Adrenalin Dealers, who provide 4 to 12-day tours of the South Island: If you get tired there's a support vehicle right behind (tel: 03 546 6936; www.cyclenewzealand. com). The Cycle Touring Company has tours of Northland for all levels of fitness (tel: 09 430 2030; www.cycletours.co.nz).

Public transport

Air travel

The domestic airlines are Air New Zealand (tel: 0800 737 000; www.airnz.com) and Qantas (tel: 0800 808 767; www.qantas.co.nz), with an extensive network of reasonably economical scheduled services to and from most domestic destinations. The services of Air New Zealand National and Air New Zealand Link (Eagle Airways, Air Nelson and Mount Cook Airline) are grouped together into one reservation system offering more than 670 flights a day to some 26 domestic destinations.

Origin Pacific (tel: 0800 302 302; www.originpacific.co.nz), an independent airline based in Nelson, operates a less frequent but budget-priced service between most main hubs, using smaller and slower aircraft than Air New Zealand or Qantas. There are also smaller commuter services, and light planes and helicopters can be chartered.

Airpasses and discounts

Alongside the standard Business Class and Economy fares, Air New Zealand has various discounted fares, most of which involve booking restrictions.

Coach tours can be a good way of getting to places such as Aoraki/Mount Cook

Overseas visitors can take advantage of the G'Day Airpass (also valid in Australia), which must be bought outside New Zealand and then used on a coupon basis once in the country (one flight sector per coupon, with prices starting from approximately NZ$700 for two coupons). Qantas also has similar passes.

Coach travel

All New Zealand's towns, cities and resorts are connected by an extensive coach (bus) network, which provides a comfortable and economical means of getting around the country. The main operators are InterCity (tel: 09 913 6100; www.intercitycoach.co.nz) and Newmans (tel: 09 913 6200; www.newmanscoach.co.nz), together providing a co-ordinated national network. For most destinations there are several daily departures and, except during holiday periods, it is not usually necessary to book your seat more than a couple of days ahead.

All the operators have various discounts or coach passes, which makes this an even more economical way to travel. The 3-in-1 Travelpass (tel: 0800 33 99 66; www.travelpass.

co.nz), for instance, allows unlimited travel throughout the country by coach, one trip by ferry and two trips by rail for eight days of travel at a cost of around NZ$612, 15 days of travel for NZ$808 and 22 days for NZ$941, all for travel within a six-month period. A 4-in-1 Pass also includes one air sector. Passes can be bought either overseas or when you arrive in the country, and may be cheaper out of season.

InterCity and Newmans have a different system, with a three-month, one-way Auckland–Wellington (or vice versa) pass for NZ$147, or Christchurch–Milford Sound for NZ$179.

Other discounts available include membership of YHA New Zealand (tel: 03 379 9970; www.yha.co.nz), which costs NZ$35 for one year and has a 15 per cent discount on InterCity and Newmans, and 20 per cent on Tranz Scenic.

Inter-island ferries
The North and South islands are linked by Interislander ferries (tel: 0800 802 802; www.interislandline. co.nz) between Wellington and Picton, with up to five departures in each direction daily. The two conventional ferries, *Arahura* and *Aratere*, take 3 hours. The *Lynx* high-speed catamaran makes the crossing in 2 hours 15 minutes. Bluebridge's Santa Regina (tel: 0800 844 844; www.bluebridge.co.nz) has a cheaper service twice a day, taking 20 minutes longer. Foot passengers should make reservations for ferry services at peak times, and car drivers should also pre-book in peak periods (December to February and other school holidays, see page 255).

Rail travel
Trains are another great way to see the countryside, and there are five main routes operated daily by Tranz Scenic (tel: 0800 TRAINS; www.tranzscenic.co.nz).

In the North Island the main services are between Auckland and

Wellington (The Overlander daytime service and The Northerner night-time service); and Auckland–Rotorua (The Geyserland Connection, by coach from Hamilton).

In the South Island, The TranzCoastal runs between Christchurch and Picton, connecting with ferries to and from Wellington.

In addition, there is the famous TranzAlpine express across the Southern Alps from Christchurch to Greymouth, which has fantastic views of the Southern Alps (see panel page 180). The TranzAlpine leaves Christchurch each morning, arrives in Greymouth early in the afternoon, and returns to Christchurch the same day.

Discount fares are available within the country, and there are also the 3-in-1 and 4-in-1 Travelpasses (see above) that include rail as well as coach travel.

259

Internal transport ranges from helicopters to old lake steamers, such as TSS Earnslaw *on Lake Wakatipu*

Communication

The media

There is no national daily newspaper in New Zealand. The largest circulation dailies are the *New Zealand Herald* (www.nzherald.co.nz—published in Auckland), followed by the *Dominion Post* (published in Wellington) and *The Press* (published in Christchurch—both www.stuff.co.nz). There are also numerous local newspapers and two Sunday newspapers.

Magazines worth looking for include *North and South* (monthly, with an emphasis on current affairs) and *Metro* (also monthly, covering mainly issues relating to Auckland).

New Zealand has four main national free-to-air television channels, all of which carry commercials: TV One (www.tvone.nzoom.com—news, sport and current affairs) and TV2 (www.tv2.nzoom. com—mainly drama and light entertainment) are both government-owned, while TV3 (www.tv3.co.nz) and TV4 (www.tv4.co.nz) combine elements of both and are privately owned. Sky TV (www.sky.co.nz—with channels devoted to 24-hour news, sport and films) is available in hotels and motels.

New Zealand's hilly terrain means that many radio stations have a fairly limited broadcasting range and this, combined with deregulation, has led to a proliferation of radio stations. Government-owned radio stations include the AM National Radio (news, drama, light entertainment and talk programmes) and Concert FM (classical music—both www. radio.co.nz). In addition, there are several Maori stations, Pacific Islands Radio and non-profit-making religious broadcasters.

Tourist FM Radio broadcasts 24 hours a day in English (88.2MHz), Japanese (100.8MHz) and German (100.4MHz).

Post offices

Towns and cities have Post Shops (www.nzpost.com. *Open* Mon–Fri 9–5, some Sat mornings), which sell stationery, postcards and other items as well as stamps. Stamps can also be purchased in other outlets such as bookshops and supermarkets. The two different types of domestic mail delivery are Standard Post (next-day delivery within town and 2–3 day delivery nationwide) and Fast Post (next-day delivery between towns and cities within New Zealand). Postcards cost NZ$1.50 to anywhere in the world (do not forget to add an Air Mail sticker).

Telephone and fax

The majority of the 4,000 Telecom public telephones in New Zealand operate on pre-paid phonecards. These cards (available in denominations of NZ$5, NZ$10, NZ$20 and NZ$50) can be bought at numerous outlets including information offices, hotels, newsagents, supermarkets and filling stations. Coin phones accept 10c, 20c, 50c, NZ$1 and NZ$2 coins.

Call charges are a flat 50c for local calls (although these are free from residential phones), and you can find out how much a call is going to cost simply by dialling the number you want without inserting the phonecard: the digital display will then tell you the cost per minute or part minute. Another option is the call-back service. Dial 013 instead of the initial 0 when making a call and an operator will ring back after you have finished to tell you how much the call has cost: The service adds an extra NZ$2.80 to the cost of the call but is useful if you need to pay a third party.

❏ **Useful telephone numbers**
National operator 010
International operator 0170
Directory Enquiries 018
International Directory
 Enquiries 0172
Telecom Help Desk 123
International access code 00
International dialling code for
 New Zealand 64

International dialling codes
Australia 61
Canada 1
Germany 49
UK 44
USA 1 ❏

There are also credit card phones (indicated by a yellow phone symbol) that accept major international credit cards.

Numbers beginning with 0508 and 0800 are toll-free numbers, so no payment is needed. Numbers starting with 02 are cellphones. Call charges to and from cellphones are generally more expensive.

Language guide

The Maori language has lent many words and phrases to New Zealand English, including the greeting *kia ora*, which means 'your good health'; it is answered with the same words. Special projects for language immersion have been started in some schools to try to halt the decline in usage of Maori, and 1995 was designated Maori Language Year.

The most obvious manifestation of Maori for visitors is in place-names, a large number of which are of Maori origin. Related to the Treaty of Waitangi settlement process, some landmarks are regaining Maori names in addition to *pakeha* ones. Examples include Aoraki/Mount Cook, Mount Taranaki or Mount Egmont and Matiu Somes Island in Wellington harbour. Many names derive from real or mythical stories in Maori history, for instance Taumatawhakatangihanga-koauauotamateapokaiwhenuaki-tanatahu, which is in Hawke Bay and records 'the place where Tamatea played his flute to his loved one'. Other place-names refer to geographical features and may include some of these commonly used words. See table below.

261

ara	path	*moana*	sea	*roto*	lake
ao	cloud	*o*	the place of	*tomo*	cave
awa	river	*puna*	spring	*wai*	water
ma (manga)	stream	*puke*	hill	*whanga*	bay
maunga	mountain	*rangi*	sky		

New Zealand English also tends to have its own idiosyncratic expressions or phrases. Some of those that may leave you puzzled include:

bach	a holiday chalet in the North Island (pronounced 'batch')	good as gold	fine, OK
bludge	scrounge, borrow	handle	beer glass with a handle
bush	the forest	jandals	flip-flops/thongs
chook	chicken	judder bars	speed bumps in the road
cocky	farmer (usually 'cow-cocky')	morning tea	mid-morning tea or coffee break
chilly-bin	portable cooler box	mozzie	mosquito
crib	the South Island equivalent of a bach	pakeha	person of European descent
crook	sick, ill	pom	an English person (mildly derogatory)
dag	an eccentric character or entertaining person	smoko	tea or coffee break
dairy	corner shop/ convenience store; it usually sells a wide range of goods	togs	swimwear
		tramping	trekking/hiking
gidday	good day, hello	wopwops	the back of beyond

Emergencies

Crime

There is a perception within New Zealand itself that crime is getting worse. But published statistics indicate that, in most categories, the crime rate peaked in the early 1990s, and has been decreasing ever since. This increase during the 1980s and 1990s may have been related to the social upheaval following economic restructuring. The lower crime rate in the last 10 to 15 years appears to reflect better economic times and lower unemployment.

New Zealand has a low crime rate by international standards, and statistically you are unlikely to be the victim of a serious crime while on holiday.

However, there is one area in which there has been a marked increase in

Despite the low crime rate, thefts from vehicles parked at beauty spots is a growing problem

crimes against visitors, and that is in the theft of valuables from cars. It is highly likely that at some point you will leave your car parked in some remote spot to go for a walk or climb up to a viewpoint. Be warned that thefts from cars parked near beauty spots or similar places are common. Take your cameras, camcorders or other valuables with you.

As in any overseas country, take common-sense precautions such as locking large amounts of money in the hotel safe, keeping a close eye on your bag or camera in crowded areas and avoiding badly lit urban areas at night. Women should not hitch-hike alone.

Embassies and consulates
Wellington
Australian High Commission, 72–78 Hobson Street, tel: 04 473 6411; www.australia.org.nz.
British High Commission, 44 Hill Street, tel: 04 924 2888; www.britain.org.nz.
Canadian High Commission, 61 Molesworth Street, tel: 04 473 9577; www.dfait-maeci.gc.ca/newzealand.
German Embassy, 90–92 Hobson Street, tel: 04 473 6063; www.deutschebotschaftwellington.co.nz.
United States Embassy, 29 Fitzherbert Terrace, tel: 04 472 2068; www.usembassy.org.nz.
Auckland
Australian Consulate-General, PricewaterhouseCoopers Tower, 186–194 Quay Street, tel: 09 921 8800.
British Consulate-General, Fay Richwhite Building, 151 Queen Street, tel: 09 303 2973.
Canadian Consulate, 9th Floor, 48 Emily Place, tel: 09 307 8516.
German Consulate, 52 Symonds Street, tel: 09 913 3674.
United States Consulate-General, Level 3, Citibank Building, 23 Customs Street East, tel: 09 303 2724.

Emergency services
Dial 111 for police, fire or ambulance.

Lost property
Lost property should be reported to the police; lost or stolen travellers' cheques or credit cards should be reported to the issuing company.

Health
New Zealand is a clean, healthy place and no unusual precautions are required while holidaying here. Tap water is safe to drink everywhere; city water supplies are chlorinated and most are also fluoridated. In some back-country rivers and lakes the parasite giardia is present, so if camping in remote areas make sure water is boiled or otherwise treated before drinking it.

The most serious potential health risk in New Zealand is from the sun. Ultraviolet radiation is particularly high, not only because of the clean, unpolluted air but also because of the increase in the hole in the ozone layer over nearby Antarctica. Take adequate precautions such as wearing a sun-hat and sunglasses, covering up vulnerable areas and using sunblock (even on overcast days the sun can burn through clouds).

There are no dangerous wild animals or poisonous snakes (but there is one very rare poisonous spider, the katipo). The most irritating insects are sandflies and mosquitoes, which can occur in relentless swarms in some areas, particularly western coastal areas in the South Island, such as Fiordland. Mosquitos do not carry diseases (such as malaria) but can still be a severe irritant. Make sure you are protected with insect repellent, particularly at dusk and/or near water.

Private and public healthcare facilities are of a high standard. Doctors and other medical facilities are listed in the front of the telephone directory; your hotel may also have an arrangement with a local doctor.

If you have an accident you are entitled to make a claim for some medical or hospital expenses under the national Accident Compensation scheme (ACC) for personal injury. Because of the existence of this scheme, actions for damages may not be brought in New Zealand courts, so it is best to ensure that your personal travel insurance covers such eventualities. The scheme does not cover illness.

Pharmacies
Pharmacies are usually open during normal shopping hours. In cities, some are open later and can be found listed in the 'Hospitals' section in the phone book, or ask at your hotel. If you are on an unusual prescription take sufficient supplies with you, since there is no guarantee that it will be available locally. To avoid potential difficulties with customs, take your prescription.

263

❏ New Zealand lies in an earthquake zone (see pages 98–99), but the likelihood of an earthquake of any magnitude occurring during your stay is minimal. If you do start to feel the earth move, shelter under a strong table or brace yourself in a doorway—do not run outside. ❏

Accommodation

Camping

New Zealand has an excellent network of well-equipped campsites in national parks, beach resorts and urban areas. Most camping grounds have facilities for campervans and caravans as well as tents, plus cabins, bunk rooms and self-contained, fully equipped visitor flats (motel-type rooms). Facilities are usually communal, with on-site launderettes in many places. Costs average NZ$8 per person for tents, with slightly higher charges for sites with power hook-ups for campervans. Several federations, such as the Cabin and Camp Association (CCA) and Kiwi Camps of New Zealand (tel: 06 753 5697; www.kiwitravelchannel.com), publish brochures with details of their members' camping grounds. The NZAA Accommodation Guide also lists campsites and motor camps.

Guest-houses can be found all over the country to suit all tastes and pockets

The Department of Conservation (DoC; www.doc.govt.nz) manages around 200 campsites in national parks and other areas, ranging from informal camping areas with limited facilities to standard camping areas and well-appointed serviced campsites. A leaflet on *Conservation Campsites* is available. from DoC offices or DoC Head Office, PO Box 10-420, Wellington.

Self-catering

A wide range of accommodation with fully equipped kitchens is available, from basic flats in campsites to fully serviced motel units. Motels represent one of the best budget options for independent visitors, with clean, comfortable units at affordable prices (around NZ$50–70, rising to NZ$100 or more).

Most motel rooms have basic tea- and coffee-making facilities, fridge, toaster and usually an electric hob and basic cooking utensils. Not all motels have fully equipped kitchens; most have television, telephone and lounge facilities, and sometimes also a bar, restaurant or swimming-pool. Reliable chains include Best Western (tel: 09 520 5418; www.bestwestern.co.nz), Budget Motels (tel: 00 800 811 22 333; www.budgetmotelchain.com.au) and Flag Hotels (tel: 0800 803 524; www.flagchoice.com.au). Motor Inns tend to be slightly smarter, with prices in the range of NZ$75–200 per day.

Hotels and lodges

Hotels—from international chains such as Hyatt (tel: 0800 44 1234; www.hyatt.com) and Sheraton (tel: 09 379 5132; www.sheraton.com), and national chains such as Scenic Circle (tel: 0800 69 69 63; www.scenic-circle.co.nz) and Pacific Park—are found in all the major cities and resort areas, with room rates ranging from NZ$175 per night upwards.

Independent hotels are a cheaper option than motels, with rooms from NZ$30 to NZ$50 per night; facilities vary widely, and in many old-style hotels the rooms are merely an adjunct to the bar.

New Zealand also has a network of top-class sporting retreats and wilderness lodges, often set in beautiful countryside and offering the services of guides. A brochure on *New Zealand in Style: Exclusive Retreats and Sporting Lodges* is available from the tourist board.

Bed and breakfast, guest-houses and country pubs

Bed-and-breakfast establishments and guest-houses all over the country provide a welcoming place to stay and the chance to meet local people.

Prices start from around NZ$45 (single), NZ$70 (double). The NZ Federation of Bed & Breakfast Hotels is at 52 Armagh Street, Christchurch, tel: 03 366 1503; www.nzbnbhotels.com; the *New Zealand Bed & Breakfast Book* (J. and J. Thomas, Moonshine Press) is also useful.

Some of the best bed-and-breakfast accommodation is in historic homesteads; nearly 30 of these are grouped together in the *Heritage Inns of New Zealand* brochure (available from visitor centres or the tourist board). Prices start from NZ$100 per night.

Country pubs often have similar facilities to the older urban hotels, at similar prices. Details are available from visitor centres.

Farmstays and homestays
Staying on a farm for a night or two is a great way to find out about the rural way of life. Bookings can be arranged through Rural Holidays New Zealand (PO Box 2155, Christchurch, tel: 03 355 6218; www.ruralhols.co.nz) and New Zealand Farm Holidays Ltd (PO Box 74, Kumeu, Auckland, tel: 09 412 9649; www.nzfarmholidays.co.nz). Charges are from NZ$50 upwards per person per night. Most visitor centres carry brochures or lists for local farmstays.

Hostels and backpackers
Budget hostel accommodation is available almost everywhere in the country.

One of the network of backpacker hostels

Beds in shared rooms start from around NZ$12–15 per night, and nearly all hostels have communal kitchens, dining areas, lounge and laundry room. The *YHA Accommodation Guide* provides details on member hostels (available from YHANZ, PO Box 436, Christchurch, tel: 03 379 9970; fax: 03 365 4476; www.yha.org.nz). There are also hundreds of privately run hostels, usually referred to as 'backpackers' or backpacker lodges: Guides include the *Backpackers Guide to New Zealand* and *Backpacker Accommodation New Zealand*.

❑ The Qualmark (www.qualmark.co.nz) is a classification system developed by the Tourism New Zealand and the New Zealand Automobile Association to encourage high standards of hospitality and service. Lists of Qualmark-rated properties are available from visitor centres and AA Travel Centres. Another quality symbol is the New Zealand Way 'fern'. Products and services with this symbol have passed a strict set of criteria, including quality of service, environmental responsibility and business achievement, all delivered in true New Zealand style. ❑

Other information

Visitors with disabilities
In general, New Zealand has good provisions for visitors with disabilities. By law, all new or redeveloped buildings must be accessible to people with disabilities, although interpretation of the law varies widely. Ramps and specially equipped toilets are usually provided in museums, theatres and other public venues. With regard to transport, it is best to phone ahead to ensure that your needs can be met. You can get full details of local services from regional disability resource centres; listings are available from the head office: Disability Resource Centre, 14 Erson Avenue, Royal Oak, Auckland, tel: 09 625 8069; www.disabilityresource.org.nz.

Opening times
Most offices and businesses are open from 8:30 to 5 Monday to Friday, with late-night shopping in the bigger

Christchurch Cathedral, one of the main Anglican places of worship

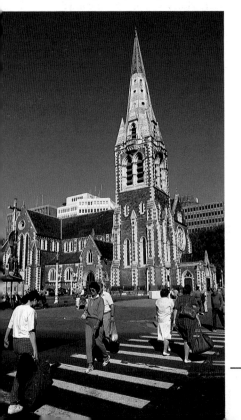

towns, usually on Thursday or Friday until 8:30 or 9PM. Some shops close at lunch-time on Saturday, while many others (particularly in resorts and larger towns) are open all weekend. Local convenience stores (dairies) are usually open from 7AM to 10PM seven days a week. Filling stations are open 24 hours in larger places, and many also have a convenience store.

Places of worship
There are Anglican, Presbyterian, Baptist, Methodist and Catholic churches or chapels in most large urban centres, plus a handful of mosques and synagogues. Hotels should be able to advise on locations and times of services.

Toilets
Public toilets can be found at major attractions, some visitor centres, filling stations, libraries, urban parks and, of course, in bars and restaurants.

Electricity
The AC electricity supply runs at 230–240 volts/50 hertz. Motels and hotels provide 110-volt/20-watt AC sockets for shavers only. Adaptors for other electrical equipment are readily available in hardware stores.

Consumer taxes
Goods and Services tax (GST) applies to all goods and services bought within the country and currently stands at 12.5 per cent. Advertised prices usually include GST.

Etiquette and local customs
New Zealanders are, on the whole, easygoing and friendly, and there are few strict rules on etiquette. Dress codes are almost universally casual, although singlets, beachwear, dirty bush clothes, flip-flops and the like may be frowned upon, and in some cases banned in pubs and restaurants. Some of the smarter restaurants also require ties for men.

Tipping is not expected, although it may be refused if you wish to reward exceptional service.

The most important aspects of etiquette relate to visiting Maori *marae*. It is very important to remove footwear on entering meeting houses (even those on display in museums), and you should always seek permission before looking around a meeting house or other building on the *marae*.

Books and films

New Zealand has a thriving literary scene and its film industry has also produced several international successes. Perhaps the most acclaimed New Zealand-born writer is Katherine Mansfield, whose short stories can be found in several anthologies, including *The Stories of Katherine Mansfield: Definitive Edition* (ed. A. Alpers, OUP Auckland 1984). One of the country's most distinguished living novelists is Janet Frame, whose autobiography *An Angel At My Table* (Hutchinson 1984) was turned into an acclaimed film by director Jane Campion. Other works by Janet Frame include *Owls Do Cry* and *Living in the Maniototo*. Maurice Shadbolt is a popular historical novelist best known for *The Season of the Jew* (Hodder and Stoughton 1986).

One of the country's most acclaimed Maori writers is Keri Hulme, whose novel *The Bone People* (Picador London 1983) won the British Booker McConnell Prize for Fiction in 1985. Another established Maori author is the prolific Witi Ihimaera, whose better-known works include *Pounamu, Pounamu* (Reed Publishing 1972) and *Tangi and Whanau: Two Classic Maori Novels* (Secker and Warburg 1994). Other Maori writers to watch for include Apirana Taylor, Hone Tuwhare and Patricia Grace, who achieved prominence with *Cousins* (Penguin Books 1992).

The first novel of contemporary writer Alan Duff, *Once Were Warriors* (Tandem Press), a harrowing tale of a poor Maori family's struggle with despair, anger and alcohol in south Auckland, caused a sensation when it was published in 1990. More recent works include *One Night Out Stealing* (Tandem Press 1992), *State Ward* (Vintage 1994), *What Becomes of the Broken Hearted* (Vintage 1996) and *Both Sides of the Moon* (Vintage 1998).

New Zealand's film industry has also received international acclaim in recent years. Jane Campion's film about a mute immigrant, *The Piano*,

was an award-winner at the 1993 Cannes Film Festival. Also outstanding are Peter Jackson's compelling *Heavenly Creatures*, starring Kate Winslet in the bizarre true story of two schoolgirl killers in 1950s Christchurch, and Lee Tamahori's *Once Were Warriors*, the prize-winning film of Alan Duff's book. Peter Jackson's *Lord of the Rings* trilogy has been an astonishing experience for New Zealand film, with New Zealand being described as 'best supporting country', Oscar winners loaning the prize statuettes to school fairs, and Wellington renaming itself (temporarily) as Middle Earth. The films were shot on locations throughout the country, with Matamata in the Waikato (Hobbiton), Tongariro National Park (Mordor), Wellington (Helm's Deep and Bree—and Jackson's home) and the Queenstown area (Isengard, Lothlórien and the Ford of Bruinen) all playing central roles. Ian Brodie's *The Lord of the Rings Location Guidebook* (HarperCollins) gives full details of all locations. The next project, due for release in 2005, is a remake of *King Kong*, with New York City re-created in a field near Welllington.

267

CONVERSION CHART		
FROM	**TO**	**MULTIPLY BY**
Inches	Centimetres	2.54
Centimetres	Inches	0.3937
Feet	Metres	0.3048
Metres	Feet	3.2810
Yards	Metres	0.9144
Metres	Yards	1.0940
Miles	Kilometres	1.6090
Kilometres	Miles	0.6214
Acres	Hectares	0.4047
Hectares	Acres	2.4710
Gallons	Litres	4.5460
Litres	Gallons	0.2200
Ounces	Grams	28.35
Grams	Ounces	0.0353
Pounds	Grams	453.6
Grams	Pounds	0.0022
Pounds	Kilograms	0.4536
Kilograms	Pounds	2.205
Tons	Tonnes	1.0160
Tonnes	Tons	0.9842

Tourist offices

Overseas

Overseas branches of the Tourism New Zealand (TNZ—www.purenz.com) can supply a wide range of information, including maps, a comprehensive *Where to Stay Guide* and a lavish *Holiday Planner* (including a brochure-ordering service for tour operators, car-rental firms, hotels and other companies with contact addresses in your home country). You can also request regional information.

Australia: Suite 3, Level 24, 1 Alfred Street, Sydney, NSW 2000 (tel: 02 8220 9000; fax: 02 8220 9099).
UK: New Zealand House, Haymarket, London SW1Y 4TQ (tel: 020-7930 1662; fax: 020-7839 8929).
USA: 501 Santa Monica Boulevard, #300, Santa Monica, CA 90401 (tel: 310 395 7480; fax: 310 395 5453).

In New Zealand

Nearly 100 tourist offices throughout the country form the Visitor Information Network, co-ordinated by the TNZ. Their friendly, helpful staff provide impartial information on everything from local attractions to adventure activities, and many are also able to handle bookings for accommodation, transport and tour operators. They also distribute free maps and brochures.

Because they are all linked to one network, visitor centres are able to access information on areas other than their own. They provide an invaluable, up-to-date service and should be your first port of call.

For their addresses and telephone numbers see the relevant entries in the A to Z section.

❏ In addition to the Qualmark rating and the New Zealand Way fern symbol, another logo to look for is the KiwiHost sign (www.kiwi-host.co.nz). This symbol means staff in the business concerned have received customer-service training, and that you can expect 'a warm Kiwi welcome, friendly attention and good service'. In general it would be surprising if you did not receive this kind of reception anyway, so do not necessarily be put off if somewhere does not have the KiwiHost logo. ❏

Visitor office, Te Anau

Hotels and Restaurants

HOTELS

£   = under NZ$75
££ = between NZ$75–$150
£££ = over NZ$150

NORTH ISLAND

Auckland

Aachen House (££)
*39 Market Road, Remuera tel: 09 520 2329/
0800 222 436 www.aachenhouse.co.nz*
A lovely Edwardian-style house, 4km (2.5 miles)
from downtown. Comfortable and welcoming;
recommended. Ideal with your own transport.
Airport Skyway Lodge (£–££)
*30 Kirkbride Road, Mangere tel: 09 275 4443
www.skywaylodge.co.nz*
One of many motels along Kirkbride Road and
McKenzie Road that has decent accommodation
within easy reach (five minutes) of the airport. All
offer free transfers if you are catching a flight. The
Skyway has a range of accommodation, from
shared rooms to self-contained family units.
It also has a pool.
Albion Hotel (££)
*corner of Wellesley and Hobson streets
tel: 09 379 4900 www.albionhotel.co.nz*
Built in 1873 and restored, with 21 moderate-sized
en-suite rooms (no views) at reasonable prices.
Ascot Parnell (££)
*36 St. Stephens Avenue, Parnell
tel: 09 309 9012 www.ascotparnell.co.nz*
A small historic house converted into a well-run and
friendly B&B, with very comfortable rooms, all non-
smoking. Parnell Village is near by.
Aspen Lodge (£)
*62 Emily Place tel: 09 379 6698
www.aspenlodge.co.nz*
Comfortable, friendly B&B, five minutes' walk from
central downtown. No private facilities, but quiet
and includes breakfast.
Carlton (£££)
*corner of Mayoral Drive and Vincent Street
tel: 09 366 3000/0800 227 586
www.carlton-auckland.co.nz*
Near the Aotea Centre, this smart hotel has
spacious rooms, all with floor-to-ceiling windows
overlooking the city and harbour.
Copthorne Anzac Avenue (£££)
*150 Anzac Avenue tel: 09 379 8509
www.copthorneanzac.co.nz*
Overlooking the harbour, with small but comfortable
rooms with balconies.
Crowne Plaza (£££)
*128 Albert Street tel: 09 302 1111/
0800 801 180 www.crowneplaza.com*
Primarily for people on business but good value. In
the middle of town, with sauna and free parking.
Devonport Villa (£££)
*46 Tainui Road, Devonport tel: 09 445 8397
www.devonportvilla.co.nz*
Superb colonial villa converted to a B&B with three
lovely guest rooms. It has lots of atmosphere, and
serves huge breakfasts. Private garden cottage near
the beach.

Hôtel du Vin (£££)
*Lyons Road, Mangatawhiri Valley
tel: 09 233 6314/0800 838 846
www.hotelduvin.co.nz*
Superb, award-winning hotel amid the vineyards of
the De Redcliffe Estate, 45 minutes from the airport.
It has palatial rooms, heated pool, tennis and gym.
Mercure Auckland (£££)
*Customs Street East tel: 09 377 8920/
0800 444 422 www.mercure.co.nz*
Near the quayside, but small rooms. Expansive
views from restaurant and some rooms.
Peace & Plenty Inn (££)
*6 Flagstaff Terrace, Devonport
tel: 09 445 2925 www.peaceandplenty.co.nz*
Elegantly restored, intimate, waterfront B&B with
five queen en-suite rooms. Breakfast is a must.
Stamford Plaza (£££)
*Albert Street tel: 09 309 8888
www.stamford.com.au*
Well-appointed rooms (ask for one on the harbour
side) and first-class service have earned this hotel
top ratings among Auckland's luxury hotels.

Northland

Far North

Kaitaia
Kaitaia Hotel (£)
*17 Commerce Street tel: 09 408 0360
www.kaitaiahotel.co.nz*
One of the oldest hotels (1837) in Northland, this
local landmark is right in the town and has a
licensed restaurant and four bars. Rooms are in
need of refurbishment, but are excellent value.
The Northerner Inn (£–££)
*North Road tel: 09 408 2800
fax: 09 408 0306*
On the main street, quiet with good-quality rooms at
reasonable prices. Pool, sauna, spa and gym.

Doubtless Bay

Mangonui
Acacia Lodge Motel (££)
*57 Mill Bay Road tel/fax: 09 406 0417
www.acacia.co.nz*
Sunny lodge on the water's edge, handy for the
village. Some rooms have spas and balconies.
Beach Lodge (££)
*Coopers Beach tel: 09 406 0068
www.beachlodge.co.nz*
On lovely Coopers Beach, 2.5km (1.5 miles) from
Mangonui. The five self-catering beachfront lodges
all have sundecks and full facilities.
Old Oak Inn (£)
66 Waterfront Drive tel/fax: 09 406 0665
This historic hotel on the water's edge was built for
whalers and sealers in the 1860s. It is now a comfortable seven-room lodge with communal facilities.

Matakohe
Old Post Office Guest House (£)
Oakleigh Road, Paparoa tel/fax: 09 431 6444
Lovely little B&B in Paparoa's converted post office.
Shared facilities, but a good budget choice and just
6.5km (4 miles) from Kauri Museum Matakohe.

Bay of Islands

Paihia
Abel Tasman Lodge (£–££)
Marsden Road tel: 09 402 7521
www.abeltasmanlodge.co.nz
In the heart of Paihia, with 25 self-contained units right opposite a sandy beach.
Bay of Islands Motel (££)
Tohitapu Road tel: 09 402 7348/
0800 402 7348 www.goldenchain.co.nz
In 1ha (2.5 acres) of grounds within easy reach of the town (2km/1 mile) and close to a swimming beach. The individual cottages are all fully self-contained and are good value.
Beachcomber Resort Hotel (£££)
1 Seaview Road tel: 09 402 7434/
0800 732 786 www.beachcomber-resort.co.nz
In a good position on the headland, with sea views from all rooms, and right on the beach. Studios, family suites and luxury suites available.
Casa Bella Motel (££)
MacMurray Road tel: 09 402 7387
0800 800 810 www.casabellamotel.co.nz
Central but quiet Spanish-style complex close to the beach. Well-furnished units with kitchens.
Cedar Suite Spas (££)
5 Sullivans Road tel: 09 402 8516
www.cedarspaspaihia.co.nz
Tucked away in woodlands south of town, this modern complex includes self-contained apartments, B&B units and a cottage with sea views.
Copthorne Resort Waitangi (££–£££)
Tau Henare Drive tel: 09 402 7411
0800 808 228 www.copthorne-bay-of-islands.nz.hotels.com
This sprawling hotel has a superb spot on the shore within the Waitangi National Trust Reserve, and has landscaped gardens and a heated pool.
Kingsgate Hotel Autolodge Paihia (££–£££)
Marsden Road tel: 09 402 7416/
0800 652 929 www.milleniumhotels.com
On the waterfront near the wharf and shops. Pool, spa and sauna. All rooms have kitchenettes. Guests have the use of dinghies and bicycles.
Paihia Pacific Resort Hotel (££–£££)
27 Kings Road tel: 09 402 8221
www.paihiapacific.co.nz
Lavish units amid landscaped gardens within walking distance of the seafront. Swimming and spa pools and floodlit tennis courts.
Swiss Chalet Lodge Motel (££)
3 Bayview Road tel: 09 402 7615
www.swisschaletmotel.co.nz
This well-run, Swiss-owned chalet has 12 spacious self-contained units with patios or balconies, plus family and honeymoon suites.

Russell
Duke of Marlborough Hotel (££)
The Strand tel: 09 403 7829
www.theduke.co.nz
An historic landmark that has been a hotel since 1827, the Duke of Marlborough has a convivial atmosphere and its seaside terraces and bar are popular local watering holes. The wood-panelled rooms all have en-suite facilities; front rooms can be noisy.

Kimberley Lodge (£££)
Pitt Street tel: 09 403 7090
www.lodges.co.nz
Charming, old-world, white-timbered mansion perched on the hill above Pompallier, with bay views. Heated pool and spa.
Motel Russell (£–££)
Matauwhi Road tel: 09 403 7854/
0800 240 011 www.motelrussell.co.nz
On a wooded hillside near the town, with a pool fed by a waterfall. Attractive, well-decorated units.
Russell Lodge (£–££)
corner of Chapel and Beresford streets
tel: 09 403 7640/0800 478 773
Surrounded by gardens, Russell Lodge has reasonably priced rooms and units (also family units, all en suite) as well as backpackers' rooms.

Whangarei
Cheviot Park Motor Lodge (££)
corner of Western Hills Drive and Cheviot Street
tel: 09 438 2341 www.cheviot-park.co.nz
AA Host property, with 15 comfortable, self-contained units, spa and swimming-pools.
Kingswood Motor Inn (££)
260 Kamo Road tel: 09 437 5779/
0800 369 469
www.nzmotels.co.nz/kingswood
A few minutes outside town. Friendly service and comfortable surroundings. Spa pool.
Pembrooke Motor Lodge (££)
corner of Hatea Drive and Deveron Street
tel: 09 437 6426/0800 736 276
www.pembrooke.co.nz
Luxurious accommodation just outside town. Outdoor swimming-pool and private spa pool.

From Coromandel to the Waikato

Coromandel

Coromandel Township
Anglers Lodge and Holiday Park (££)
1446 Colville Road, Amodeo Bay
tel: 07 866 8584 www.anglers.co.nz
Just 18km (11 miles) north of town in a bush setting beside the sea. One- or two-bedroomed units, with cooking facilities. Pool, spa, tennis, boats for rent.
Coromandel Colonial Cottages (££)
1737 Rings Road tel/fax: 07 866 8857
www.corocottagesmotel.co.nz
Eight spacious and well-appointed units (each sleeping up to six) just outside town. Barbecue, playground, billiards, swimming-pool.
Karamana (1872) Homestead (££)
Whangapoua Road tel: 07 866 7138
www.karamanahomestead.co.nz
This lovely Victorian homestead in a tranquil valley just outside town has just four rooms.

Pauanui
Mercure Grand Puka Park Resort (£££)
Mount Avenue tel: 07 864 8088
www.pukapark.co.nz
This exclusive lodge has 48 superb balconied 'tree hut' chalets built into the wooded hillside, each secluded from its neighbours. The main building has log fires and a sophisticated atmosphere.

271

Hotels and Restaurants

Thames
Coastal Motor Lodge (££)
608 Tararu Road (SH25) tel: 07 868 6843
www.nzmotels.co.nz/coastal
Modern, self-contained, cottage-type units in a
garden setting overlooking the Firth of Thames,
2.5km (1.5 miles) north of the middle of the town.
Shortland Court (££)
corner of Jellicoe Crescent and Fenton Street
tel: 07 868 6506/0800 474 700
www.bestwestern.co.nz/shortland
A Best Western hotel 1km (0.5 mile) from the town;
nine large family units at reasonable prices.

Whitianga
Buffalo Beach Resort (£)
Eyre Street tel/fax: 07 866 5854
www.holidayparks.co.nz/buffalo
Fully equipped units, plus tent and campervan
sites, handy for the shops and ferry.
Cosy Cat Cottage (££)
41 South Highway tel/fax: 07 866 4488
www.cosycat.co.nz
Comfortable little B&B that will be appreciated by
cat lovers—the whole house is full of cat statues
and other feline memorabilia.
Mercury Bay Beachfront Resort (££)
111–113 Buffalo Beach Road
tel: 07 866 5637 www.beachfrontresort.co.nz
Directly on the beach, with rooms opening onto
gardens (with spa pool) and the sea. Eight fully
equipped units plus one luxury unit. Boats, fishing
rods and bicycles are free to guests.

Bay of Plenty

Katikati
Fantail Lodge (£££)
40 Rea Road tel: 07 549 1581
www.fantaillodge.co.nz
Twelve luxury suites and 12 villas, surrounded
by orchards.

Rotorua
Boulevard Motel (£–££)
corner of Fenton and Seddon streets
tel: 07 348 2074 www.boulevardrotorua.co.nz
The 33 units range from small studios to family
suites. Facilities include swimming-pool, spa baths,
putting green and games room.
Eaton Hall Guest House (£–££)
1255 Hinemaru Street tel: 07 347 0366
www.eatonhallbnb.cjb.net
This pleasant two-storey wooden building is one of
the handiest of Rotorua's B&Bs. The house has an
interesting interior and a welcoming atmosphere.
Lake Plaza (£££)
1000 Eruera Street tel: 07 348 1174/
0800 801 440 www.lakeplazahotel.co.nz
Near the Polynesian Spa and Government Gardens,
handy for downtown attractions. Well-appointed
rooms (the best overlook the lake).
Grand Tiara Hotel (£££)
Fenton Street tel: 07 349 5200
www.grandtiara.co.nz
Close to the Whakarewarewa Thermal Area on the
fringes of the city. The 122 rooms have IDD, TV,
minibar; eight suites with spa bath, separate

lounge and balcony. The best rooms overlook the
golf course from the top two floors. On-site
services include shops, health club, heated pool,
sauna, restaurants and bar.
Princes Gate Hotel (££–£££)
1057 Arawa Street tel: 07 348 1179
www.scenic-circle.co.nz
Next to the Government Gardens in the central
area, this is one of the leading boutique hotels in
New Zealand. The 22 luxurious, old-fashioned
rooms are complemented by eight suites. Heated
pool, spa, tennis court, health complex, restaurant
and bar.
Sequoia-Acacia Lodge Motel (£–££)
40 Victoria Street tel: 07 348 7089/
fax: 07 346 1104
A French-style motel near the middle of town. The
18 ground-floor units have kitchen facilities and
there are some family units. Sauna, mineral pools.
Solitaire Lodge (£££)
Lake Tarawera Road tel: 07 362 8208/
0800 SOLITAIRE www.solitairelodge.com
In a spectacular setting on a wooded peninsula
overlooking Lake Tarawera, Solitaire Lodge is a
sophisticated hideaway catering for up to 20
guests. All suites have king-size beds. The lounge
and dining area have wood fires, with the emphasis in the restaurant on New Zealand game and
fine wines. Private beach, spa pool. Free use of
windsurfers, dinghies, fishing tackle and yachts.

Tauranga/Mount Maunganui
Ambassador Motor Inn (£–££)
91 5th Avenue, Tauranga tel: 07 578 5665
www.ambassador-motorinn.co.nz
The Ambassador Motor Inn is just five minutes'
drive from downtown. It has 20 comfortable
units (some with spa baths). Attractive pool and
spa complex.
Hotel Armitage (££)
9 Willow Street, Tauranga tel: 07 578 9119
www.armitage.nz-hotels.com
In the downtown area, with good facilities (restaurants, heated pool, satellite TV in 81 rooms).
Specially commissioned Maori sculpture in foyer.
Ocean Waves Motel (££)
74 Marine Parade, Mount Maunganui
tel/fax: 07 575 4594 www.oceanwaves.co.nz
Seven modern, self-contained units with one or
two bedrooms, across the road from the beach.
Handy for the heart of town and 1km (0.5 mile)
from the mountain.
Tauranga Motel (££)
No. 1 Second Avenue, tel: 07 578 7079/
0800 109 007 www.taurangamotel.co.nz
Very central: 12 units are on the waterfront, and
the 14 newer units all have water views.

Whakatane
Camellia Court Motel (£–££)
11 Domain Road tel: 07 308 6213/
www.camelliacourt.co.nz
Handy for downtown; 12 well-maintained and
spacious units with full facilities.
Whakatane Motor Camp & Caravan Park (£)
McGarvey Road tel: 07 308 8694
On the banks of the Whakatane River. Powered and
tent sites and basic cabins. Swimming pool, spa.

The Waikato

Hamilton
Alcamo Hotel (££–£££)
290 Ulster Street tel: 07 839 0200/0800 802 468 www.scenic-circle.co.nz/alcamo
Stylish hotel with 56 luxury suites (complete with spa baths) and a presidential suite. Pool, restaurant and conference facilities.
Glenview International Hotel (££)
200 Ohaupo Road tel: 07 843 6049/0800 453 689 www.glenviewinternational.co.nz
Between the city and the airport, the Glenview has well-appointed rooms (some with kitchens), and a waterbed suite. Swimming-pool.
Le Grand Hôtel (££–£££)
corner of Victoria and Collingwood streets tel: 07 839 1994 www.legrandhotel.co.nz
A lavish, old-world style development built inside a former commercial building, with palatial rooms, 28 de luxe, 3 executive and 7 business suites.
The Monastery (££)
Newell Road tel: 07 856 9587 www.lodgings.co.nz/monastery.html
Built as a private home in 1906, this became a monastery in 1952 and in 1990 was moved here, to the edge of the Waikato River. There are just four guest rooms.
Tudor Motor Lodge (££)
24 Thackeray Street tel: 07 838 2244/ 0800 883 667 www.tudormotorlodge.co.nz
An AA Host property near the business district, but quiet. All 24 serviced units have kitchen facilities.

Waitomo
Caves Motor Inn (£–££)
SH3 Waitomo Junction tel/fax: 07 873 8109
Ten minutes from the caves, with 20 spacious and cosy units, plus cabins and backpackers' rooms.
Waitomo Caves Hotel (£–£££)
Waitomo tel: 07 878 8204/ 0800 782 994 fax: 07 878 8205 www.waitomocaveshotel.co.nz
Charming hotel built at the turn of the 20th century, with a country club atmosphere. Comfortable guest rooms and good-value economy rooms; separate backpackers' accommodation. Public rooms include a lounge, cocktail bar and restaurant.

East Coast

Gisborne
Cedar House (£££)
4 Clifford Street tel: 06 868 1902 www.cedarhouse.co.nz
This 1909 mansion has four rooms (two en suite). Breakfast is to be savoured!
Teal Motor Lodge (££)
479 Gladstone Road tel: 06 868 4019/ 0800 838 325 www.teal.co.nz
Set in large landscaped gardens with a salt-water pool, near the central city. The units have one or two bedrooms and kitchen facilities.
Thomson Homestay (£)
16 Rawiri Street tel: 06 868 9675/ 0800 370 505 fax: 06 868 9675
Five minutes from the city is this modest but pleasant homestay, with no private facilities.

Hastings
Angus Inn Hotel (££)
Railway Road tel: 06 878 8177/ 0800 109 595 fax: 06 878 7496
The largest hotel in Hawke Bay, with a pool, spa and sauna. Sixty-one hotel rooms and 12 motel units with self-catering facilities.
Ebbett Park Lodge Motel (£–££)
616 Gordon Road tel: 06 878 9860 www.nzmotels.co.nz/ebbett
Next to an extensive park—14 quiet units at reasonable prices. Swimming-pool, playground.
Hawthorne Country House (££)
SH2, Pakipaki tel/fax: 06 878 0035 www.hawthorne.co.nz
Built in 1908, this B&B has five en suite rooms. Hotel has native timber panelling and floors.

Napier
Albatross Motel (£)
56 Meeanee Quay tel: 06 835 5991 fax: 06 835 5949
Overlooking Ahuriri Lagoon on Napier's Westshore, this is a well-priced modern motel.
Bella Tuscany on Kennedy (££)
371 Kennedy Road tel: 06 843 9129 www.bellatuscany.co.nz
Long-established motel five minutes from central Napier. Self-contained units with kitchen facilities.
County Hotel (£££)
12 Browning Street tel: 06 835 7800/ 0800 843 468 www.countyhotel.co.nz
Converted from the former council offices, with 11 business rooms and a 'Vice-Regal' suite.
Edgewater Motor Lodge (££–£££)
359 Marine Parade tel: 06 835 1148 fax: 06 835 6600
Seafront hotel with studio units and executive suites. All upstairs rooms have balconies.
Mon Logis (££–£££)
415 Marine Parade tel: 06 835 2125 www.babs.co.nz/monlogis
Superb old hotel in the heart of Napier, with the highest standards of French hospitality. Just four rooms, all en suite. No smoking, no children.
Quality Inn Napier (££)
311 Marine Parade tel: 06 835 3237 fax: 06 833 5312 www.napiertravelinn.co.nz
A superior seafront hotel, popular with business people, with 59 well-appointed rooms with tea- and coffee-making facilities.

Central North Island and the West Coast

New Plymouth
Amber Court Motel (££)
61 Eliot Street tel: 06 758 0922/ 0800 654 800 www.ambercourtmotel.co.nz
A few minutes' walk from the heart of the city and close to Pukekura Park. Units are good quality, with kitchens, and sleep from two to seven; some have spa baths. Large heated pool.
Shoestring Backpackers (£)
48 Lemon Street tel/fax: 06 758 0404 www.backpackers.co.nz
Single, twin, double and dormitory rooms, plus sauna. Short walk from town and Pukekura Park.

273

Hotels and Restaurants

Ohakune

The Hobbit Motor Lodge (££)
corner of Goldfinch and Wye streets
tel: 06 385 8248/0800 843 462
www.nzmotels.co.nz/hobbit
Well-positioned motel with a wide range of units.
Spa pool, lounge with wood fire, restaurant and bar.

Powderhorn Château (££–£££)
Mountain Road tel: 06 385 8888
www.powderhorn.co.nz
Close to the Turoa ski field, this traditional-style ski chalet has 30 well-furnished rooms. The public areas have wood fires, and there are bars and two restaurants. Lively *après-ski* atmosphere.

Taupo

Anchorage Resort Motel (££)
Lake Terrace, Two Mile Bay tel: 07 378 5542/
0800 991 995 www.taupomotel.co.nz
Beside Lake Taupo, the Anchorage has luxurious units (some with spas) in a two-floor block surrounding a heated pool. It also has a sauna, gym, mineral pools, conference and games rooms.

Cedar Park Motor Lodge (££)
Two Mile Bay tel: 07 378 6325
fax: 07 377 0641
This lodge is across the road from the lake, with 24 self-contained, two-bedroom family units. Heated pool, spa pools. Boat ramp near by.

Le Chalet Suisse Motel (££)
3 Titiraupenga Street tel: 07 378 1556
www.lechaletsuisse.co.nz
Five minutes' walk from the town, with 17 modern units, most with lake views (executive units have spa baths). Large heated pool, spa.

Gillies of Taupo (££)
77 Gillies Avenue tel/fax: 07 377 2377
www.beds-n-leisure.com/gillies-lodge
A traditional hotel with nine rooms, all with private facilities. Bar and restaurant. In-room TV and radio on request.

Huka Lodge (£££)
Huka Falls Road tel: 07 378 5791
www.hukalodge.com
Originally a fishing lodge in the 1920s, Huka Lodge is now one of the leading exclusive retreats in the country. There are 20 individual lodges near the banks of the Waikato, with spacious bedrooms and glass-ceilinged bathroom. Library, cocktail lounge with wood fire, heated pool, all-weather tennis court.

Wairakei Resort (£££)
SH1, Wairakei tel: 07 374 8021
www.wairakeiresort.co.nz
Taupo's top resort is set in 60ha (148 acres) of woods and parkland in the Wairakei thermal valley. There are two heated pools, tennis, golf, children's playground, restaurants and bars.

Tongariro

Whakapapa Village
The Grand Château (£££)
Mount Ruapehu tel: 07 892 3809
www.chateau.co.nz
This impressive local landmark has elegant, Victorian-style rooms with IDD phones, TV, fridge and other modern comforts. The hotel also has a pool, sauna, tennis, golf course and cinema.

The Skotel Alpine Resort (£–££)
Mount Ruapehu tel: 07 892 3719/
0800 756 835 www.skotel.com
This attractive ski lodge claims to be the country's highest hotel, with spectacular views of the cone of Mount Ruapehu. The 37 well-appointed rooms include self-contained units and hostel beds.

Wanganui

Avenue Motel (££)
379 Victoria Avenue tel: 06 345 0907
www.theavenuewanganui.co.nz
Very comfortable units with good facilities; family units also available. Swimming pool, restaurant.

Braemar House (£)
2 Plymouth Street tel/fax: 06 347 2529
www.braemarhouse.co.nz
Nicely decorated and furnished house (dated 1895) near the river, surrounded by lawns. Budget twin or double rooms and backpackers' bunks.

Burwood Motor Inn (££)
63 Dublin Street tel: 06 345 2180/
0800 202 063 www.burwoodmotel.co.nz
Close to the central city. Twenty self-contained units with kitchens, eight luxury suites with spa baths and ten studio units. Pool, sauna, spa.

Lower North Island

Palmerston North
Aztec Motel (££)
109 Ruahine Street tel: 06 356 7125/
0800 828 082 www.bestwestern.co.nz/aztec
Only 3km (2 miles) from The Square, with 16 ground-floor units ranging from one-bedroomed studios to family accommodation with fully equipped kitchens. Large garden and pool.

Rose City Motel (££–£££)
120 Fitzherbert Avenue tel: 06 356 5388/
0508 356 538 www.rosecitymotel.co.nz
Close to the middle of the city, 26 modern, spacious units (sleeping up to five), most with double spa baths. Sauna, spa pool, squash court, and children's play area available.

Wellington
Abel Tasman Hotel (££)
169 Willis Street tel: 04 385 1304/
0800 843 827 www.abeltasmanhotel.co.nz
Small hotel in the heart of the city with basic rooms at reasonable rates. Also studio units with kitchens.

Apollo Lodge Motel (££)
49 Majoribanks Street tel: 04 385 1849
www.apollo-lodge.co.nz
Reasonably priced rooms in a convenient location.

The Chancellor Wellington (£–££)
213 Cuba Street tel: 04 385 2153
www.trekkers.co.nz
Mostly a backpackers' hostel, but also has basic double or twin rooms (with or without en suite) at very moderate prices. Spa, restaurant and bar.

Downtown Backpackers (£)
corner of Waterloo Quay and Bunny Street
tel: 04 473 8482
www.downtownbackpackers.co.nz
Basic, low-priced rooms in the heart of the city opposite the railway station—in the old Waterloo Hotel, where Queen Elizabeth II once stayed.

Duxton Hotel (£££)
148–176 Wakefield Street tel: 04 473 3900/
0800 655 555 www.duxton.com
Central top-class hotel with views over the harbour.
Several bars and restaurants, gym and business
services.
InterContinental Wellington (£££)
Grey Street tel: 04 472 2722/
0800 442 215 fax: 04 472 4724
The city's top hotel, in the heart of the central
business district. Over 200 rooms, and seven
suites (with spa baths). Indoor heated pool,
health centre, spa, several restaurants and bars.
Museum Hotel—Hotel de Wheels (££)
90 Cable Street tel: 04 802 8900
www.museumhotel.co.nz
Close to the harbour across from Te Papa, the
Museum of New Zealand. The unusual name
comes from the fact that it was put on wheels
and moved to its present position after being
threatened with demolition to make way for the
museum. The rooms (all refurbished) are of a high
standard and very good value for the city.
Richmond Guest House (££)
116 Brougham Street tel: 04 939 4567
wwww.richmondguesthouse.co.nz
Twenty comfortable rooms, on a B&B basis, only
ten minutes' walk from the downtown area and
very close to Basin Reserve cricket ground.
Tinakori Lodge (££)
182 Tinakori Road tel: 04 473 3478
www.tinakorilodge.co.nz
Delightful old house with nine comfortably
furnished rooms (most share bathrooms). Huge
breakfasts served as a buffet. Complimentary tea,
coffee and newspapers available in the
conservatory overlooking a bushland reserve.
West Plaza Hotel (££–£££)
110–16 Wakefield Street tel: 04 473 1440/
0800 731 444 www.westplaza.co.nz
The hotel has 102 rooms and seven suites,
all with en suite bathroom and shower.
Rooms also have tea- and coffee-making
facilities, satellite TV, direct-dial phones and
more. Good location.

SOUTH ISLAND

Marlborough and Nelson

Abel Tasman National Park
Abel Tasman Marahau Lodge (££)
Marahau Beach Road, RD2, Motueka
tel: 03 527 8250
www.abeltasmanmarahaulodge.co.nz
Further down the hill from the Ocean View Chalets
(see below), these plush luxury units are very
comfortable and handy for the start of the Abel
Tasman Coastal Track (see pages 174–175).
The Awaroa Lodge & Café (£)
PO Box 163, Takaka tel: 03 528 8758
www.awaroalodge.co.nz
Tucked away in Awaroa Bay on the Abel Tasman
Coastal Track, this lovely lodge is just 300m
(330 yards) from the shore and has twin/double
rooms as well as backpackers' accommodation.
Access is by foot, by sea or by air.

Ocean View Chalets (££)
Marahau Beach Road, RD2, Motueka
tel: 03 527 8232
www.accommodationabeltasman.co.nz
Overlooking Marahau Beach at the start of the
Abel Tasman Coastal Track, these timber chalets
have all amenities, including TV, phones and
balconies with wonderful views.

Blenheim
Charmwood Rural Retreat (££)
158 Murrays Road tel: 03 570 5409
www.charmwood.co.nz
A three-bedroom farmstay (private facilities) with
swimming and spa pools, ducks, hens and a cat.
Hotel D'Urville (£££)
52 Queen Street tel: 03 577 9945
www.durville.com
Good central hotel in the historic Public Trust building. Nine themed rooms, wine bar and brasserie.
Montana Lodge Motel (££)
71 Main Street tel: 03 578 9259/
0800 117 799 www.manz.co.nz/montana
Peaceful atmosphere and yet centrally located.
The 12 comfortable units sleep up to six people.
The Peppertree (£££)
SH1, Riverlands tel: 03 520 9200
www.thepeppertree.co.nz
A 1901 homestead with five large bedrooms (all en
suite, some with balconies) and a lovely farmhouse
kitchen for breakfast. Garden with pool, veranda.
Scenic Circle Blenheim Country Hotel (££)
corner of Alfred and Henry streets
tel: 03 578 5079/0800 696 963
www.scenic-circle.co.nz
Very comfortable, privately owned lodge close to
the middle of town; 54 rooms, licensed restaurant.

Golden Bay
Kahurangi Luxury Retreat (£££)
RD2, Takaka tel: 03 524 8312
www.kahuranginz.co.nz
This attractive lodge has a wood fire, lounge and
restaurant. Balconied rooms with great views.
Sans Souci Inn (£)
Richmond Road, Pohara Beach
tel/fax: 03 525 8663 www.sansouciinn.co.nz
A short walk from Pohara Beach, this rustic-looking
house (with thick clay walls and grass roof) has six
rooms and shared kitchen; meals also available.

Kaikoura
The Old Convent (£–££)
Mount Fyffe Road tel: 03 319 6603/ 0800
365 603 www.theoldconvent.co.nz
Rooms full of character (all en suite) in a peaceful
atmosphere 3km (2 miles) from town, overlooking
Kaikoura and the mountains. French cooking.
Panorama Motel (££)
266 The Esplanade tel: 03 319 5053/ 0800
288 299 www.manz.co.nz/panorama.kaikoura
Aptly named, this modern and clean beachfront
motel has superb mountain and ocean views.
White Morph Motor Inn (££–£££)
92 Esplanade tel: 03 319 5014/
0800 803 666 www.whitemorph.co.nz
A modern motel, with 19 high-quality units and four
luxury suites (with spa baths). Licensed restaurant.

27*

Hotels and Restaurants

Marlborough Sounds
Punga Cove Resort (£–£££)
Punga Cove tel: 03 579 8561
www.pungacove.co.nz
Superb little hideaway resort tucked into the hillside above Punga Cove, Endeavour Inlet (under an hour by water taxi from Picton). Chalets have balconies overlooking the Sounds; smaller chalets (with en-suite facilities) sleep two to three. Backpackers' accommodation and tent sites also available.

Nelson
Beachcomber Motor Inn (££)
23 Beach Road, Tahunanui tel: 03 548 5985
www.beachcomber.co.nz
Minutes from the airport and the central city, this complex is close to the beach and golf and tennis facilities. The 47 spacious units include 11 family units with kitchens. Bar and restaurant.
California House Inn (££–£££)
29 Collingwood Street tel: 03 548 4173
www.californiahouse.co.nz
A gracious colonial villa (1893) with oak panelling, stained-glass windows, a comfortable guest lounge with wood fire and verandas. The four guest rooms are furnished in period style and have en-suite facilities. Californian breakfasts are a speciality.
Mid City Motor Lodge (££)
218 Trafalgar Street tel: 03 546 9063/
0800 264 324 www.goldenchain.co.nz
In the heart of the city and yet with very quiet rooms. The lodge has 15 self-contained units that sleep up to four people.
South Street Cottages (££)
1 South Street tel: 03 540 2769
www.cottageaccommodation.co.nz
One of several historic cottages on South Street in the middle of the city, this charming old cottage has just two bedrooms.

Picton
Marlin Motel (£–££)
33 Devon Street tel: 03 573 6784
www.marlinmotel.com
Quietly located motel, handy for the ferry, with spacious and well-maintained units.
Yacht Club Restort Hotel (££)
corner Waikawa Road and Wellington Street
tel: 03 573 7002/0800 991 188
www.theyachtclub.co.nz
Two minutes from the town, affordable and good quality. Executive rooms have circular beds and video screens. Pool, spa, sauna, gym.

The West Coast

Fox Glacier
Fox Glacier Resort Hotel (££)
corner of Cook Flat Road and SH6
tel: 03 751 0839/0800 273 767
www.resorts.co.nz/fox.html
Nice hotel, dating from 1928, with 57 warm rooms and full facilities.
Glacier Country Hotel (££)
SH6 tel: 03 751 0847/0800 730 847
www.scenic-circle.co.nz/glaciercountry
A modern hotel with 51 rooms, all with the usual facilities; restaurant, bar and lounge with wood fire.

The Homestead (££)
Cook Flat Road tel: 03 751 0835
B&B in a 100-year-old farmhouse on a working sheep and cattle farm, 500m (550 yards) from town. There are just three bedrooms (two en suite).

Franz Josef Glacier
A1 Rata Grove Motel (£–££)
Cron Street tel: 03 752 0741
www.ratagrove.co.nz
Close to the main street, this friendly motel has some of the most comfortable rooms (from studios to family units) in the township.
Château Franz (£)
8 Cron Street tel/fax: 03 752 0738
www.chateaufranz.co.nz
Convivial backpackers' lodge near the village, with double/twin rooms as well as bunk rooms.
Glacier View Motel (££)
SH6 tel: 03 752 0705/0800 484 397
www.goldenchain.co.nz
Just north of Franz Josef, this is the motel with the best views of the glacier. Fourteen self-contained, ground-floor units.
Westwood Lodge (££)
SH6 tel: 03 752 0112
www.westwood-lodge.co.nz
Just 2km (1 mile) north of town; superb views. Six en-suite rooms, lounge, full-size billiards room.

Greymouth
Kingsgate Hotel (££)
32 Mawhera Quay tel: 03 768 5085
www.kingsgategreymouth.co.nz
In the town overlooking the Grey River and Great Wall of Greymouth (flood barrier). The 100 rooms include superior suites. Restaurant and bar.
Oak Lodge (££)
Coal Creek, Main North Road
tel: 03 768 6832/0800 357 100
www.oaklodge.co.nz
A smart B&B/homestay; some bedrooms have four-poster beds, and all have en-suite facilities. Pool and tennis court.

Lake Brunner
Lake Brunner Lodge (£££)
Mitchells, RD1, Kumara
tel/fax: 03 738 0163 www.lakebrunner.com
On the forested shores of Lake Brunner. Nine plain but spacious bedrooms (front ones overlook the lake). Fishing, hiking, hunting and bird-watching.

Lake Moeraki
Wilderness Lodge Lake Moeraki (£££)
SH6, Lake Moeraki tel: 03 750 0881
www.wildernesslodge.co.nz/lakemoeraki
An eco-lodge in stunning surroundings. Complimentary naturalist-guided trips to beaches to see penguins, fur seals and other wildlife.

Hokitika
Airport Tudor Motel (££)
123 Tudor Street tel: 03 755 8193/
0800 883 671 www.airporttudor.co.nz
In a peaceful location close to the middle of town, with spacious, fully self-contained units.

Southland Hotel (£–££)
111 Revell Street tel: 03 755 8344
www.southlandhotel.com
Near the seafront, with a range of budget rooms
through to self-contained units with spa baths.
Teichelmann's B&B Inn (£)
20 Hamilton Street tel: 03 755 8232
www.teichelmanns.co.nz
Friendly B&B, quiet but near the heart of town. Six
rooms, four en suite.

Paparoa National Park
Punakaiki Cottage Motels (££)
SH6, Punakaiki tel: 03 731 1008
fax 03 731 1118
Comfortable studios or more spacious units, right
on the beach and close to the blowholes.

Westport
Bella Vista Motel (££)
314 Palmerston Street tel: 03 789 7800/
0800 493 787 www.bellavistamotels.co.nz
Modern units range from small studios to larger,
fully equipped units with Jacuzzi.

Canterbury

Akaroa, Banks Peninsula
Akaroa Village Inn (££)
Beach Road tel: 03 304 7421/ 0800 695
2000 www.akaroavillageinn.co.nz
A sprawling complex with a wide range of rooms
(some sleeping eight). Restaurant and indoor pool.
Driftwood and Wai-Iti Motels (££–£££)
64 Rue Jolie tel: 03 304 7484/0508 928 373
www.driftwood.co.nz
Twelve self-contained units In spacious grounds on
the water's edge (sleeping up to eight).
Grand Hotel (£)
6 Rue Lavaud tel: 03 304 7011
fax: 03 304 7304 www.grandhotelakaroa.co.nz
Built in 1860 and refurbished to high standards:
12 rooms, 2 bars, beer garden and restaurant.
L'Hôtel (££)
75 Beach Road tel: 03 304 7559
fax: 03 304 7455
Very attractive rooms and harbourside studios. Ten
units (all en suite) sleeping up to four.
Oinako Lodge (£££)
99 Beach Road tel/fax: 03 304 8787
www.oinako.co.nz
Historic house furnished with antiques. Each en-
suite room is individually themed and priced
accordingly. Well worth a stay.

Arthur's Pass
Wilderness Lodge Arthur's Pass (£££)
SH73, Arthur's Pass tel: 03 318 9246
www.wildernesslodge.co.nz/arthurspass
An eco-lodge on a 3,000ha (7,400-acre)
sheep station; quality with nature discovery
and conservation.

Christchurch
Alexandra Court Motel (££)
960 Colombo Street tel: 03 366 1855/
0508 367 223
www.bestwestern.co.nz/alexandracourt
Quiet location, but handy for the central city and
airport. Large units (with kitchens) sleep up to six.
The Charlotte Jane (£££)
110 Papanui Road tel: 03 355 1028
www.charlotte-jane.co.nz
Outstanding B&B in a 1891 villa—luxury bedrooms
and stylish public rooms. Highly recommended.
Crowne Plaza Christchurch (£££)
corner of Durham and Kilmore streets tel: 03
365 7799 www.christchurch.crowneplaza.com
The city's most exclusive hotel, overlooking
Victoria Square. Its 296 rooms have good facilities. Restaurants and bars, gym, sauna.
The George Hotel (£££)
50 Park Terrace tel: 03 379 4560/
0800 100 220 www.thegeorge.com
This 'boutique' hotel has 54 tastefully furnished
rooms and suites, with views over Hagley Park
and the River Avon, two licensed restaurants and
a bar.
The Grange Guesthouse (££)
56 Armagh Street tel: 03 366 2850/ 0800
932 850 www.thegrange.co.nz
Close to the central city, this charming Victorian
mansion has superior B&B accommodation.
The Manor (££)
82 Bealey Avenue tel: 03 366 8584
www.themanor.co.nz
This wonderful old mansion has a kauri staircase,
wood-carvings and antiques. Ten bedrooms (eight
en suite), cosy bar and a restaurant.
Windsor Hotel (££)
52 Armagh Street tel: 03 366 1503/ 0800
366 1503 www.windsorhotel.co.nz
Rambling old hotel on the heritage tram route with
pleasant rooms with shared bathrooms.

Hanmer Springs
Greenacres Chalets & Apartments (££)
86 Conical Hill Road tel: 03 315 7125/
0800 822 262 www.greenacresmotel.co.nz
To the north of the resort, five minutes' walk
from the thermal pools. One- and two-bedroom
villas, plus fully equipped luxury apartments.
Hanmer Resort Motel (££)
7 Cheltenham Street tel: 03 315 7362
0800 777 666 fax: 03 315 7581
Right in the heart of Hanmer Springs, across from
the thermal pools. Studio, family or executive
units, most with individual courtyards or balconies
and all with fully equipped kitchens.

Aoraki/Mount Cook National Park
The Hermitage Hotel (£££)
Mount Cook Village tel: 03 435 1809/
0800 686 800 www.mount-cook.com
The grand old lady of the national park, with
unsurpassable views of Aoraki/Mount Cook and
the surrounding mountains. The hotel's monopoly
has allowed it to set prices way above those with
similar facilities.
Mount Cook Chalets (££–£££)
Mount Cook Village tel: 03 435 1809
www.mount-cook.com
These comfortable chalets are the only mid-priced
alternative to The Hermitage in Aoraki/Mount Cook
National Park itself. Unfortunately, they are only
open in summer. The 19 units sleep up to five.

Hotels and Restaurants

Mount Hutt

The Homestead, Mount Hutt Station (££)
RD12, Rakaia Gorge, Methven
tel: 03 302 8130 www.tmounthuttstation.co.nz
Comfortable and peaceful accommodation on this up-country station. Fishing, hunting and other activities available. Restaurant and house bar.

Timaru

Bay Motel (£)
9 Hewlings Street tel: 03 684 3267/
0800 150 014 fax: 03 684 3267
Four fully equipped units close to Caroline Bay in a quiet location off the main road.

Grosvenor Hotel (££–£££)
Cairns Terrace tel: 03 688 3129
www.nztravel.co.nz/grosvenor
Refurbished grand old (1875) whitestone hotel close to the main shopping area and the waterfront.

The Deep South

Dunedin

Bentley's Hotel (££)
137 St. Andrew Street tel: 03 477 0572/
0800 266 336 fax: 03 477 0293
www.bentleyhotel.co.nz
Close to the Octagon, above-average accommodation with all facilities. Cocktail bar, restaurant, café.

Cargills Hotel (££–£££)
678 George Street tel: 03 477 7983
www.cargills.co.nz
Near the Octagon, with a courtyard garden. Motel-type rooms (some with waterbeds or spa baths) to executive suites. Lounge bar, restaurant.

The Chancellor (££)
310 Princes Street tel: 03 477 1145/
0800 275 337 www.thechancellor.co.nz
Victorian hotel near the Octagon, with individually decorated bedrooms (all facilities) and four suites.

Leviathan Heritage Hotel (£–££)
27 Queens Gardens tel: 03 477 3160
0800 773 773 www.dunedinhotel.co.nz
Landmark hotel dating from 1884 with 80 good-value basic rooms or self-contained studios, 12 executive suites and backpackers' dorms.

Invercargill

Ascot Park Hotel (££–£££)
corner of Tay Street and Racecourse Road
tel: 03 217 6195/0800 272 687
www.mainstay.co.nz
In park-like surroundings five minutes from the city, the hotel has 72 de luxe rooms and 24 above-average motel units. Bar and brasserie.

Victoria Railway Hotel (£–££)
corner of Esk and Leven streets
tel: 03 218 1281
Right in the heart of the city, this listed historic building (1896) has 20 rooms (10 en suite).

Queenstown

A-Line Hotel (££)
27 Stanley Street tel: 03 442 7700
www.scenic-circle.co.nz
Alpine-style hotel, with lake views. All 82 rooms are comfortable and well appointed; best value are the large two-storey units at the front.

Earnslaw Lodge (££)
77 Frankton Road tel: 03 442 8728
www.earnslawlodge.co.nz
An inviting, modern complex with 20 studio units. Rooms on the upper levels have the best views.

Gardens Parkroyal (£££)
corner of Marine Parade and Earl Street
tel: 03 442 7750/0800 801 111
www.zqn.co.nz/gardensparkroyal
A de luxe hotel right on the waterfront next to Queenstown Gardens. All rooms have lake views.

Millbrook Resort (£££)
Malaghans Road, Arrowtown tel: 03 441
7000/0800 800 604 www.millbrook.co.nz
Just 19km (12 miles) from Queenstown, this resort has large, two-storey villas in the middle of a championship 18-hole golf course.

Parkroyal Queenstown (£££)
Beach Street tel: 03 442 7800
www.zqn.co.nz/parkroyal
The resort's premier hotel—many of its 139 de luxe rooms and suites overlook the lake.

Queenstown House (££)
69 Hallenstein Street tel: 03 442 9043
www.queenstownhouse.co.nz
This B&B near the town has 15 rooms (all en suite). Peaceful, with good views from every room.

Queenstown Lodge (£)
Sainsbury Road, Fernhill tel: 03 442 7107/
0800 756 343 www.qlodge.co.nz
An unusual lodge with views over the lake. Rooms range from shared bunk rooms to private rooms.

Stewart Island

Shearwater Inn (£)
Halfmoon Bay tel: 03 219 1114
www.stewart-island.co.nz/shearwater
This complex has basic hostel accommodation, single, double and family rooms. Restaurant.

South Sea Hotel (£–££)
Halfmoon Bay tel: 03 219 1059
www.stewart-island.co.nz
The 16 reasonably priced rooms in this old-fashioned hotel all have shared facilities.

Stewart Island Holiday Homes (£)
Elgin Terrace, Halfmoon Bay tel: 03 219 1057
Peaceful setting five minutes' walk from the town. Two self-contained units with four bedrooms and two bathrooms sleep up to ten. Bay views.

Te Anau

Edgewater XL Motel (£–££)
52 Lakefront Drive tel: 03 249 7258/
0800 433 439
Next to the lake, 15 units with full kitchen facilities, very reasonably priced. Free canoes.

Holiday Inn Te Anau (£££)
Lake Front Drive tel: 03 249 9700/
0800 223 687 www.holiday-inn.com
Central hotel with 112 rooms, all with private facilties. Pool, spa, sauna, restaurants and bars.

Te Anau Holiday Park (£)
Te Anau–Manapouri Road tel: 03 249
7457/0800 4 TEANAU
www.teanauholidaypark.co.nz
Well-positioned motor park near the lake shore and town, with a range of accommodation, plus tent and campervan sites.

Mount Aspiring Hotel (££–£££)
Mount Aspiring Road tel: 03 443 8216/
0800 688 688 www.wanakanz.com
A well-run inn with 32 studio units and four junior suites (all with en-suite facilities), 2km (1.25 miles) from the town, with lake and mountain views.

Wanaka
Te Wanaka Lodge (££)
23 Brownston Street tel: 03 443 9224
www.tewanaka.co.nz
This lodge (built from traditional materials) in the main town has 12 reasonably priced units (with cooking facilities) and two guest lounges.

RESTAURANTS

£   = under NZ$20
££   = between NZ$20–$30
£££ = over NZ$30

NORTH ISLAND

Auckland

Auckland
Cin Cin on Quay (££–£££)
Auckland Ferry Building, 99 Quay Street
tel: 09 307 6966 www.cincin.co.nz
Popular and busy restaurant reputed to be one of Auckland's best. Outdoor area overlooking the harbour. The menu has cordon bleu dishes as well as pizzas from the wood-burning oven.
Collins House (£££)
20 Greenhithe Road tel: 09 413 9322
Converted from one of the oldest cottages in the area, this is an attractive restaurant in a rural setting in Greenhithe. The chef specializes in French food.
Esplanade (£–£££)
1 Victoria Road, Devonport tel: 09 445 1291
www.esplanadehotel.co.nz
Spacious wine bar with wood décor and views over the harbour. Interesting food and extensive wine list as well as local and imported beers.
Hammerheads (££–£££)
19 Tamaki Drive, Mission Bay
tel: 09 521 4400 www.hammerheads.co.nz
Large and popular seafood restaurant and bar with a wide-ranging and tempting menu; chilli skate wings, lamb and chargrilled fish and shellfish.
Iguaçu (££)
269 Parnell Road tel: 09 358 4804
www.iguacu.co.nz
Fine brasserie, popular with young corporate types, with outdoor and conservatory dining.
Kermadec (££–£££)
1st floor, Viaduct Quay, Lower Hobson Street
tel: 09 309 0412 www.kermadec.co.nz
The owners promise the freshest fish—and it should be fresh, since they own a fishing fleet. Oysters, *sashimi* and skilfully prepared fish.
The Loaded Hog (£–££)
Viaduct Quay, Hobson and Quay streets tel: 09 366 6491 www.menus.co.nz/loadedhog
Busy brewery restaurant and bar—their own beers are brewed on the premises—serving fun food in a lively atmosphere.

Mad Dogs & Englishmen (££)
41 Albert Street; tel: 09 379 6004
One of a chain of English-type pubs, serving traditional English beers and food. Good value.
Metropole (££–£££)
223 Parnell Road tel: 09 379 9300
A casual but stylish restaurant in Parnell. The menu ranges from interesting bar snacks to classic dishes and less traditional fare.
Mexican Café (£–££)
67 Victoria Street West tel: 09 373 2311
www.mexicancafe.co.nz
Fun and friendly Mexican cantina, a great place for fine, varied vegetarian dishes. They serve great margaritas, too.
Mikano (££–£££)
1 Solent Street, Mechanics Bay
tel: 09 309 9514
The Mikano is noted for its snappy service, fabulous outlook and wonderful food. For seafood alone there is a choice of seven types cooked in five different ways, plus many other delights.
Poppadom (££)
471 Khyber Pass Road tel: 09 529 1897
www.poppadom.org
Acclaimed Indian restaurant with traditional dishes and a full Tandoori menu; lunch-time buffets are good value.

279

Northland

Doubtless Bay

Mangonui
Mangonui Fish Shop (£)
The Wharf tel: 09 406 0478
The place to eat fish—fresh shellfish, fish and chips and seafood salads.

Bay of Islands

Paihia
Bistro 40 Restaurant & Bar (£££)
Bayswater Inn, 40 Marsden Road tel: 09 402 7444 www.paihia.com/restaurants/bistro40
Attractive restaurant in a converted homestead (1884) with an outside patio. Wide-ranging menu. Open evenings only.
Saltwater Café (££)
14 Kings Road tel: 09 402 6080
This large eatery, with a bright and contemporary décor, specializes in seafood, beef and lamb, but is also particularly good for desserts.

Russell
Duke of Marlborough (£–££)
The Strand tel: 09 403 7829
www.theduke.co.nz
There are several options in this historic waterfront hotel, with pub food in the bar or more elegant dining in the Sommerset Restaurant.
The Gables (££)
The Strand tel: 09 403 7618
www.gablesrestaurant.co.nz
Popular restaurant in an 1847 building on the seafront, serving New Zealand produce and seafood. Reservations recommended.

Whangarei
Killer Prawn Bar & Restaurant (£–£££)
Strand Plaza, 28 Bank Street
tel: 09 430 3333 www.killerprawn.co.nz
Trendy central bar with an extensive menu from
New Zealand and the Pacific Rim. Prawns are
obviously the house dish, but bar snacks and
breakfasts (weekends only) are also available.
Reva's on the Waterfront (£–££)
Quayside tel: 09 438 8969
www.revas.co.nz
Popular hang-out with international 'yachties'.
Plenty of choice, from pasta to Mexican and
seafood. Live music Wed, Thu and Fri.

From Coromandel to the Waikato

Coromandel

Coromandel Township
Coromandel Hotel (£–££)
Kapanga Road tel: 07 866 8760
Historic pub just outside the middle of town, open
for lunch, with bistro dining every evening.
The Peppertree (£)
31 Kapanga Road tel: 07 866 8211
Try the local seafood here—the oysters and
mussels are very tasty.

Pauanui
Mercure Grand Puka Park (£££)
Mount Avenue tel: 07 864 8088
www.pukapark.co.nz
The lodge has the acclaimed Miha restaurant with
an innovative menu of New Zealand and international cuisine. Bistro food in the Puka Café.

Thames
Majestic Family Restaurant (£–££)
640 Pollen Street tel: 07 868 6204
This restaurant specializes in seafood and steak,
as well as takeaway meals.
Sealey Café (££)
109 Sealey Street tel: 07 868 8641
Arguably the best place to eat in town, this
Victorian villa with courtyard serves light lunches
as well as more substantial meals.

Whitianga
Snapper Jacks (£)
corner of Albert and Monk Streets
tel: 07 866 5482
A popular fish and seafood restaurant that has
a take-away section. It also sells fresh seafood
as well.

Bay of Plenty

Rotorua
Aorangi Peak Restaurant (£££)
Mountain Road, Mount Ngongotaha
tel: 07 347 0046
Just a short drive from the city, the Aorangi Peak
has panoramic views across the lake and the township. House specials here include steak, venison,
teriyaki and scallop tempura, and there's also a
range of vegetarian dishes. A great place for a
special night out.

Fat Dog Café (££)
1161 Arawa Street tel: 07 347 7586
Open until late, this is a buzzing place with good
food and plenty to see—both people and
decorations on the walls.
The Fishspot (£–££)
1123 Eruera Street tel: 07 349 3494
Fresh fish and seafood, as well as steaks and a
dessert menu. Licensed/B(ring)Y(our)O(wn).
Happy Days Buffet Restaurant (££–£££)
Grand Establishment, 1129 Hinemoa Street
tel: 07 348 2089
A restaurant serving straightforward meals such as
steaks, grills, chicken and fish.
Mitas (££)
1114 Tutanekai Street tel: 07 349 6482
www.mitas.co.nz
Enjoy Asian fusion food surrounded by art, antiques
and other collectables from Southeast Asia.

Tauranga
Bella Mia (££)
73a Devonport Road tel: 07 578 4996
Cosy pizzeria/ristorante with an Italian proprietor/
chef, serving pasta dishes and pizzas, and also
meat and fish.
Harbourside Brasserie & Bar (££–£££)
Old Yacht Club Building, Strand extension
tel: 07 571 0520 www.harbourside-tga.co.nz
Overlooking the harbour, with excellent seafood and
grills, and desserts and coffee served to midnight.
Shiraz (££)
12 Wharf Street tel: 07 577 0059
Middle Eastern cuisine at reasonable prices.
Often busy, so it's best to book. Small covered
courtyard.

The Waikato

Hamilton
Caffè Centrale (£–££)
10 Alma Street tel: 07 838 1013
An atmospheric Italian, Mexican and Kiwi restaurant
with a huge menu and equally huge portions. A
good-value, fun place to eat.
Sahara Tent Café & Bar (£–££)
254 Victoria Street, tel: 07 834 0409
www.hamiltoncity.co.nz/saharatent
Good Middle Eastern food, with a selection of
gourmet pizzas.
Turtle Lake Garden Café and Restaurant (£££)
Cobham Drive, tel: 07 856 6581
www.hamiltoncity.co.nz/turtlelake/index.html
Lunches, dinners and casual meals overlooking
Turtle Lake in Hamilton's Botanic Gardens.
Valentines (£–££)
corner of Anglesea and Clarence streets
tel: 07 839 1990
One of a chain of licensed buffet restaurant offering
a smorgasbord of over 120 fixed-price dishes
(prices are higher at dinner).

East Coast

Hastings
@108 Cafe and Wine Bar (£–££)
108 Market Street South tel: 06 878 8596
Pleasant little wine bar with a wood fire and a

terrace. Open six days a week for bar snacks or more substantial meals.

Vidal Winery Restaurant (££–£££)
913 St. Aubyn Street East tel: 07 876 8105
On the Vidal Estate winery, this popular brasserie has rustic décor and serves light meals, steaks and blackboard specials. Jazz brunch on Sunday.

Napier
Chambers Restaurant (££)
Country Hotel, 12 Browning Street, Napier tel: 06 835 7800
A silver-service restaurant, which serves international cuisine. Open 7 days a week.

Gumnuts (££)
The Provincial Hotel, corner of Emerson Street and Clive Square tel: 06 835 6934
An imaginative vegetarian menu sits alongside steaks, lamb and seafood. There's a children's menu and also tempting desserts.

Pierre sur le Quai Restaurant (£££)
62 West Quay, Ahuriri tel: 06 834 0189
Slightly out of town on the quayside, this elegant restaurant is rated as one of Napier's top dining-out venues. Reservations are essential.

Westshore Fish Cafe (£)
112a Charles Street, Westshore, Napier tel: 06 834 0227
A little distance from the main town, but worth a visit for the fish.

Central North Island and the West Coast

Lake Taupo
The Bach (££)
2 Pataka Road, Lake Terrace tel: 07 378 7856 www.thebach.co.nz
Gourmet food and spectacular lake views make this a very popular restaurant. There is also an à la carte menu and dining on the deck or lawn in summer.

Edgewater Restaurant, Manuel's Copthorne Resort (£££)
243 Lake Terrace tel: 07 378 5110 www.copthornemanuelstaupo.nz-hotels.com
One of Taupo's top restaurants, which serves imaginative and well-presented New Zealand dishes. The plush dining-room overlooks the lake.

Prawn Farm (£)
Huka Falls Road, Wairakei Park tel: 07 374 8474 www.prawnpark.co.nz
Round off a visit to the geothermally heated prawn farm (see page 124) by sampling the excellent produce at Prawn Farm. Booking advisable.

Walnut Keep (£–££)
77 Spa Road tel: 07 378 0777
Popular restaurant with an inventive chef who serves international cuisine. The only significant drawback is the lack of a view.

New Plymouth
Andre L'Escargot (£££)
37–41 Brougham Street tel: 06 758 4812 www.andres.co.nz
A French restaurant in an historic building, with an extensive wine list.

Wanganui
Liffiton Castle Restaurant (££–£££)
26 Liffiton Street tel: 06 345 7864
Complete with moat, antique fittings, lively atmosphere and good food, served smorgasbord-style.

Rutland Arms (££–£££)
corner of Victoria Avenue and Ridgway Street tel: 06 347 7677
In the heart of the city, this atmospheric restaurant has a range of interesting dishes.

What Cafe (££)
Victoria Court, 92 Victoria Avenue tel: 06 348 4484
A friendly cafe, with great home-baking.

Lower North Island

Wellington
Chevy's (££)
97 Dixon Street tel: 04 384 2724
The neon cowboy outside advertises the essentially American nature of this diner. Spare ribs, burgers, nachos, chicken wings and steaks.

Chocolate Fish (£)
497a Karaka Bay Road, Seatoun tel: 04 388 2808
Popular with the *Lord of the Rings* crew when they were in town—and everyone else on a sunny day. Highly recommended for alfresco brunch.

281

Cobar (££)
Eastern Bays Marine Drive, Days Bay, Eastbourne tel: 04 562 8882 www.cobar.co.nz
Catch the ferry from Wellington for a waterside lunch or enjoy the sunset over dinner.

Dockside (£–££)
Shed 3, Queen's Wharf tel: 04 499 9900
A busy and trendy eating place on the waterfront, Dockside serves everything from breakfasts through to late-night snacks (daily 7AM–3AM).

Fishermans Table (££)
245 Oriental Parade tel: 04 801 7900 www.fishermanstable.co.nz
Family restaurant giving excellent value for money and with stunning views over the harbour.

Shed 5 Restaurant (£££)
Shed 5, Queen's Wharf tel: 04 499 9069 www.menus.co.nz/shed5
One of a clutch of waterfront restaurants. Seafood specials as well as lamb and venison, pasta and poultry. Great for brunch at weekends.

The White House (££–£££)
232 Oriental Parade tel: 04 385 8555 www.menus.co.nz/whitehouse
Excellent New Zealand cuisine in a superb waterside setting.

SOUTH ISLAND

Marlborough and Nelson

Blenheim
D'Urville Wine Bar & Brasserie (££)
52 Queen Street tel: 03 577 9945 www.durville.com
International cuisine and a range of local wines. Serves local produce, including seafood.

Hotels and Restaurants

Hunter's Vintner's Restaurant (££)
Rapaura Road tel: 03 572 8803
www.hunters.co.nz
First-class dining within the family-owned vineyard.
Paddy Barry's Irish Pub (£–££)
51 Scott Street tel: 03 578 7470
www.angelfire.com/artimitatesguinness
Friendly pub with a pleasant veranda, reasonably priced pub food and draught Guinness.
Paysanne Café and Bar (£–££)
1st floor, Forum Building, Market Place
tel: 03 577 6278
Convivial wine bar serves light snacks and meals; also daily blackboard specials, and gourmet pizzas.
Seymours (££–£££)
Scenic Circle Blenheim Country Hotel, corner of Alfred and Henry streets tel: 03 578 5079
www.scenic-circle.co.nz
Elegant restaurant. Gourmet Marlborough foods, plus over 70 local wines. Live bands Fri and Sat.

Kaikoura
Caves Restaurant (££)
Main Highway South tel: 03 319 5023
Reasonable value local seafood as well as snacks and light meals in generous portions.
White Morph Restaurant (££–£££)
94 Esplanade tel: 03 319 5676
www.whitemorph.co.nz
Set in an historic home, serving fresh fish and seafood. Devonshire cream teas served all day.

Nelson
Broccoli Row (£–££)
5 Buxton Square tel: 03 548 9621
Mediterranean-style vegetarian restaurant. Blackboard menu, outdoor dining, sumptuous desserts.
Chez Eelco (££)
296 Trafalgar Street tel: 03 548 7595
Forty years ago this was Nelson's only café—Eelco's daughter now runs it in a tasteful, casual way, complete with art gallery. Lunch only.
Pomeroy's (£–££)
276 Trafalgar Street tel: 03 548 7524
Central café/wine bar serving coffee and cakes, plus delicious snacks. Extensive wine list.
Victorian Rose (£–££)
281 Trafalgar Street tel: 03 548 7631
Old English-style pub with a good range of beers. Meals and snacks, plus live entertainment.

Motueka
Gothic Gourmet Restaurant (££–£££)
208 High Street tel: 03 528 6699
Unmissable, pink-painted converted church with an interesting menu, including scallops and medallions of lamb. Informal and children's menus.
Hot Mamas (£–££)
105 High Street tel: 03 528 7039
Busy bistro serving Mexican food and traditional NZ fare at café prices. Live bands at weekends.

Picton
Expresso House (£)
58 Auckland Street tel: 03 573 7112
This small cottage comes with a courtyard behind. It serves excellent coffee and is handy for the ferry.

The West Coast

Fox Glacier
Fox Glacier Resort Hotel (£–££)
Fox Township tel: 03 751 0839
www.resorts.co.nz
A licensed restaurant specializing in local delicacies; bar with snacks.

Franz Josef Glacier
Batson's Tavern (£)
corner of Cron and Cowan streets
tel: 03 752 0740
A convivial pub offering a good range of bistro meals.
Blue Ice (£–£££)
Main Road tel: 03 752 0707
A cheerful restaurant with mountain views and jazz music. The cosmopolitan menu includes Westland salmon, venison casserole, lobster and vegetarian dishes. Tasty desserts and great espresso coffee.

Hokitika
Café de Paris (£–££)
19 Tancred Street tel: 03 755 8933
As its name suggests, fine French-style food in a relaxed atmosphere.
Tasman View Restaurant (££–£££)
Southland Hotel, Revell Street
tel: 03 755 8344 www.southlandhotel.com
Overlooking the windswept Tasman Sea, this chic restaurant specializes in west-coast foods. Friday smorgasbords are good value.
Trapper's (££)
Revell Street tel: 03 755 6854
Very unusual restaurant which grew out of the Hokitika Wildfoods Festival, with a changing menu that features wild venison, chamois, thar and wild boar, plus even more exotic meats such as crocodile, kangaroo and water buffalo.

Canterbury

Akaroa, Banks Peninsula
C'est la Vie (£–££)
33 Rue Lavaud tel: 03 304 7314
Intimate little café/bistro serving mainly French food as well as cakes and desserts.
Harbour 71 (£–££)
71 Beach Road tel: 03 304 7656
Seafood is the special of this restaurant, together with chicken dishes.
Ma Maison (££)
2 Rue Jolie tel: 03 304 7658
Good for fish and steak; right on the waterfront.

Christchurch
Canterbury Tales (£££)
Crowne Plaza Christchurch, corner of Kilmore and Durham streets tel: 03 365 7799
www.christchurch.crowneplaza.com
Formal restaurant with a medieval theme, winner of many awards and generally considered one of the best in the South Island. Freshest Canterbury produce, complemented by an extensive wine list.
Christchurch Tramway Restaurant (££)
Cathedral Square tram stop tel: 03 366 7511
www.tram.co.nz

Dine and tour in the elegant surroundings of a restored Melbourne tram, adapted to seat 36. The à la carte menu is small but interesting.

Dux de Lux (£–££)
corner of Hereford and Montreal streets
tel: 03 366 6919 www.thedux.co.nz
Close to the Arts Centre, this popular place has an excellent self-service vegetarian restaurant (considered one of the best in town), a cocktail bar and the Tavern Bar with beers brewed on site.

Indochine (££)
209 Cambridge Terrace tel: 03 365 7323
www.indochine.co.nz
Asian restaurant and cocktail bar. It's known for its pressed duck with mandarin sauce and dim sum.

Lone Star Café (££)
26 Manchester Street tel: 03 365 7086
www.lonestar.co.nz
Tex-Mex food in a carefully contrived Wild West atmosphere. Lots of fun, reasonable value. Other branches are in Dunedin, Queenstown and Invercargill.

Sign of the Takahe (£££)
Dyers Pass Road, Cashmere Hills
tel: 03 332 4052
In a mock-baronial castle 20 minutes' drive from the city, this restaurant is best known for its crayfish, but also has other seafood dishes, such as whitebait, mussels and scallops.

Strawberry Fare (£–££)
114 Peterborough Street tel: 03 365 4897
Divine desserts are wonderful at this restaurant, served at any time of day. They also have savoury meals from brunch through to dinner. There is another branch in Wellington.

The Tap Room (££)
124 Oxford Terrace tel: 03 365 0547
A craft beer bar serving Monteith's beers from the West Coast, complemented by unusual food specials and a full wine list.

The Deep South

Dunedin

Bacchus Wine Bar and Restaurant (££–£££)
1st floor, 12 The Octagon tel: 03 474 0824
Overlooking the Octagon, this smart wine bar has good food plus an extensive selection of imported and New Zealand wines.

Bell Pepper Blues (££)
474 Princes Street tel: 03 474 0973
www.bellpepperblues.co.nz
The place to eat in Dunedin. Fine dining Pacific-rim style, including venison, beef and lamb. Booking advisable.

The Palms (£–££)
18 Queens Gardens tel: 03 477 6534
Cosy café in an atmospheric old building, with a blackboard menu as well as staples such as chicken, lamb and fish.

Queenstown

The Bathhouse (££)
28 Marine Parade tel: 03 442 5625
www.bathhouse.co.nz
Right on the edge of Lake Wakatipu, with good food, excellent service and equally good views.

Berkels Gourmet Burgers (£–££)
19 Shotover Street tel: 03 442 6950
Burgers as simple or as complicated as you like (with Camembert, horseradish, chilli and more). Wide range of beers and wines.

Boardwalk Seafood Restaurant & Bar (££–£££)
Steamer Wharf tel: 03 442 5630
www.boardwalk.net.nz
On the first floor of the complex, this stylish restaurant is known for its fresh seafood and New Zealand produce such as venison, lamb and beef.

The Bunker (££)
Cow Lane tel: 03 441 8030
A haven from the bustle of Queenstown, reminiscent of a gentlemen's club. In- and outdoor dining, with an inventive menu and impressive wine list.

The Cow (£)
Cow Lane (off Beach Street) tel/fax: 03 442 8588 www.thecowrestaurant.co.nz
A Queenstown institution since 1976, The Cow serves spaghetti and pizza. The open fire helps make it a popular place in winter.

Dux de Lux (££)
14 Church Street tel: 03 442 7745
This restaurant and bar often has live music during the evenings.

Fishbone Bar & Grill (££)
7 Beach Street tel: 03 442 6768
www.entertainmentnz.com/nz/fishbone
One of Queenstown's best-priced fish restaurants, with chargrilled seafoods and other delicacies straight from the slab. There is also a fresh fish counter. Licensed and BYO.

Gantley's (££–£££)
Arthurs Point Road, Arthurs Point
tel: 03 442 8999 www.gantleys.co.nz
It's worth the short trip north for the internationally renowned wine list alone. The French-influenced food is outstanding, and the atmosphere of this 1863 former inn completes the experience.

Lone Star Café (££)
14 Brecon Street tel: 03 442 9995
www.lonestar.co.nz
Chargrilled steaks, Cajun dishes, Dixie chicken and spare ribs are some of the many southern dishes on offer in this popular chain restaurant. Generous portions and a fun atmosphere.

Minami Jujisei (££–£££)
45 Beach Street tel: 03 442 9854
www.entertainmentnz.com/nz/minamijujisei
This is reputed to be one of the finest Japanese restaurants in New Zealand, with an excellent sushi bar and traditional *tatami* room. There's also a Western-style dining-room.

Skyline Restaurant (££–£££)
Brecon Street tel: 03 441 0101
www.skyline.co.nz
Fabulous views from the gondola complex, with an international menu in the brasserie (evenings only) or a huge spread (including carvery) in the buffet. Lounge bar—great for cocktails—and a café.

Vudu (££)
23 Beach Street tel: 03 442 5357
www.vudu.co.nz
A casual café noted for its fresh food, good coffee, comfy chairs, good-value breakfasts and organic and vegetarian dishes.

Index

Index

Index/Acknowledgements

288

Author's Acknowledgements

The author would like to thank the following for their assistance: The Palzer family, Ocean View Chalets, Marahau; Grant and Judie Smith, Wanaka Motor Inn, Mount Hutt Station; Stefanie and Brent Ritchie, Punakaiki Cottage Motels; Jean and Don Goldschmidt, Aachen House, Remuera; Kevin and Lois Kelly, Taiparoro House, Tauranga; Lake Plaza Hotel, Rotorua; Clint and Jill Tauri, Te Anau Motor Park; Garrick and Maureen Workman, Hobbit Motor Lodge, Ohakune; Bart and Theresa Blommaert, Ascot Parnell; Bernadette Walker, Wains Boutique Hotel, Dunedin; The Wairakei Resort, Lake Taupo; Mercury Bay Beachfront Resort, Whitianga; Bruce and Aileen Stone, Cheviot Park Motor Lodge, Whangarei; Napier Travel Inn, Hawke's Bay; Harry Sellarsby, A-Line Hotel, Queenstown; Russell and Rosalie Mathews, Grandvue, Picton; Ellenor and Leslie King, Rata Grove Motel, Franz Josef; Avenue Motor Inn, Wanganui. Also thanks to Peter Peck of Fiordland Travel, Queenstown; Neil Ross, Dart River Safaris, Queenstown; Graham Allen of Mount Cook Line, London; Karen Jones, Tranz Rail, London; Kiwifruits Bookshop, London. Finally, thanks to Angela Becket and Adrienne Wilde in Tauranga and to Graham and Jill Hubble in Auckland for their generous hospitality.

Publisher's Acknowledgements

The Automobile Association wishes to thank the following photographers, libraries and associations for their assistance in the preparation of this book:
ALAMY 133, 137 **ALLSPORT UK LTD** 146a (M. Hewitt), 146b (S Bruty), 147a (C. Mason), 147b (S. Bruty); **AUCKLAND CITY ART GALLERY** 51a; **BRUCE COLEMAN COLLECTION** 34a (M. Carwardine), 98b (G. Cubitt), 105a (F. Furlong), 105b (F. Furlong), 156 (M. Carwardine), 167 (M. Carwardine), 216/7 (L. Lee Rue), 236b (G. Cubitt); **MARY EVANS PICTURE LIBRARY** 34b, 35, 38t, 38b, 39b; **FOCUS NEW ZEALAND PHOTO LIBRARY** 18b, 20, 20/1, 22/3, 23, 24b, 44, 46b, 54, 60, 64/5, 74/5, 80, 92, 101, 102/3, 107, 111, 127, 138, 145, 155, 163, 166a, 185b (carved by Neil Brown), 187a, 187b, 244, 250; **FIORDLAND TRAVEL** 235; **FOOTPRINTS COLOUR LIBRARY (Nick Hanna)** 136b, 224, 234b; **GREENPEACE COMMUNICATIONS LTD** 19 (Miller); **L. C. HAZLEY** 228/9; **HULTON GETTY** 27b, 32b, 37, 40, 42a, 43, 45, 150, 171, 237; **NATIONAL MARITIME MUSEUM, LONDON** 32/3, 116a, 117; **NATURE PHOTOGRAPHERS LTD.** 213 (B Burbidge); **NEW ZEALAND TOURISM BOARD PHOTO LIBRARY** 114, 185a; **OTAMATEA KAURI AND PIONEER MUSEUM** 77; **POPPERFOTO** 42/3, 99, 112/3, 112b; **ROB SUISTED/NATURE'S PIC IMAGES** 154, 154/5; **THE RONALD GRANT ARCHIVE** 57c; **SPECTRUM COLOUR LIBRARY** 46a, 120, 149, 176/7, 180/1, 182a, 182b, 223a; **TAHI DESIGNS** 57; **TE PAPA TONGAREWA MUSEUM OF NEW ZEALAND** 151
The remaining photographs are held in the Association's own library (AA PHOTO LIBRARY) and were taken by Paul Kenward with the exception of page 4 (Andy Reisinger), page 14/15a (Adrian Baker), pages 17, 57b, 76/77, 122 (Andy Belcher), pages 13, 22b, 59, 86, 88, 104, 106/107, 223b, 236a (Mike Langford) and pages 195, 227, 242, 259, which were taken by Nick Hanna.

Contributors
Original copy editor: Barbara Mellor
Revision verifier: Michael Mellor